From Montmartre to the Latin Quarter
by Francis Carco

Edited with Annotations and an Introduction
by Rob Couteau

Afterword by Christopher Sawyer-Lauçanno

Translated from the French by Madeleine Boyd

Born in Nouméa, New Caledonia in 1886, Francis Carco arrived in Paris during the winter of his 24th year, in January 1910. Making a beeline for the soon-to-be legendary cabaret, Le Lapin Agile, he was quickly accepted into the inner circle of a Parisian bohemia. There, on La Butte Montmartre, he rubbed shoulders with the likes of Picasso, Modigliani, Utrillo, Max Jacob, Pierre Mac Orlan, Apollinaire, and many of the other leading lights of a Parisian avant-garde. As the author of over 100 books, Carco's talents were plentiful. He composed poetry, literary fiction, plays, and biography, and was even known as a witty and engaging *chansonnier*. But throughout each of these creative expressions his manner remains that of a poet: utilizing a personal vision to unravel and portray the spiritual enigmas that life presents. He was also possessed by a prescient perception and published the first critical essay on Modigliani, whose work he began to collect during a period when other French critics merely scoffed at the contributions of this modern master. Likewise, his early essays on Utrillo, forged by his personal interactions with the painter, remain modern classics filled with a unique perspective. But certainly, his most developed and enduring talent was that of a memoirist. In *From Montmartre to the Latin Quarter* he evokes the rich, hallucinatory marvels of Montmartre, Montparnasse, and the Latin Quarter during the 1910s and early Twenties. The work also serves as a poignant memorial to all those artists and writers who were sacrificed during the Great War, their young, promising lives nipped in the bud before they reached their highest potential. *From Montmartre to the Latin Quarter* is a record of deep friendship in which memory serves as the most potent talisman of the heart. This newly revised edition features an in-depth Introduction and over 300 annotations that serve to greatly expand the context of this lively chronicle.

In 1922, Carco was awarded Le Grand Prix du Roman for his novel *L'Homme traqué* ("The Hunted Man"), and in 1937 he was elected to the Académie Goncourt. During WWII, Carco fled to Switzerland with his Jewish wife, Éliane Négrin. Upon returning to France, he was elected to the board of directors of the Comité national des écrivains, the institution that determined which writers were to be blacklisted due to their shameful collaboration with the Nazi regime.

Francis Carco in Agen, France

Contents

Francis Carco

Francis Carco's "Proximity to Genius":
An Introduction by Rob Couteau

"Carco was very young then, almost a boy, but he was knowing and had already considerable experience of life. Perpetually on the defensive and jeering, with a vicious, observant eye, he took in everything. I first knew him when he was living with Édouard Gazanion. Then one day I saw him at the Lapin Agile. Leaning on a table, he was singing and imitating, with great talent, I must say, a comic café-concert singer singing a popular song of the day [...] We really enjoyed ourselves at the Lapin Agile, and when Carco used to perch on a table and do his bawdy song act, our enjoyment knew no bounds." – Fernande Olivier, *Picasso and His Friends*

One of the most remarkable passages in Francis Carco's *From Montmartre to the Latin Quarter* concerns his love and respect for the visionary labors of Amedeo Modigliani.

Carco brings us back to a time when he's poor and struggling (but struggling with great joie de vivre) in Paris. Having taken the vows of poverty to pursue his craft, he knows something about an artist's quotidian challenges. But, being French, at least he can hope for some eventual support from the broader French institutional networks. For a foreigner living in Paris in the interwar years, there was the additional obstacle of widespread xenophobia – particularly within the native art community – as well as an ever-mounting anti-Semitism. (A point worth mentioning here, since Modigliani was a Sephardic Jew from central Italy.)

No wonder that the dealer Modigliani finally ended up with was himself a foreigner, the Polish-born Jewish poet Léopold Zborowski, who underwent great personal sacrifice to support Modi and to represent his work – even though he had no prior experience in this profession. [1]

And what an unusual dealer he was! This is how Carco describes a visit to Zborowski's lair:

> When one went to see Zborowski, he would run down to buy a candle and, setting it in the neck of a bottle, he would take you into a narrow room without furniture, bare, desolate, in a corner of which the painter's canvases were heaped. Lighted by the candle, Zborowski showed his treasures, stroking them passionately with his hands and devouring them with his eyes, then, fascinated, he would spit with disgust, talk agitatedly and curse the fate which crushed Modigliani. The more agitated he was the more naturally would the words come to his mouth to express his strange and splendid feeling before those nudes, those figures, those portraits painted without any care for schools, but in which the painter's pure and blinding art were manifested.
>
> "Such poetry!" Zborowski would say ecstatically.

This final exclamation might appear to be clichéd until one remembers that Zborowski devoted his life to poetry – and then abandoned his craft once he recognized a higher poetry working within the painting of this modern master. Thus, we shouldn't underestimate the role of this poet's eye: for, at that time, besides Zborowski and Carco, there were few who were

---

[1] For more about how poorly the foreign-born artists living in Paris were treated, many of whom were placed under observation simply because they were "foreign," see Annie Cohen-Solal, *Picasso the Foreigner: An Artist in France, 1900-1973*, New York: Farrar, Straus, and Giroux, 2023. As just one example, on 18 June 1901, the Préfecture de police subjected Picasso to a decades-long surveillance. After he was denied citizenship in April 1940, the painter was in grave danger of being deported to Franco's Spain. And, "Like those of other non-French painters, his works were excluded from the opening of the Museum of Modern Art in August 1942." Frederic Spotts, *The Shameful Peace*, London: Yale University Press, 2008, p. 152.

capable of comprehending what, exactly, Modigliani was up to. "In any age," says Picasso, "there are only a handful that can truly see."

One can certainly add Picasso and Max Jacob to that handful, but most of the French dealers wanted nothing to do with Modigliani.[2] While so many in the Parisian art world were not only rejecting but also insulting and berating Modi's work, "Zbo" was bestowing upon it the highest term of value: *poetry*. And for him, it's even a tactile poetry – he can't restrain himself from touching the canvas, like a lover mesmerized under flickering candlelight.[3]

Via Zborowski's monologue, Carco chronicles the difficulties that are facing Modigliani. As Zbo laments his inability to interest other dealers in Modi's work, he utters words that will prove to be prophetic:

> "How stupid they are ... They are not yet accustomed ... But you shall see ... later ... not even later – soon ... they'll pay high prices for those canvases they don't want now ... they'll all want Modigliani's ... and

[2] Among the exceptions were Paul Guillaume and Berthe Weill. Having hailed from a family of Alsatian Jews, Weill would have been regarded as an outsider, or even as a "foreigner," by many of her Parisian contemporaries. During the Dreyfus affair, Degas would glare at Weill and spit on the pavement in contempt whenever he passed her shop. Weill describes her early life as "difficult" and her family as being "very poor" until her mother received a modest inheritance from an aunt.

[3] Here I'm reminded of Renoir's encounter with Modigliani, in which he advised the younger painter: "Paint with joy ... with the same joy that you would make love to a woman." When Modi failed to respond, Renoir added (much to Modigliani's chagrin): "I always caress the buttocks for days and days before finishing a canvas." Charles Douglas, *Artist Quarter: Reminiscences of Montmartre and Montparnasse in the first two decades of the twentieth century*, London: Pallas Athene, 2021, p. 276.

meanwhile, he has no money, he is unhappy, he fills one with pity."[4]

Again, one might write this off as the braggadocio of a dealer attempting to trigger a sale. But watch what follows. When Carco – despite his meager resources – offers to purchase a painting, Zborowski refuses to sell it:

> "Well," I said to him, "sell me that nude, will you?"
> "You love it?"
> "It is very beautiful."
> Zborowski uttered a shout of joy […]
> "To you," he decided, "I won't sell ... I shall give it. Here ... I give it to you ... because you love it."
> "And the money for Modigliani?"
> "No ... Take it, I am so pleased you love it ... Forget the money question ... Don't bother about that ... Tomorrow a man is coming to buy some clothes ... he'll give twenty francs. That will be enough ..."

For Zborowski, better than cash in hand is this affirmation that he's just received: that the writer believes in Modi's work,

---

[4] "The most important point to consider in the schism between the École des Beaux-Arts and the independent academies is the fact that foreigners were not eligible to compete for the crowning prize of the academic system, the prestigious Prix de Rome, which was essential for obtaining official teaching positions and state commissions. To obtain this prize, French students at the École des Beaux-Arts were encouraged to look at antiquity as seen by past French masters. Conformity to an idea of the 'French tradition' was stressed above all. Foreign artists may have been taught to value antiquity and the classical tradition in the independent academies, but because they were outside of the French system, they did not need to interpret it as had past French masters and could be more diverse in their interpretation. Thus, the restriction that kept them outside of the French system also acted as a liberating force." Kenneth Wayne, *Modigliani and the Artists of Montparnasse*, New York: Harry N. Abrams, Inc., 2002, pp. 25-26.

that it's a thing of beauty, a masterpiece worthy of love. And so, one begins to wonder: What kind of a dealer *is* this?

> And he came with me to my house, carrying that magnificent picture and refusing even at the last minute to accept a very small sum which, not being rich, I tried to force upon him.
>
> It was my first picture, but the concierge who cleaned my room, in the quai aux Fleurs, almost fell dead the next day when she discovered that nude above my bed.

This last remark is far from incidental; for the meddlesome, suspicious concierge is the living embodiment of those who have *yet to see*. And those who are quick to judge, denounce, or berate anyone in possession of such earth-shattering vision, which, if acknowledged, would turn that petty little world on its head. Which eventually, it did.

But meanwhile, the mocking laughter of this gossipmonger – who even invites the other tenants of the building into Carco's room, while he's away, so that they, too, can ridicule the painting – foreshadows what will soon follow:

> Unhappy Modi! Almost five years were necessary before, one after the other, the finest [aficionados][5] and the most enlightened decided to have him in their collections. Meanwhile they would not listen to Zborowski, they laughed in his face, or else they did not receive him, offended that anyone should try to mock them in that way. Zborowski did not mind. He would leave the painting, come back, and talk and talk, until the day when, following my own taste, I wrote in a Swiss review called the *Éventail* an article which

[55] Boyd translates "les amateurs" as "amateurs" rather than the more appropriate "aficionados." This has been corrected throughout the text.

> brought Zborowski two or three Swiss collectors who, thanks to the exchange, bought some nudes of Modigliani for almost nothing.

Carco is referring to his review of Modigliani's one-man show held at Galerie Berthe Weill. The inclusion of four nude portraits attracted so many gawking bystanders – shocked by the public display of such "immodestly" posed figures – that the police arrived (from a headquarters across the street) and forced Weill to remove the provocative canvases.

Although Carco appears to brush aside the importance of this review, in fact his essay helped to build a firm foundation of recognition for the beleaguered painter. As Modigliani scholar Kenneth Wayne writes: "Carco's was the only article devoted solely to Modigliani during his lifetime.... Written before Modigliani's untimely death and, hence before a romantic myth developed around him, this article is one of the purest, most sensitive, and insightful pieces of writing ever penned about the artist and his work by someone close to him."[6]

And so, Zbo's beneficence toward Carco, although engendered by the purest of intentions, also served to nurture within the writer an even deeper appreciation of Modi's work, resulting in an essay that brought some important recognition from abroad.

Perhaps the Polish poet wasn't so naive after all. Perhaps his way of doing business, as impractical as it seems, was guided by a "poetic logic" that few other dealers have access to.[7] For, consider what follows – in what I regard as the story's climax:

[6] Kenneth Wayne, *Modigliani and the Artists of Montparnasse*, p. 67. See Francis Carco, "Modigliani," *L'Éventail*, Geneva: Librairie Artistique Kundig, 15 July 1919, pp. 201-209.

[7] Since Zborowski was an avid gambler, one might argue that he was also following the "logic" of a roulette wheel, i.e., he was willing to gamble all his chips on Modi's winning number.

Carco invites us into his little pauper's flat, guarded by that narrow-minded Cerberus who might as well be blind. But who would suspect that within this innocuous habitation there dwells such a luminous magical treasure?

> The one I had in my room filled me with delight and yet not one of my friends admired it. They all called me mad, an idiot, an imbecile ... I let them joke as much as they liked and without asking their advice I began to save some notes from my slender resources for which Zborowski sold me other paintings by Modi and shouted it to the housetops.

Once again, Zbo's gift has paid itself off. For, after living with that first fine portrait, Carco couldn't help but to purchase additional works. As a result, we're now privy to one of the most enthusiastic tributes ever penned about Modi and his alluring women:

> What delight I felt in the mornings, in the quai aux Fleurs, when I woke, amongst those nudes with milky and orange flesh, under their blinking eyes and their magnificent forms! Two windows in a corner offered through their light the clean fresh landscape of the Seine. The shrill cries of tugs, the smoke, the panting of the motors upon the river surrounded me like a dream. In the summer, especially, when the open windows let a warm sun come in with the smell of the big trees, golden and rustling, from the point of the Île Saint-Louis, a light drunkenness would seize me. With half-closed eyes, I saw the blue sky, the mirroring waters which threw to the ceiling a thousand circles within circles and sometimes – the moving flight of pigeons – a warm and soft caress, folding and unfolding wings whose shadows hardly appeared. Everything was delightful to me. Everything kept me late in bed in a

serene immobility when the beautiful burning day's youthfulness and my own faced each other and thought of nothing. What could I have wished more charming and more agreeable! I had these nudes in my home like a lover, they were women I loved and I felt alive beside them. And they were alive: their presence excited me, as the sun rising high in the sky filled my room with wonderful fire.

If I tasted the full measure of that happy tide, which is to real love what music is to poetry, I owe it to Modigliani; because at the same time, I imagined his dreadful life, his passion to paint, and I closed my eyes. He was standing there, looking at me and asking me as he did one winter's night, when half drunk:

"You? ... You love my painting ... Hey? And why? Do you understand it? ... You love it? ... As you love women? … So! So! So! ... Yes ... That's it ..."

Every morning the same delight was waiting me, or else, when I had bought something new, I would wake ten times during the night to light my lamp and grow absorbed in the inexpressible contemplation. It was like an enchantment, but such a singular one, so subtle, so voluptuous that, in remembering it, I almost regret those days when I owned nothing and I was the richest man alive amongst my paintings and the scattered pages of my first novels.

One would be hard-pressed to find such a scintillating piece of prose about the treasures that fell from Modigliani's brush. Particularly striking is the bizarre contrast that Carco creates between the poverty of his humble abode and the priceless gems glowing upon the peeling walls. I might add that to be alone with such a painting – especially one engendered by a modern master – is an experience that transcends the frame of mere words. But the real topper is that he's alone with a masterpiece that has yet to be recognized as one.

Carco's writing normally contains an abundance of visual ingredients, but oddly enough he neglects to include any specific details about these portraits except to remark upon their "milky and orange flesh." And yet, when I read this passage, the Modiglianis immediately came to life and assumed a palpable, enticing presence.

Perhaps that's because what Carco really portrays here is his own enchantment. Not only are these sensuous figures perfectly framed by the shimmering light, oscillating sound, and delicate fragrance that enters and fills the intimate space; they also subtly shift from objects of art into sentient creatures: the new lovers of this otherwise impoverished tenant, who grows "wealthy" in their beatitude.

"Not from earthly riches but from the milk of human kindness comes true beatitude" – but even more so, from the milky flesh of sensual delight.

*

When I first discovered *From Montmartre to the Latin Quarter* I was impressed by how it reads not only as a heartfelt memoir but also as a collective memorial to the dead. Their shadows flicker across the page as we trace their footprints moving in and out of Carco's life. I was also struck by how the culminating scenes of this chronicle lead to the opening lines of fellow *montmartrois* Louis-Ferdinand Céline's novel, *Voyage au bout de la nuit.*

Carco's book was published in 1927. Céline began work on *Voyage* only two years later, in 1929, completing it in 1931. Carco's memoir ends and Céline's novel begins with the same swirling mass of people taking to the street as war is declared and a blind and ferocious "patriotism" sweeps men directly into a dustbin of death. In both accounts the protagonists express a dim, cynical view of the war; yet they join in the charade anyway, without hesitating to enlist. Carco confesses:

> I was like the others, that is to say, I had no control over my actions. I was prey to a kind of folly and pushed on heedlessly through the streets which again became animated and were filled with thick, black waves of sacred fury.

He briefly stops at the Café Cyrano (fittingly, the brasserie of the Surrealists), where he meets with friends for a drink. Afterward, back on rue Blanche, they witness an assault: three thieves attack several young men, and for a moment Carco and his entourage are also threatened: "Suspicious individuals surrounded us for a moment and then ran away." How quickly the jingoistic patriotism has devolved into a noxious, petty criminality! "Everywhere in the mob pockets were picked shamelessly, there were battles and slowly the enthusiasm diminished."

Carco weaves his way through emptying streets, but suddenly the crowds well up again; gangsters intermingle with howling partisans; songs are feverishly sung; students parading with lanterns and waving flags "shouted like madmen: 'To Berlin! To Berlin!'" as "an echo of a thousand voices answered them." He then utilizes an ingenious device to unravel the meaning behind such frenetic, mindless actions:

Carco zooms in on the rippling flags – that ultimate symbol of boisterous nationalism – as they exert an increasingly hypnotic effect upon the minions streaming below. But all the while, they mask an insidious reality. He describes them as "billowing with a hellish palpitation" until they spread "like an immense shroud and swayed mockingly":

I think I see them still at the top of their poles unrolling their sinister and capricious caresses. They floated gracefully, twisted suddenly. Under their folds, moving like a scythe amongst the ripe corn, one would have said that already many young foreheads bent down brushed by an invisible hand.

But they soon stood up again, those smooth foreheads which death had marked before their time. They stood in front of him with a ferocious confidence that made me weak and hopeless. I saw flags no longer, but a horrible shroud with a long train red with blood. Why did not a voice come from that human flock to denounce the abominable and useless massacre which tomorrow was going to take place on the fields where the smell of earth and fruits is the only one permissible? One voice only would have been enough perhaps to change all that or, at least, to give to the immense gift of all those lives in their flower a more poignant and deeper significance ...

And there was no one, there was no one ... Only shouts, songs, more shouts, unheard clamorings ...

The voice of reason is silenced by the bellowing of the herd, as eager as ever to jettison itself off a cliff.

Compare this to the opening lines of *Voyage au bout de la nuit*. Ferdinand Bardamu (Céline's fictional alter ego) and his pal Arthur are seated at a café *terrasse*, sardonically debating the merits of the war:

But just then, who should come marching past the cafe where we're sitting but a regiment with the colonel up front on his horse, looking nice and friendly, a fine figure of a man! Enthusiasm lifted me to my feet.

"I'll just go see if that's the way it is!" I sing out to Arthur, and off I go to enlist, on the double.

"Ferdinand!" he yells back.

"Don't be an ass!" I suppose he was nettled by the effect my heroism was having on the people all around us.

It kind of hurt my feelings the way he was taking it, but that didn't stop me. I fell right in. "Here I am," I says to myself, "and here I stay."

I just had time to call out to Arthur: "All right, you jerk, we'll see" – before we turned the corner. And there I was with the regiment, marching behind the colonel and his band. That's exactly how it happened.

We marched a long time. There were streets and more streets, and they were all crowded with civilians and their wives, cheering us on, bombarding us with flowers from café terraces, railroad stations, crowded churches. You never saw so many patriots in all your life! And then there were fewer patriots ... It started to rain, and then there were still fewer and fewer, and not a single cheer, not one.

Pretty soon there was nobody but us, we were all alone. Row after row. The music had stopped. "Come to think of it," I said to myself, when I saw what was what, "this is no fun anymore! I'd better try something else!" I was about to clear out. Too late! They'd quietly shut the gate behind us civilians. We were caught like rats.[8]

By subtle, gradual degrees, the crowd's ebullient fervor is transformed into a tomblike silence, reflecting the narrator's grim sense of isolation: "We were all alone," "the music had stopped."

[8] Louis-Ferdinand Céline, *Journey to the End of the Night*, Ralph Manheim, trans., New York: New Directions, 1983, pp. 5-6. (Originally published as *Voyage au bout de la nuit*, Paris: Denoël et Steele, 1932.) On 25 October 1914, while serving in the 12th Cuirassier Regiment, Céline was wounded in the arm by enemy fire near Ypres. As a result of being thrown by an exploding shell, he suffered from severe tinnitus and chronic migraines for the rest of his life.

As literary historian Nicholas Hewitt notes in his meticulously researched work on Montmartre's cultural history, the regimental band that "whisks Bardamu away … implicitly alludes to the Pied Piper of Hamelin." Carco's narrative is even more explicit: "a kind of exaltation took hold of us, threw us into the street like everybody else and made us join with ardor all the other young men who were going, without knowing it, singing, to their death." And in Carco's account we encounter a similar shift in mood and action:

> Then, little by little, the streets became calmer. They were almost deserted when I arrived home, at nine o'clock, in the quai aux Fleurs, where I took from a drawer my draft papers, my military book and about twenty francs which, with the small change I had in my pocket, were all my riches at the time.

As is all too often the case, the poor will sacrifice life and limb in a conflagration that will serve to make the rich even richer.[9]

Hewitt concludes that, rather than being a realist or naturalist novel, *Voyage* exhibits all the telltale signs of an "eighteenth-century *voyage imaginaire*," or "imaginary journey." He raises the additional possibility that it functions as a "ghost story." Besides providing a Pied Piper motif, the regimental band

> also functions, however, in a way similar to the White Rabbit in that favorite text of the Surrealists, Lewis Carroll's *Alice in Wonderland*, who ensures a transition to the dreamworld which becomes the novel's space. In other words, Bardamu may either be presumed to be "dead" – in which case the novel employs the

[9] "Food shortages and lack of coal … made the winter of 1917 difficult. Workers' strikes broke out in revolt against high profits made by the war industry and a surge in prices for ordinary goods." Henri Colt, *Becoming Modigliani*, Laguna Beach, CA: Rake Press, 2024, p. 177.

> format of the ghost story – or undertaking an "imaginary voyage" in which the episodes of the war … are all projections forward into a dream …

In a subsequent paragraph, he continues:

> The status of *Voyage au bout de la nuit* as a ghost story is reinforced not only by the recurrent references by Bardamu to himself as a "ghost," but also by the initial description of Robinson, likened to the dead infantry major they encounter lying in a river. The ghost theme climaxes on All-Saints Eve, when Bardamu and Tanya … walk up to the place du Tertre and witness the extraordinary, and patently fantastical, spectacle of the "cavalcade des morts" – all the past characters in the novel, transformed into ghosts and flying over the Montmartre skyline.[10]

Céline's novel is riddled with figures of the dead who momentarily appear in Ferdinand's uncanny visions.[11] But whereas the ghosts in *Voyage* are mostly imaginary personages and don't necessarily reflect actual characters from the author's life, the specters that haunt Carco's memoir are very real indeed. The spectacle of a "cavalcade des morts" flying over place du Tertre would, in Carco's case, include poets such as Jean Pellerin, André du Fresnois, Apollinaire, and other friends and colleagues who struggled to creatively express themselves, only to be prematurely nipped in the bud. So many of these artists and writers perished from shrapnel, enemy fire, mustard gas, the impact of exploding shells, or wounds that grew

[10] Nicholas Hewitt, *Montmartre: A Cultural History*, Liverpool, UK: Liverpool University Press, 2017, pp. 252-253. See also Hewitt, *The Life of Celine: A Critical Biography*, Hoboken, NY: Wiley-Blackwell, 1991.

[11] Céline utilizes this device in his later work as well, helping us to suspend disbelief by having his protagonist conclude that such hallucinations are merely the result of "fever."

infected as they trudged through unsanitary, tubercular, mud-filled trenches. As was the case with André du Fresnois, some of their corpses were never even recovered.

Hewitt's notion of Bardamu "undertaking an 'imaginary voyage' in which the episodes of the war ... are all projections forward into a dream" calls to mind Carco's portrait of his friend du Fresnois in the memoir's penultimate chapter. For there, as well, the episodes of war are projections forward, into an imagined voyage that nonetheless culminates in a fatal and objective *reality*. This is what I mean:

André is standing on a chair in the street, mesmerized by a chanting mob that has become seduced by war fever,

> his whole being one with that mob, he, who ordinarily was so disdainful of crowds and who was ruled by the mind only, communed with the mob and consented to his own sacrifice. Then Jean Pellerin took hold of my arm, tightened his grip and pointed to our friend.
>
> "Look at him," he said in a low tone ... "Look ... He won't come back!"

"André!" Jean shouts, trying to snap him out of it. But when he fails to respond, Jean

> climbed up beside André du Fresnois on the same seat, drew him towards him and for more than an hour held him in a brotherly embrace and du Fresnois may have understood for he stopped shouting.
>
> Beside me, deaf to the applause, which came from the terrace of the Napolitain, like a continual fire of machine-guns, André du Fresnois's sweetheart was standing mute and motionless. Did she also have in that awful moment the presentment that André would soon be killed? [...]

> I must not be accused of having written these lines after du Fresnois's disappearance. He was already no longer amongst us! The look I saw behind his misty glasses impressed me so that it still haunts me and recalls to me the time when I first felt it.

The poignancy of the scene is amplified tenfold once we realize that André will be killed in combat in 1914 and that Jean will die from tuberculosis contracted during the war, in the summer of 1921. In the midst of this clangor and commotion their silent, loving, brotherly embrace remains one of the most touching cameos engraved in Carco's reminiscence. With lines that might easily have inspired Céline, Carco laments:

> I stir only ashes with my recollections – very fragile ashes which are lifted on the night wind and shaped like disembodied spirits – ghosts …

The impersonal imagery of wind and ash, and the rhythmic phrasing that imitates direct speech, anticipates Céline's prose style in the years ahead. The comparison between the two that's usually drawn, however, focuses more upon Carco's use of argot[12] in his depiction of *la pègre* or underworld, particularly in very early works such as *Jésus-la-Caille* (a practice soon taken up, with even greater effect, by Céline). As Carco's biographer points out, the eponymously named protagonist, a gay hooker who experiments with bisexuality, is "a type not previously treated at such length in novels dealing with this stratum of society … Carco does not either consider La Caille's sentiments as intrinsically abnormal or differentiate their quality from that

---

[12] See for example Jean-Jacques Bedu, *Francis Carco: Au coeur de la bohème* Éditions du Rocher, Monaco, 2001, p. 148, who writes of how Céline "drew inspiration and stylistic richness from [Carco's] novels, culminating in the success of *Voyage au bout de la nuit.*" (My translation.)

of the ordinary heterosexual."[13] At times bordering on pulp fiction, *Jésus-la-Caille* (1914) anticipates the French noir genre with its seedy bars, corrupt *flics*, brutal pimps, and endearing *filles de joie*.

Following the gender-bending portraits in *Jésus-la-Caille*, in 1916 Carco published *Les Innocents*, a novel depicting his former mistress, the author Katherine Mansfield, engaged in a lesbian affair with the British writer Beatrice Hastings. Carco's biographer informs us that *Les Innocents* was "censored for military reasons" – as if exposure to a tale about lesbian love might somehow be more dangerous than entering the trenches without a gas mask.

Another one of these noiresque novels worth mentioning is *Rien qu'une femme* (1921). It's the story of a boy named Claude who falls in love with Mariette, a servant at his mother's hotel. After their affair is exposed, Claude's domineering mother banishes Mariette from the premises, which leads the insouciant young lady into a life of prostitution. Her new vocation serves to further inflame Claude's ardor, turning him into a jealous yet impassioned cuckold. In an unexpected twist at the end, Mariette pairs with Claude's father, who, using Mariette's own money, sets her up as the proprietress of a cozy little bar (with the father working the bar deck), where she can live out her dream of making a safe and secure landing into the *bourgeoise*. Considered to be one of Carco's major works, *Rien qu'une femme* maintains a tightly spun literary texture from beginning to end. In another strange parallel with Céline, the English-language version of the work, titled "Only a Woman,[14] was translated by Ralph Manheim, whose unparalleled rendition of Céline's

---

[13] Seymour S. Weiner, *Francis Carco*, New York: Columbia University Press, 1952, p. 80. Published just a few years before Carco died, Weiner enjoyed the benefit of composing this biography with Carco's collaboration.

[14] Francis Carco, *Only a Woman*, Ralph Manheim, trans., New York: Berkley Publishing, 1953.

Voyage (and of Céline's later work) will probably remain forever unsurpassed.

While Céline was by far the greater writer, he lacked Carco's sentimental awareness with its focus on personal loss, enduring friendship, and joyous camaraderie. Céline as loner and miscreant would never have completed Carco's vignette in this same manner:

> And yet however far it may be from Montmartre to the Latin Quarter, the same ghosts are there, everywhere, alive and smiling and quick to touch me with the heady bitterness that rises from the past. But for them, I should not have been tempted to write this book. Should I have needed to set down here, like a guide, the record of our follies and of the places we used to haunt?

Indeed, Carco's account is a portrait not only of people but also of these "ghost" landscapes that exist only in memory. For, even if their physical structures endure, everything else has been radically altered:

> Alas! See what remains: memories, and some empty places. [...] The young men who have succeeded us are all there. May it be long before they find more sorrow than pleasure in counting over their friends!

This sentence marks the end of Carco's first chapter, thus setting the tone for the journey that lies ahead. But after all the adventures that subsequently unfold, in the final chapter we travel full circle, back to the theme of personal loss and the assuaging yet bitter phenomenon of memory:

> Memories? Yes ... Nothing more. Gay or sad, as light as the smoke I had seen mixed with the atmosphere, from

> the height of the small Blercourt cemetery, they have
> no other power than to evoke for the friends of my
> youth years which never will be given back to us.

After describing the billowing smoke of the Blercourt crematorium – where Carco's brother was interred after he lost his life in the war – Carco adds, almost as an afterthought:

> I have tried to show them much as they were at the
> time when I knew them.

Such an understated remark is pure Carco: a simple declaration of love between him and his fallen comrades, linked through the intercessor of memory.

*

Following these somber passages, the memoir concludes with a coda devoted to the final days of Modigliani. I find the placement of this segment to be rather fitting; for, with this gesture, he links the death of the artist (a martyr sacrificed to his vocation upon Montmartre's hill of martyrs) to the sacrificial slaughter of the young men of the Great War.

Carco's intimate association with Modigliani and with the artists and writers of Montmartre and Montparnasse lend these concluding pages a special resonance. The capstone is the portrayal of Modi's funeral procession. It's a unique personal memory, but Carco also notes its broader implications. For this is not only the death of a friend; it's also the end of an era, an end to Bohemia itself:

> From everywhere came comrades, dealers, humble
> people, owners of dives and models. They were all
> thunderstruck. With Modi, the last bohemian of his

generation – which had not been coddled by life – bohemia in the best sense of the word was disappearing.

But as far as Carco's imagination may take him, it remains overshadowed by the genius of Picasso. As if looming on the metaphoric apex of Montmartre and gazing down from the crown of the Butte (even though he's actually standing beside Carco in the vicinity of Père-Lachaise), it's Picasso who will deliver the crowning insight:

> Behind the hearse which, through a supreme irony, was covered with very expensive flowers and wreaths, an astonishing crowd followed. There were many painters, women, writers, the whole of Montmartre, the whole of Montparnasse, all united in a supreme homage to the memory of the departed friend who, during [his life of happenstance and disorder], had been deprived of more things than anyone else. Anecdotes were told. People talked about the work he left behind and following the procession, I saw in the ranks the friends of the unlucky Modi. They had all succeeded since the old days. They had all grown older and fatter. Some of them were celebrated, others were going to be: Picasso, Salmon, Max Jacob, Blaise Cendrars ... All were there. They denied nothing in the past. On the contrary. With Modi they were burying their youth, and the policemen who, on the way, clicked heels and saluted, perhaps were the same who, so many times, had taken Modi to the police station and who now certainly had no idea that their salute appeared in our eyes a rather belated but public reparation.
>
> It was Picasso, who, as always, drew from that spectacle the lesson it had for all of us, because, turning to me, and pointing first to the hearse where

Modigliani rested under mountains of flowers, and
then to the policemen at attention, he said softly:
"You see, he gets his revenge!"[15]

Only Picasso would have possessed the wit to recognize the meaning behind this final moment and to seize upon it with his painter's eye: the central focal point of a portrait unfolding before them, panorama-like, on the street. But it was Carco's genius to be there, at that precise moment, standing beside the master and chronicling the event. Perhaps it's this unerring "proximity to genius" that best summarizes his principal creative contribution.

As is the case with so many anecdotes in this memoir, the author's personal connection to the protagonists of that time and place allowed him to collect unique and vital information, which later formed the keynotes of various biographies. But even while relating incidents of a less consequential nature, his reminiscence is full of delightful surprises. A few that come to mind:

[15] Although there are many firsthand accounts of Modigliani being arrested for public intoxication and disturbing the peace, his police records have yet to surface. There may be a simple explanation for this. When the Nazis were pulling out of Paris, the Gestapo absconded with many of the files stored at the Prefecture de Police. Modi's dossier would have been tucked away in this burgeoning archive, which included extensive paperwork on foreigners and alien residents. And although his principal records have disappeared, thanks to the dogged pursuits of my assistant, Céline Cardon, we recently located a dossier labeled *Les amis d'Amedeo Modigliani* (file 359 W 57726) and a second police file titled *Alam Archive legale Amedeo Modigliani* (359 W 64823). We are now in the process of obtaining permission to view these records.

Sometimes the contents of the old dossiers are rather fragmentary. For example, a file on Modi's friend Charles Beadle, which Céline also obtained, contains merely a single sheet bearing the author's name, suggesting that the rest of his file was either pilfered or destroyed.

– When Max Jacob tries to trip up a young man who falsely claims to be a world traveler, Max informs him: "There is an alarm clock on the top of each mountain in Switzerland." His deadpan delivery is so impeccable that all the young fellow can say is: "It is quite possible."

– While remarking upon the "extraordinary radiance" that "hovered around" Picasso, Carco quotes one of Pablo's Zenlike aphorisms: "When you paint a landscape, it first must look like a plate."

– Despite the many commendable things that Carco relates about Apollinaire, for some reason this passage devoted entirely to his girth remains my favorite:

> His extreme stoutness, though it made him puff at the slightest effort, gave him an air of great authority. A gourmand in the best sense of the word, enormous, appetizing to look at, he broke between his teeth the bones served to him, sucked them, covered himself with grease and, then, telling some story about a painter, made his chair groan under his weight without worrying about his fate. What did he have to fear? He looked like some big laughing god, so steady upon his base that, even if the chair broke, he had his big hassock to soften the shock. The more he ate, the gayer he became, with a physical gaiety which shown all over him.

– Finally, sounding a more somber note, there's Carco's conversation with Mac Orlan and Max Jacob, when

> we remarked that only when a poet is abandoned by the whole world and battered by the bitterest or the tenderest of disillusionment, does he know why he was born and what fate has in store for him.
>
> At that time we all suffered from a deep and

> incurable disillusionment, but as recompense we had
> our friendships and experiences…. All of us paid with
> our best years for the sad knowledge of life and only
> the stronger amongst us have been able to stand it.

*

Though he was a man of many talents – poet, chansonnier, novelist, biographer – Carco's work as a memoirist remains his most enduring achievement. ("A blend of fact and fancy, his memoirs are perhaps the richest of his writings, and surely, in his works, outstandingly affecting.")[16] And under the category of "memoir" I would include his critical writing on artists, which, to his credit, often transcends the stultifying boundaries that one typically encounters in that genre (and in art "history" in general, much of which should be reclassified as works of rather unimaginative fiction). It's precisely because he injects himself so directly into these critical accounts – judging the artwork in accordance with his own personal reaction to it – that he succeeds so well.[17]

But in fact, Carco was not alone in this approach. Malcolm Gee reports that most French books about modern art during this epoch maintained a conservative viewpoint and focused on artists whose output "conformed in many ways to a traditional view of art – it was figurative, 'painterly,' and conformist in its subject matter – while possessing certain modern and 'progressive' characteristics."

---

[16] Seymour S. Weiner, *Francis Carco*, p. 147.

[17] Weiner makes the astute observation that, regardless of the literary form that Carco inhabits – poetry, fiction, drama, or essay – the body of his work remains "truly united," because "In all forms we have the conception of the poet. Whatever the subject, whatever the technical ordonnance, the interpretation is personal, poetic." Ibid., p. 192.

The other major feature of books on modern art was one common to all forms of criticism during this period – its concentration on the individual artist. Few books attempted to analyze a type of art, rather than an individual's output, expressive of his personal gift.... It was common to make a distinction between poets and professionals as critics of painting, usually in favor of the former. Up to a point, it was accurate to split up the body of art critics in this way: Apollinaire, Salmon, and Francis Carco, for instance, all writers who played a role as critics, had ambitions and attitudes which were different from those of 'professional' critics like Louis Vauxcelles or Waldemar George. Their education was less academic and they did not aspire to the editorship of learned reviews or to museum posts; often their relationship with the artists was closer, and their style of writing about them more effusive and less analytic.[18]

But Carco adds to this a deeply informed awareness of how painters such as Utrillo, Modigliani, and Vlaminck are linked to tradition while simultaneously transforming it.[19] By describing his interactions with these artists while plumbing the essence of their creations, he enables us to see things that would otherwise remain beyond our grasp.

For example, take this passage in which we're unexpectedly led to the subject of Utrillo:

[18] Malcolm Gee, *Dealers, Critics, and Collectors of Modern Painting: Aspects of the Parisian Art Market between 1910 and 1930*, New York: Garland, 1981, pp. 125-126.

[19] E.g., "The Fauves ... have become a part of [tradition] in the same violent measure that they once opposed it, for it is thanks to this fabric of actions and reactions that such things ultimately equilibrate themselves." Francis Carco, *Vertès*, Rosamond Frost, trans., New York: Athenaeum Publishing Co., 1946, p. 85.

> ... it was not only the women I loved but, most of all, the black streets, the low cafés, the cold, the fine rain upon the roofs, the bars, the chance meetings, and in the bedrooms an air of sad abandon which tightened my heart. The tragic winter nights, so dark and so pathetic, fascinated me and gave me such sensations that, perfectly insensible to other attractions than theirs, I intoxicated myself, as with a bitter wine, with my own misfortunes.

At first we assume that he's speaking only of himself. But then we realize that this "self" has also been projected upon the surrounding landscape – or shall we say, is eerily *reflected* within it. And then, without warning, the paragraph breaks and we encounter a painter who does the same thing with pigment that Carco has just attempted to accomplish with words:

> Has not Utrillo expressed in his work that secret and cruel obsession which during a certain period of his life pursued him more than any other? It has laid its weight on our teens with a heavy load and has marked the men of my generation with such a mysterious sign that without it they would have no means of recognizing themselves.

"The men of my generation"! The words are shaped with a tone of such world-weariness; who would guess that Carco was only thirty-nine years old when this memoir was first completed, on 6 December 1925? But in the aftermath of a world war that filled the air with so many specters – in France alone, 1.4 million dead and 4.2 million wounded – he's speaking in a way that perhaps only those of that time and place can truly understand.

In Utrillo it can be seen at once, as he has cherished his illness and has dissected it so minutely that he could not deny it. Recall the perspectives, deserted for the most part, of his Paris streets and of the suburbs. There shines upon the walls, upon the houses with closed shutters, upon the brown windows of bistros a fixed light which comes from nowhere, except from those dream regions which no one dares talk about. And what anxiety there is, an anxiety that cannot be captured, what an ambiguous, fleeting, unattainable presence, what a piercing call! It seems that, at the precise minute when he could have helped us, the only human being alive in the world had just turned around the corner of those plaster houses and disappeared forever. Why has he not heard?

He pauses for a moment to further describe Utrillo's painting, *Champeau washhouse*, zooming in an enormous sign that floats horizontally across the composition, reading: "Lavoir Champeau." Then he concludes:

> … you look at it, you approach it with curiosity, as if, from behind the shutters someone were watching you, and you act as if you had not seen him. But is one sure of anything? Isn't it rather that other self, which every man spends his life crushing down, who before this canvas awakes as if by enchantment? Those places are so familiar to that other self! He knows them. I mean to say, he recognizes them and the emotion that seizes him – at that moment – is one which only a few human beings can feel […]

Here, Carco adroitly places his finger on the pulse that drives us right up to the canvas's edge and draws us in – to the fundamental visions that buoy one's soul. This is certainly not the discourse of ordinary art history; but it is the plain and simple truth. (He was writing about Utrillo in this same manner as early as 1921; for example, he speaks of a painting in which both the sky and "a kind of inner fervor illuminate the severe horizon and the desolate perspectives.")[20] The memoir passage continues:

> I felt then a fear and an uneasiness which I did not analyze, and in the streets where I roamed very late, I had the impression of being swept into the confused and blind totality of existence which stalks about at night, in secret, haunts desperately, comes and goes ... borne by the wind. I can't express myself better [...]

That's not to say that Carco possessed infallible taste or that his critical acumen was always on point. Among his more egregious breaches of discernment we would have to include his assessment of Cubism as "essentially Jewish in its origins" (a remark that rightfully irked his friend Max Jacob) "and destined by its development ... to be of less aid in the triumph of art than to an exchange of ideas and theories where art took second place." (Malcolm Gee notes that Carco's attitude to painting "combined the modernism of Salmon with the anti-intellectualism of Vauxcelles.")[21] And how could the same man who collected Picassos have ever considered the daubs of the illustrator Marcel Vertès to be worthy of his attention? Carco's effusions over these meritless sketches are, at best, embarrassing (not least because the high caliber of his writing

[20] When Carco's collection went on the auction block in 1925, the list included more work by Utrillo than by any other artist. The fourteen Utrillo lots included a drawing, a pastel, six lithographs, and six oil paintings. Several of these are reproduced in Carco's early tribute to the painter, *Les Peintres Français Nouveaux N°. 8: Utrillo* (1921; part of series of booklets published by La Nouvelle Revue Française), which is the source of this quote. (My translation.)

[21] Malcolm Gee, *Dealers, Critics, and Collectors of Modern Painting*, p. 141.

style overshadows its inferior subject matter).[22] Perhaps there's no accounting for taste! But there's also no accounting for his prescient ability to recognize – so far in advance – the genius of men such as Utrillo, Modigliani, and Max Jacob. Or of Apollinaire, whom he regarded not only as an avant-garde poet but also as an innovative essayist whose critical work would remain enduring.

We should also bear in mind that Carco's fundamental preference was always centered round a "modern" art that also highlighted traditional ingredients. For example, his inclination always leaned more toward Picasso's Rose and Blue Period rather than the more avant-garde formulations of Cubism. A similar dynamic was at work regarding his interest in Derain, Vlaminck, and the Fauves. As Nicholas Hewitt has remarked, "Fauvism increasingly pointed in two directions." One reflected "the Fauves' appreciation of Jarry's vitality and iconoclasm and their flirtation with anarchism in the early 1900s …" But certain Fauvist works also "testify to both a nostalgia for a lost golden age and a movement toward classicism."[23] (The latter tendency would remain closer to Carco's sensibilities.)

The same could be said regarding the work of Utrillo (nostalgia) and Modigliani (classicism). That is, a pull in two directions at once: an anchoring to a classical tradition (and, in Modi's case, even to antiquity) but also a propulsion forward, into a future unknown. It was often this type of creation – so finely balanced on a cusp of dual polarities – which attracted Carco's attention. But this may also explain why some of the more traditional visual artists that he chronicles in his memoir now remain largely forgotten. One also suspects that these tributes are rooted just as much in a passion for friendship as

[22] See Francis Carco, *Vertès*.
[23] Nicholas Hewitt, *Montmartre*, pp. 120-121.

they are in whatever aesthetic interest the work may have held for him.

*

Carco doesn't only concern himself with cultural figures. His richly textured interactions with both ordinary people and the denizens of the underworld are featured throughout his writing, especially in his fiction. One episode that stands out in the memoir is a simple tale that reveals much about his empathy for the poor and downtrodden, who comprise a great swath of the Parisian landscape. At the chronicle's midpoint Carco reminisces about his early days in the capital, shortly after he arrived there in 1910:

> Paris with its brasseries, its cafés, its carriages, its perpetual and feverish animation frightened me. I did not know many people, and when I sat in the bars and looked at the women, they inspired in me more astonishment than desire and I did not dare go near them. One of them whom I met at the Taverne du Panthéon and whom I secretly admired, was very much amused by my shyness.

This seasoned Latin Quarter prostitute must have taken one look at young Carco and sized him up accordingly – as a country bumpkin with Parisian stardust beclouding his precocious vision. Carco paints her thus:

> She was a [brunette], very [loose], who smoked luxurious cigarettes with gold tips, and who, far from [sticking to her prices], accepted when the café was closing, anything that was offered. It never occurred to me to take advantage of such a reduction in price and one evening the woman herself spoke to me,

explaining that her feet were hurting her and asked me for three francs so that she could take a carriage to go home.

He dutifully surrenders the cash but then witnesses a little miracle: "I saw the charming borrower forget all about her feet, and run as fast as she could to a bakery, where women of her kind went on feasting the whole night."

Although remorseful over neglecting his own basic needs, the young pilgrim is quick to acknowledge that he's learned a lesson: "That incident taught me more about those women than a whole night spent with one would have, because I missed the three francs dreadfully the next day." Then he goes into detail about what, exactly, those francs might have purchased to ease his alimentary woes. For, at this point, the author is still quite poor:

> At that time one could eat three square meals for that sum, and even drink and smoke as well. In the rue de la Montagne-Sainte-Geneviève [...] our meals cost twelve sous. Bread, ten centimes; meat, thirty centimes; vegetables, fifteen; hot chocolate, one sou, so that from three francs there was enough left for luxury.

Typical for those enduring such a marginal existence, every franc must be carefully considered: one must learn to master a form of microeconomics that is not yet taught at the London School of Economics. By sharing such minutia, the author is also ensuring that we grasp the full measure of his suffering. He concludes: "But I thought philosophically, one must learn, and I did not trouble myself anymore about it." This completes the first part of a triptych depicting his down-and-out lifestyle.

On another night, at first he's blessed with the possession of a gold coin that will render its bearer "a week of ease." With said lucre in hand, he crosses the Petit Pont (site of the oldest and shortest bridge in Paris) and wanders into the *parvis* of Notre-Dame:

A fine winter rain was wetting the pavements and the roadway, the dark shrubs shone along the quay and in a line around the *parvis*, and the gaslights were glowing. No one was abroad at such a time, except a *garde-républicain* who, to keep warm, was stamping his feet in his sentry box and grumbling under his long coat. He saluted me as I passed near him and as I turned around to greet him in return, the coin I held in my hand escaped me and rolled I don't know where.

"Oh, how stupid!"

"What is the matter?" asked the *garde*.

"I had ten francs …"

"Ten francs!"

"Yes," I said, very much upset, "and now it's gone …"

"You must look for it," said the *garde* as he stopped stamping his feet on the bottom of his box. "It can't have rolled very far …"

Next, he's approached by "a miserable beggar" who volunteers to help him locate his precious booty:

He was down on his knees, feeling in the dirty water, searching on the ground, his fingers moving along slowly in the mud.

"We'll share, hey," he asked, "you promise?"

"Of course."

"Well, then, old man, have patience!"

A great moment! And one after another my matches went out, while the indefatigable beggar carefully explored the pavement. Soon, other individuals as blue with cold as he was, and intrigued by our conduct, had joined us. They came out from under the shrubs which are at the foot of Charlemagne's statue and, hearing what was the matter, began looking also. Some women came as well and also searched in the rain. I was tired and unhappy at the site of all those miserable people who, for five francs, silently prayed luck to be good to them and were watching each other covertly. Suddenly I could not stand it anymore. I gave up the search and went home very sadly.

"How pitiful!" I thought.

The invisible coin works like a lure to attract the heretofore-invisible presence of the homeless and destitute, hidden beneath the shrubbery of an otherwise glamorous city. They are its sub-rosa spectacle – Picasso's Blue Period come to life, just barely – with flesh tinted an icy hue from the freezing cold. Instead of being repulsed by them, when the filthy beggar sticks his hand into a wretched gutter ("his fingers moving along slowly in the mud") and advises Carco to "have patience!" Carco turns to us and announces that this is, indeed, "A great moment!"[24]

But he finally departs: not out of disgust, but due to unbearable sadness. His heart is pained by the sight of all those individuals, "blue with cold," who are forced to shelter beneath that heroic bronze figure of Charlemagne, and who, "for five francs, silently prayed luck to be good to them and were watching each other covertly."[25]

[24] Describing Carco's emotional connection to the prisoners in the penal colony administered by his father, Carco's biographer says: "there was implanted early a responsive feeling of innate sympathy for those generally deemed repellent." Seymour S. Weiner, *Francis Carco*, p. 14.

[25] During the early 1900s, a young Swiss doctor named Carl Jung wandered through the streets of Paris in a state of near shock over the notorious scenes of social injustice. As he would later recall: "In Paris, two phenomena touched me deeply: one was the beautiful art and the other was *la misère qui a froid, la misère noire* [the misery that is cold, the black misery].... Paris

When he returns home and begins to undress, the treasured coin emerges from a crease in his "old trousers" and falls to the floor. And this is where the petals of the story really unfold, revealing an essential ingredient in Carco's character:

> I kept for a long time a painful recollection of those ten francs which I used instead of dividing them. I am still ashamed when I think about it. I asked for the beggar the next day of the passersby, at the same time, at the same place, but nobody was able to give me any information. Necessity kept me from insisting anymore. Days and years have passed and if now I think of that night only rarely, it is still very difficult for me to cross the Petit Pont without feeling a tightness around my heart ...

A third and final vignette is also instructive, for it portrays the depth of the author's impoverishment: an experience that links him directly to the tattered figures that trigger such mercy:

> Everywhere in that damp quarter the same impression follows me, for no matter where I go I see myself penniless and tormented by a smell of warm chestnuts which aggravated my hunger. [...] I had not always

made an enormous impression on me. On the one hand such beauty and on the other such terrible squalor. Actually, I found myself in a terrible state. I'd never seen anything like it before. The whole of human misery ... I was completely occupied with dark thoughts about the suffering of humankind, about the gaping black abyss. Feelings of a *grande compassion* surged in me.... That people could find Paris *amusant* baffled me. I was far too affected by the social tragedy.... Paris was either wonderfully beautiful, tasteful and elegant – or it was a pit of squalor. I found it very difficult to bear.... I would not wish to have missed this time of poverty. It taught me to appreciate the simple things." Aniela Jaffe, *Reflections on the Life and Dreams of C. G. Jung*, Einsiedeln, Switzerland: Daimon Verlag, 2023, pp. 25-26.

the twelve sous which my friends paid for their meals at the Montagne and I had often to go without eating.

He spends three days fasting in bed, "under a gable in the garret where I had taken my abode," but then he wanders out at night, trembling in the bitter cold. He feels "done up, vanquished, lost":

> Unsteady on my legs, wandering here and there, lightheaded, I soon landed on a bench in the boulevard de Sébastopol [...] I was looking without seeing, listening without hearing, to the trams and the heavy market trucks rumbling by, when an old woman who had been haunting the neighborhood for a while came and sat down beside me.
>
> She was a sordid creature with an old boa around her neck, its feathers flying in the wind, a ridiculous hat, mittens and a canvas bag. What did she want? Either I could not understand the words she said or else she was crazy. I drew away slowly.
>
> "Well, are you coming," she said, looking hard at me. "Well? Come along ..."
>
> She scanned my face, shook her head and asked:
>
> "[You look clean, though.] What is the matter? It does not please you? ..."
>
> "No, no," I said ... "Go away!"
>
> And as she was hesitating:
>
> "Don't you see," I cried suddenly, "that I am hungry?"
>
> "What?"
>
> "Oh, leave me alone!"
>
> The old woman came closer and then, convinced I did not lie, went away silently and came back two minutes later with a big hunk of warm and appetizing bread which she laid without a word upon the bench.

The poet who knows so well how to describe beggars now portrays himself as one, lending us a clue about the wellspring of his empathy for the impoverished souls of Paris.

*

Much of this emotional awareness was fostered by Carco's flânerie through the underbelly of the City of Light, but I'm convinced that it also germinated from deeper – and more painful – roots in his past. Thanks to Seymour Weiner's groundbreaking biography, we have at our disposal a few relevant facts about the alienation that Carco suffered as a child: a victim of his father's iron fist during those very early, impressionable years.

Born on 3 July 1886 in Nouméa, New Caledonia, François Carcopino-Tusoli was the son of a thick-skinned Corsican named Jean-Dominique and of his Niçoise wife, Marie-Antoinette Roux. New Caledonia was "home" to thousands of prisoners; and, in many ways, Francis could be considered as one of them. His father was the administrator in charge of the penal colony in Nouméa; and, judging from the information that Carco shares with his biographer, Jean-Dominique never once considered sparing the rod to spoil his child. But which category of prisoner would Carco fit into?

Weiner provides a brief history of the colony and of its prison population, which was composed of three main groups. First, there were the *déportés* or political prisoners, including "four thousand Communards of 1871," who "furnished the backbone of the labor supply in the pioneer days of New Caledonia." The second group was composed of *relégués* or "habitual criminals judged to be of 'perversité incurable.'" The third group, *transportés*, were "serious offenders" who, along with the *relégués*, were "condemned to hard labor."

At the time of Carco's birth, there were between five to seven thousand prisoners in the penal colony administered by the Inspector of the Domains of the State – Carco's father. If Jean-Dominique had been gifted with the vision of divine omniscience, he would have been aghast at how his son sympathized with – and even admired – such characters of habitual and incurable perversity, memorializing their Parisian counterparts in his later works of poetry and prose. (One of his novels is even titled *Perversité*.)

"Serious offenders" are also richly portrayed in Carco's fiction; and the view the author takes is that the nature of their dramatic arc through life is more or less inevitable, given their dismal background, narrow set of choices, and tendency to react impulsivity to certain events, thus guaranteeing their own victimization. In this sense, many are "foredoomed."[26]

Regarding the *déportés* or political prisoners, one wonders if Carco gave them thought during the dire days of the Nazi Occupation. As Nicholas Hewitt points out, while some of Carco's friends, such as Roger Dorgelès and Mac Orlan, were borderline collaborators, Carco avoided such pitfalls while maintaining his friendships with those on the Left.[27]

[26] "Carco's predilection is not, however, with his characters' actions, but with their impulses. One reason for his fascination with this world of criminals and parasites and profiteers on mankind's baser instincts is its elemental character. These people follow their instincts, though they themselves do not well comprehend what motivates them, nor can they express articulately why they act as they do. The science of the author is to make comprehensible what is obscure to them. He examines them with passionate interest, but he does not claim to be omniscient. There is much that remains obscure, unexplained." Ibid., pp. 171-172, 184.

[27] "Dorgelès and Mac Orlan, like many of their Montmartre peers, adopted a conservative political stance as the interwar period progressed, which led them to a modest level of collaboration during the Occupation, an activity which Carco, who had friends on the left, like Aragon and Elsa Triolet, was able to avoid." And Mac Orlan was even a supporter of Franco! See Nicholas Hewitt, *Montmartre*, p. 204.

Furthermore, during the Occupation, Carco and his Jewish wife, Éliane Négrin, were forced to seek exile in Switzerland.

One can only imagine what the Nazis would have thought of *Jésus-la-Caille*, with its sympathetic portrayal of underworld characters and its flamboyantly bisexual protagonist, all of whom the Nazis would have regarded as mere "degenerates." For that matter, one wonders what Carco's father thought about all this. Perhaps we have a clue in a passage that appears later in the memoir. When an American reporter asks Carco, "What is the thing that has astonished you most?" he responds:

> "The thing which has astonished me most? Well," I said, "I think my being able to earn my living by telling stories which my parents would not have tolerated at table."

In any case, based on biographical information, we can plainly discern three principal forces at work in shaping our young writer:

One is his daily exposure to the prisoners, even if they were viewed only from a distance as they were marched through the street. Carco's biographer describes a remarkable form of communication that existed "between the convicts and the children": a "mute affection expressed by a smile or a wink, which these men, bereft of home and family, displayed as much as they dared towards the youngsters." We should bear in mind that this information recorded by his biographer must be coming directly from Carco, who still held the memory dear. Weiner also displays an acute awareness of Carco's situation when he adds:

> Instinctively young Francis felt the uncritical hungering affection of these men, and felt, too, that regardless of their position in society, as human beings

they were akin to the most proper in his sphere.... His own conduct, so censured by his family, may have made him feel a personal affinity for these lawbreakers.

Then he reaches a startling conclusion: "At times these men must have seemed more tender and kind than his own father."

Another preeminent developmental force is the sympathetic treatment that Carco receives from his mother and from the native servants that share his home, several of whom possess delightfully eccentric qualities. The strange stories these islanders tell, the warmth of their personalities, and their "exotic" (i.e., non-French) manner must have planted influential seeds in his character.

The third – and most potent – formative force was the domineering nature of his father, who seemed determined to do everything in his power to turn his son against him. In a rather unsettling passage we learn all we need to know about this terrifying figure:

> Jean-Dominique was an industrious, ambitious, very methodical person. It was only by chance he had been offered a position in New Caledonia rather than a post elsewhere. Even in the Pacific, or perhaps all the more so because he was in the Pacific, he was determined to live the careful and logical life of a sensible man in a secure position offering a comfortable future. His duties, which required him to visit various prison camps and to frequent criminals, disposed him the more strongly to conduct his home according to conservative bourgeois principles. Strong tempered, autocratic, the dominant influence in the home, he had a powerful nature.
>
> The disciplined rhythm of the domestic routine had its insidious counterpart in the spectacle of prisoners

tramping in ordered file through the streets to and from labor assignments. The fetish made of conformity at home clashed with the wild-growing natural surroundings. Strict obedience, exacted by paternal authority, contrasted strongly with the stories of violence and revolt related by the servants. Especially bewildering for the child were his father's abrupt shifts in humor, veering from dispassion to vehemence. Francis had the intimate feeling that his father was fundamentally violent, but as ruthless with himself as with others. In this atmosphere the boy was unable to establish a harmonious equilibrium. He found that he was a rebel in spirit and mentality, that he could not seem to do the right thing in the right way at the right time, that there was a serious deficiency and distortion in his values. Peccadilloes were punished with severe beatings and strong censure. Most of the time a mutually antipathetic attitude prevailed. But where another child might have submitted, at least on the surface, young Francis did not knuckle under.

The father would fly into a terrible rage at the lack of conformity and the insubordination in his son and would beat him to the point of their mutual exhaustion. There were times when he came close to infanticide, so hotly was he spurred on by the mute resistance of his own flesh and blood. Years later he was to avow to Francis that he had never known another child to have been beaten as much as his own son. But just as Fortunato submitted to the decision of Mateo Falcone,[28] so Francis, like the true Corsican he considered himself to be, never revolted physically against the punishment ordered for him. It became a point of honor with him to take these beatings without a murmur. Pride in moral resistance was augmented

---

[28] A reference to "Mateo Falcone" (1929), Prosper Mérimée's short story set in Corsica, in which a father kills his son as retribution for an act that the father deems as treasonous.

by a growing pleasure in the giving and receiving of suffering. In the obscure depths of his sensual nature a perverse taste for hurt made him enjoy the dejection and loneliness of being an outcast. He found that there was pleasure in the intense feeling of anguish at being rejected, at his fall from his father's good graces – an aspect of the algolagnia which was later to be exteriorized in his art. He sought refuge for his unhappiness and a palliative to his hate in the escape offered by his more sympathetic surroundings. Lying in the grass, he would sob out his pain alone. In spite of resentment and anger, he felt murkily that there was a very close temperamental affinity between him and his father, and that the father was offering him as a sacrifice to exercise the latent devil in himself. To his oldest child he was indeed a bewildering personality.[29]

This "bewildering personality" is a textbook example of what we would now refer to as a *personality disorder*. The abrupt and extreme mood swings (alternating between icy antagonism and boiling rage); the condemnation of all those who fail to behave in exactly the fashion he expects and demands; and a deeply engrained sadism that shapes the hollow core of his being are all telltale signs of pathological narcissism and sociopathy. The sociopath refuses to allow independence of thought or action in anyone but himself, censuring and condemning all those who fail to mirror his preordained expectations.

If Jean-Dominique had been a fictional character in a novel, his middle name would be perfectly fitting. The term *dominate* is from the Latin *dominatus,* past participle of *dominari,* from *dominus,* "master"; akin to Latin *domus* "house." Therefore, the meaning of the name *Dominique* or *Dominicus* is "Lordly," "of the Lord," "belonging to God," or "of the Master." Quite a lot for the "master of the house" to live up to.

[29] See Seymour S. Weiner, *Francis Carco*, pp. 4-14.

But if a child refuses to submit and to follow the script, where does he go when faced with such terrors? He can either run away from home (an action that may get him into even more dire straits), or he can stand there and make himself numb, bury his authentic self in an act of emotional detachment, and wait for that moment when, later in life, the self may be safely exhumed and given a chance to manifest its authenticity and uniqueness – freed from the destructive milieu of the parental world and its demand to accommodate pathology.[30]

In refusing to respond to the father's abuse – by just standing there and stubbornly taking it without a whimper – Carco was accomplishing two things. He was insulting his paterfamilias via an act of nonviolent resistance; and he was attempting to escape into an inner world. That world is where the artist belongs, where he finds his deepest haven, and where he is essentially reborn. But it's not a place where one can find material sustenance or the type of worldly experience, enriching friendship, and external support that truly nourishes the soul.

As he grows older, such an abused child may be attracted to those marginal, outlier spaces where he can temporarily elude the surveillance of the parental eye and nurture his emotional independence. But unless he can forge a suitable vocation, the escape into such liminal spaces may result in a second type of prison: chronic exile from the institutions of the broader conventional world.

Consider for a moment the hobo poet Villon, whom Carco adored and wrote about in his quasi-fictional biography, *Le roman de François Villon* (1926). Like Villon, Carco feels most at "home" in the taverns and brothels, where he even recites Villon to his friends, the hookers. In portraying his gambol along the road to excess, Carco describes a street that "was not

---

[30] For more on the protective interment and eventual exhumation of the authentic self, see Alice Miller, *Prisoners of Childhood*, New York: Basic Books, 1979, whose terminology is utilized here.

very prepossessing. Some *bistrots*, some dark little shops, some hotels and third-rate houses of prostitution succeeded each other from left to right and its damp pavements, its panes thick with dirt, its untidy and unclean shop windows gave it all together a very unpleasant appearance." Yet,

> it was in that street we met at night as friends of the girls and of the harpies who exploited them. We were very poor clients but we were welcome, they offered us drink [...] In exchange for stories and songs the white wine was poured ad libitum [...] A thick air filled the room, between its plastered walls, under the gas jets on the ceiling which lighted the room crudely. But what did it matter! We were under cover. We listened to the rain falling and to the verses of François Villon [...] Must I be frank? No other place pleased us as much. [...] Where could we have gone? There was not much choice for us. Here or there, I mean, in the brasseries or in the strange shops of the Quarter, we would have found very much the same people.

Unlike Villon, even when he was down and out in Paris, Carco never ended up homeless. He was drawn to the legends of the street; he romanticized the rain-slicked cobblestone and the blinking lights advertising the dance halls, not to mention the blood-red glow of curtains drawn in the rooms of the *grandes horizontales*; yet he always managed to stay afloat, even if just barely. But how did all this psychological baggage affect his artistry?

To cite just one example, we might examine the thematic connection between *Perversité* (1925) and *Rien qu'une femme* (1921). In a single word, it's the motif of cuckoldry. But a more convoluted dynamic is also at play: the notion that relationships are based on one partner physically and psychologically dominating the other. Instead of empathy there's a power complex, which eclipses and destroys any capacity to experience actual love. Hence, cuckoldry is simply one manner of expressing the domination / submission polarity.

Without a doubt, this was implanted within Carco as a result of being mistreated by Jean-Dominique, who subjected him to such brutality that Carco developed a certain taste for sadomasochism. Carco's mother was also completely under the thumb of her husband. Therefore, this was the model of "relationship" that was imprinted within the young boy's psyche as being "normal."

There was also an event in Carco's early life that shaped the expression of this power complex on the erotic level. In his 1938 memoir, *À voix basse*, Carco describes how, when he was an adolescent, he would visit a coquette who would allow him to watch as she dressed in lingerie and prepared to meet her lover. Carco would burn with desire, but he wasn't allowed to do anything. He could only passively observe until she abruptly dismissed him. The connection between this actual event and the overarching theme of *Rien qu'une femme* is clear:

> Carco has claimed that his personal experiences with venal lovemaking of a voluptuous nature were limited to (regretfully) passive attendance at the toilette of a local belle. She would invite him to her room and let him look on in rapt hunger while she prepared to go to an amorous rendezvous. Carco permits himself the metaphor of saying that the fire in the room "burned with all my senses" while she perversely allowed her slip to slide along her body to nestle in a little swirl of silk at her feet, and would then slowly strip off her stockings. The sinuous contortions of her arms as she arranged her hair before dressing fascinated him. When she was ready to leave, she would dismiss him with a pert tap on his flushed cheek. By then it was time for him to go home where he was obliged to

remain for the night. All the heartache and febrile longing of these envies and these desires found their expression later in the fictional reminiscences of *Rien qu'une femme*.[31]

We can plainly see how the author transposed his experience into a plotline that unfolds between Claude and Mariette. Just as Mariette's life of prostitution fuels a seething, all-consuming jealousy that inflames Claude's submissive desires, in *Perversité* we encounter a similar situation in which the protagonist, Emile, is forced to listen to the woman he loves (his sister, Irma) having sex with other men. Irma psychologically dominates Emile while she, in turn, is controlled, dominated, and abused by her pimp, Bébert.

Emile is gradually overwhelmed by his unconscious craving for incest, which at first makes itself felt as an obscure urge: an imposing presence whose meaning is only dimly perceived and haltingly acknowledged, but never understood for what it truly is. Fantasizing about Irma's "slightest movements" and attempting "to follow and anticipate them," "Emile welcomed these images with a feeling that he dared not analyze." Then comes their gradual transposition onto other, more acceptable female "presences," which "substituted themselves in his mind for Irma's." Until finally, "when Irma came home with a man, he strained his ears to listen." As with the chief protagonist of

---

[31] Weiner, *Francis Carco*, p. 43, citing *À voix basse* as the source of this information. In an interview published in *Les Nouvelles Littéraires* on 30 January 1932 Carco is quoted as saying that, from *Rien qu'une femme* onward, "I have always continued to write in the first-person; believe me, there is no ploy involved: the identification between the character who speaks and myself is absolute." And since, technically speaking, his novels are actually composed in the third-person, regarding them (figuratively) as first-person confessions is particularly revealing. ("J'ai toujours continué à écrire à la première personne; croyez bien qu'il n'y à l à aucun procédé: l'identification entre le personnage qui parle et moi-même est absolue.") Ibid., p. 235, n. 44.

Rien qu'une femme, in *Perversité* Emile acknowledges that his suffering is "full of obscure delights."[32] Although Irma and Emile never act upon their mutual but unspoken desire, Emile's initial reaction is essentially identical to that of a scorned lover confronted with infidelity – and it eventually leads to homicidal revenge.

Rien qu'une femme's open-ended conclusion poses the possibility that Claude may himself become a pimp, as it's the only thing he's properly wired for. This raises the intriguing notion that pimps are, in fact, cuckolds, because their women offer sexual satisfaction to other men. Yet the pimps pretend not to be, because, supposedly, their partners engage with others only for monetary gain, while retaining their true love for the pimp. (Some prostitutes are even known to reserve a special area on their flesh that only the pimp may kiss or caress.)

In any case, the portrayal of power and subservience remains a predominant theme in Carco's novels. In this context we should revisit a quote from Carco's biographer: "It became a point of honor with him to take these beatings without a murmur. Pride in moral resistance was augmented by a growing pleasure in the giving and receiving of suffering. In the obscure depths of his sensual nature a perverse taste for hurt made him enjoy the dejection and loneliness of being an outcast. He found that there was pleasure in the intense feeling of anguish at being rejected, at his fall from his father's good graces – an aspect of the algolagnia which was later to be exteriorized in his art." E.g., in the dramatis personae of *Perversité*, *Rien qu'une femme*, and works of fiction such as *Jésus-la-Caille*, which centers around a streetwalker who's rejected and abandoned by her violent pimp, then beaten and mistreated by a bisexual lover. The latter is the novel's eponymous protagonist who's ironically named after the

[32] Francis Carco, *Perversity*, Jean Rhys, trans., Chicago: Pascal Covici, 1928, pp. 109-110, 113.

tormented, tortured, and crucified god of love. Ever-brewing in the background of each of these tales is a "suffering full of obscure delights" counterpointed by a sadist's "mysterious attraction"[33] to inflicting pain.

But these are more than just portraits of conquest and defeat. Pushed to their existential limits, the protagonists exist, like Emile, "in a strange world" replete with fears and "modest pleasures." And instead of accruing insight into their own unconscious motivation, they confront themselves either as shadows in an opaque mirror or as depersonalized specters witnessing an incipient self-destruction, wrought largely through blind acts of compulsion.

As noted earlier, judging from the information that Carco has rendered to his biographer, it's safe to say that Jean-Dominique was a raging, pathological narcissist – or even something worse, verging on the psychopathic. As a result of numerous clinical studies, we now know that such brutal physical discipline can lead to chronic clinical depression: one that may stretch over the course of a lifetime.[34] We also know that Major Depressive Disorder features suicidal ideation in approximately 48% of the cases.[35] Viewed from another angle, it "accounts for up to 87% of completed suicides."[36]

[33] Ibid., p. 180.

[34] "Corporal punishment is associated with increased anxiety and depressive symptoms in adolescence. However, our study goes further to demonstrate that corporal punishment might impact brain activity and neuro-development." Elsevier, "Corporal Punishment Affects Brain Activity, Anxiety, and Depression," *Science Daily*, 16 November 2022, sciencedaily.com, quoting Kreshnik Burani.

[35] Elyas Basha, et al., "Suicidal Ideation and Its Associated Factors among Patients with Major Depressive Disorder at Amanuel Mental Specialized Hospital, Addis Ababa, Ethiopia," *Neuropsychiatric Disease and Treatment*, 21 May 2021, pp. 1571- 1577, dovepress.com.

[36] Hong Cai, et al., "Prevalence of Suicidality in Major Depressive Disorder," *Frontiers in Psychiatry*, 16 September 2021, frontiersin.org.

Although he lacked such clinical tools and insights, Carco's biographer noticed how the shadow of depression was cast across the writer's life. He says that Carco suffered from "fits of weakness" and, at times, "felt completely exhausted, incapable of the slightest exertion."

> The characteristic was a physical inability to engage in any activity, coupled with intellectual and spiritual vacuity. It was as though he 'blacked out.' Then he would pretend illness and remain in bed until renewed interest and energy were consciously felt. Although he was ashamed of these depressions and attempted to surmount them, they were beyond his control. First felt at Toulouse, they were to occur periodically throughout later years.[37]

Not surprisingly, Carco records his melancholy in various parts of his chronicle, although he never recounts his father's abysmal behavior. But years later, perhaps in response to this psychological quagmire, in his typically understated fashion Carco remarked: "My father and I never had anything to say to one another."[38]

All this is not to psychologize the writer but to place his plight in a broader context. One thing that such clinical research will never explain, however, is why some young men are psychologically destroyed by their fathers while others proceed to resurrect themselves, fashioning a new world of creativity and a new sense of identity. Bearing all this in mind, we may view the memoir in a new light. Especially revealing is this unapologetic confession of youthful folly:

---

[37] Seymour S. Weiner, *Francis Carco*, p. 46. Carco was in Toulouse during the summer and fall of his nineteenth year.
[38] See Ibid., p. 19.

How many times, as I went back to my room at dawn, I suffered from loneliness and lack of courage. I would have given half of my life to get rid of that emptiness within me, that emptiness which made me tolerate in others and commit myself a thousand excesses! ... There was in me ... such a desire to escape from my life that it seemed to me that I acted, thought, and slept in a dream. It was a great torment. I saw my disorder clearly; I judged myself accurately. I pitied myself, but at the same time, my youth triumphed and far from making a decision, I was carried away by my pleasures, and they blinded me.

Given the broader context of the challenges that faced him even as a little boy, it's no wonder that Carco developed a hearty thirst for sensual pleasure and for the assuagement of pain that it brings, even when its effects are only temporary and superficial. One can also view Carco's tendency to indulge in sentimentality in a similar light: the alienation and sense of separation that he experienced in early life is later counterbalanced by the affection he feels for his comrades,[39] especially those employed in the "underworld" smithies, forging works of literature and art.

Figuratively speaking, when a father tells his son to "go to the devil" or to "go to hell," this is precisely where such a lad may end up: in that subalary cacodemonic realm where one meets the most interesting ladies and gentlemen. Indeed, *le milieu de la pègre* (the criminal underworld) is where Carco was drawn and where, by rubbing shoulders with those ladies and gents of such ill repute, he would find his most enduring inspiration.

[39] "Carco has made almost a fetish of friendship; he has devoted some of his most moving works to the evocation of friends. Indeed, he feels that the only triumph over death, the only prolongation of life offered to man is through the memory that he leaves behind him." Ibid., p. 181.

Rather than offering a sanctuary of mentorship, if a father embodies such physical and psychological danger, then his son is offered only one of two options. He can either imitate this pathology, with its need to overpower others rather than bond with them through acts of empathy; or he can utterly reject this model of behavior and seek a new pattern of mentorship. In the latter case, in rejecting the paterfamilias, this means developing a new world philosophy, a new way of living. This is part of what Carco was seeking when he ventured to Paris and slipped into the penumbra of those delightfully shady circles.[40]

But before we go too far in drawing connections between artistic flowerings and the dank psychic soil that nurtures them, a word of caution is provided by Carco himself: "Since Villon – and indeed before him, if you count the monstrous couplings of demons, male and female, which embellish certain cathedral portals – there has existed a lewd tradition which should not always be taken literally for its total, cynical, and disturbing indecency. In the Middle Ages the spectacle of earthly voluptuousness was only treated in this suggestive fashion the better to contrast it with the Heavenly ecstasies promised the Blessed."

In so many ways, Carco's "disturbing indecency" remains our enduring blessing.[41]

---

[40] Although Francis had hardly spoken to his father over the years, when he visited him at his deathbed he discovered that Jean-Dominique had carefully followed Carco's career: "'Every time they talked about you in the newspapers,' my mother informed me, 'he carefully kept the article. Two drawers of the furniture are full of them ... Did you not know? He was never very expressive. Yet, he was proud of your success. Without entirely approving ... your existence is so different from ours.'" Whatever feelings Jean-Dominique harbored for his son remained carefully stored away in those drawers. Carco left without seeking a reconciliation, and two days later his father passed away. (See Carco, *Bohème d'artiste*, p. 209.)
[41] Francis Carco, *Vertès*, p. 11.

The Francis Carco Modigliani Collection

"I finally met Carco, with whom I'd been corresponding for five years [...] He's very nice, very fat, with an excessively disdainful smile [...] He has a lot of paintings at home, Modigliani, Utrillo, Derain, Asselin, well chosen." – Swiss artist Maurice Barraud, writing to his friend and fellow painter Charles Chinet, 1924

As Malcolm Gee observes in his thesis on the Parisian art market, Carco's desire to purchase paintings wasn't merely a hobby:

> His period in Montmartre had brought him into contact with painters, and led him to take an interest in contemporary art. Also, like other writers of his generation, he had taken up art journalism as a way of earning a living. By 1913, he was art critic on a small paper, *L'Homme Libre*; then he was taken up by Louis Vauxcelles and given work on *Gil Blas*. Vauxcelles also took him to visit artists – he first met Utrillo in this way. Quite soon, he began to buy paintings. This was a natural thing for someone in his position to do. He was interested in developing the image of a writer, and was also genuinely anxious to play an active cultural role outside the sphere of writing. His first acquisitions seem to have been Utrillos bought either just before or soon after the outbreak of war. This led him to discover, or rediscover, the other painters of the Ecole de Paris: Modigliani, Kisling, Soutine and Pascin. Most of the paintings he bought at this time cost him very little; after the war, his increased means allowed him to buy from other, better-known artists, notably Derain, Dufy and Vlaminck. At the same time, he realized the interest and advantage of encouraging the growing interest in the Ecole de Paris: he helped Alphonse Bellier establish himself as a specialist auctioneer in

modern painting, with advice, contacts, and, very probably, paintings. In 1925, this activism reached a high point when Bellier auctioned Carco's own collection. This auction, together with Georges Aubry's a few months earlier, constituted the first conclusive signs of the evolution of taste in favor of contemporary independent painting.... The sale itself was a Parisian occasion, widely reported in the press....

The movement which these sales both marked and helped to create affected other members of the artistic professions. Jane Renouardt, for instance, a well-known actress and theatre proprietor, actually began to buy art at the Carco sale (she bought an Utrillo and a Modigliani). Sacha Guitry seems to have extended his collecting to the Ecole de Paris at about this time; and Henri Bernstein, a successful playwright who had built up, and auctioned, a collection of Impressionist painting before the war, began buying contemporary work in sales the same year.

Gee adds that Carco's auction grossed 208,250 francs: "far more" than the estimate. In March 1925 this was the equivalent of $10,787 – about $192,528 in 2024 currency.[42]

What else do we know about Carco's Modigliani collection? When I posed this question to Modigliani expert Kenneth Wayne, he kindly tracked down both the 1925 auction catalog and the 1939 catalog in the online Institut national d'histoire de l'art. The 1925 brochure lists nine of Carco's Modiglianis: six drawings and three paintings. The 1939 booklet lists just one lot from the Carco Collection: a Modigliani oil painting. Both

[42] *Dealers, Critics, and Collectors of Modern Painting*, pp. 192-193. Gee identifies the prices and buyers of about twenty of Carco's lots. The overall sales figure of 208,250 FF appears on p. 193, n. 1; but elsewhere he quotes the price as 208,150 francs. Gee's sources include "French dealers, critics, and collectors." He was also in contact with such notable figures as Pierre Cabanne, Paulette Jourdain, and Daniel-Henry Kahnweiler.

auctions were held at the Hôtel Drouot, a premiere art auction house in Paris.

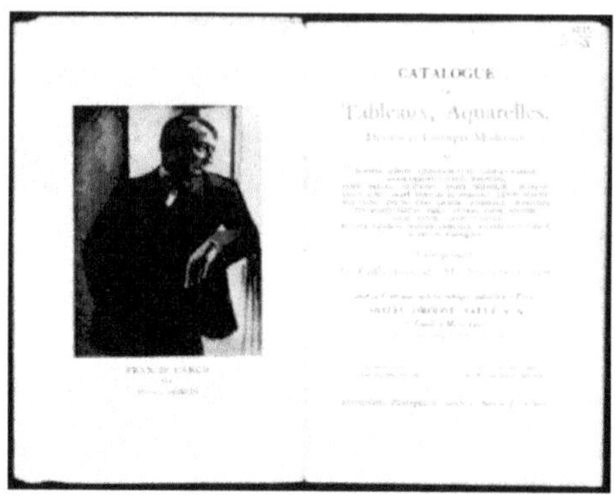

Hôtel Drouot auction catalog, 2 March 1925, with a frontispiece illustration of Maurice Asselin's oil painting, *Portrait de Francis Carco*, 92 x 73 cm.

Wayne also referred me to the Modigliani "Bible" – the Ceroni catalogue raisonné – as the paintings (which are reproduced in the catalogs) correspond to Ceroni N° 193 (from the 1939 auction), and Ceroni N°ˢ 41, 111, and 185 (from the 1925 auction).

The 1939 sale[43] identifies Carco as the owner of *Nu blond* (N° 158 on the auction block). Thanks to the photo, there's no doubt about which nude blonde it is – the same one that's reproduced in his memoir. Also known as *Standing Nude* or *Blonde Nude with the Dropped Chemise* or *La Môme Haricot Rouge*[44] (1917), it must have been one of his favorites, as it also serves as a frontispiece

[43] The 2 March 1939 auction, "following the amicable liquidation of the Galerie Druet," was held on an ominous date: just six months later, on 3 September 1939, England and France would declare war on Germany. The "liquidation" of goods – and of human lives – was in the air.

[44] Arthur Pfannstiel, *Modigliani et son oeuvre: étude critique et catalogue raisonné*, caption for plate 38. According to Marevna, "Haricot Rouge" was Jeanne Hébuterne's nickname. Although the identity of the model remains unknown, some have speculated that it's a portrait of Modigliani's mistress, Simone Thiroux, who bore a striking resemblance to Jeanne.

for his book, *Le Nu Dans La Peinture Moderne* (1924). In that text, Carco's love of this portrait is expressed in a moving tribute.

He begins the passage with a quote from André Salmon: "Modigliani is our only painter of the nude." He proceeds to delineate all the reasons this is so, culminating in this vivid assessment:

> Here the young girl … stands smiling, holding her shirt down to her thighs, and the most delicious flesh tones blend, knead with an adorable lightness to whip with mother-of-pearl and pink, rub with amber, fluff with blondness this triumphant freshness that an exquisitely attenuated light of an April morning caresses more than it sculpts. Between the light and the skin, there is this impalpable velvety garment, this 'frozen' translucent flower, but where the lighting plays with all its shimmering: all this mixed, melted, less painted than sprayed on the canvas.

Carco compares the living, breathing, animate forms incarnated by Modi's enlivening brush to the daubs of the more academic painters that have preceded him: "It is impossible, after having had the opportunity to admire a nude figure by Modigliani at length, to look without laughing at the cold, sandpapered nudes of the art academies – or even at some otherwise praiseworthy museum paintings: bodies made of inflatable rubber, breasts stacked like tiered cakes, buttocks of trembling jelly." But now, instead of all this,

> A breath exhales from his nudes, the very breath of life…. Doubtless, there are more numerous, more consistent works than his. But where is there a more interesting and expressive one? Where is the image in which the fervor of living is better incarnated, where the higher reasons for pleasure and voluptuousness will find such a vibrant, rich accord, a more precise and elevated justification?[45]

The 1925 catalog is of even greater interest for our purpose, as its contents are devoted entirely to Carco's collection, which includes quite a roster of artists. The sheer volume of the sale is impressive – a total of 101 lots:

> Catalog of paintings, watercolors, drawings and modern prints, by Maurice Asselin, Georges Bottini, Charles Camoin, Emilie Charmy, Coubine, Daragnès, André Derain, Dignimont, Daniel Dourouze, Dufresne, Raoul Dufy, André Dunoyer de Segonzac, Louise Hervieu, Max Jacob, Kisling, Chas Laborde, Mainssieux, Modigliani, Luc-Albert Moreau, Pascin, Picasso, Rodin, Soutine, André Utter, Maurice Utrillo, Suzanne Valadon, Mathieu Verdilhan, Maurice de Vlaminck, Henry de Waroquier, composing the collection of M. Francis Carco whose public auction will take place in Paris, Hôtel Drouot, room N° 6, on Monday March 2, 1925, at two o'clock very precisely.

The three Modigliani oil paintings on sale are featured in black-and-white reproduction:

[45] See Francis Carco, *Le Nu Dans La Peinture Moderne*, Paris: Crès et Cie, 1924, pp. 112-118.

– Portrait d'homme, 1914. Later titled *Portrait of Diego Rivera*. (Lot Nº 62, corresponding to Ceroni Nº 41.) Purchased by Paul Éluard for 3600 FF (see Malcolm Gee, appendix section, p. 180).

– Le Modèle, 1916. (Lot Nº 63; Ceroni Nº 111.) Purchased by the silent film actress Jane Renouardt for 12,200 FF (Gee, app. sec., p. 178).

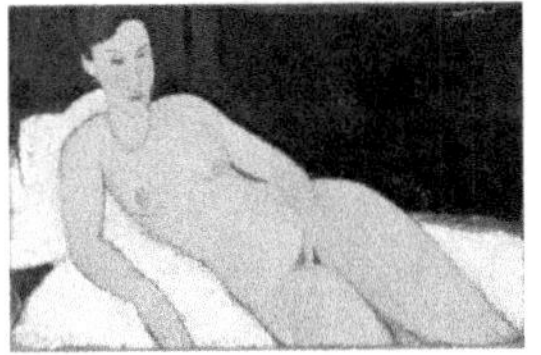

– Nu couché, 1917. Later titled *Reclining Nude with Coral Necklace*. (Lot Nº 64; Ceroni Nº 185.) Purchased by Felix Fénéon for 18,500 FF (Gee, app. sec., p. 180).[46]

[46] The sales of *Le Modèle* and *Nu couché* are reported in the 15 March 1925 *Beaux-Arts* journal, which also records the purchase of Carco's Utrillos by Madame Menginou and by actress Jane Renouardt. See Seymour de Ricci, "La vente Carco," p. 96.

Nu couché is a big nude, measuring 65 x 100 centimeters.[47] The online resource "Secret Modigliani," which cites Ceroni, notes that the back of this canvas is signed "Modigliani. / 3 Joseph Bara. / Paris. / 1917." (Zborowski resided at 3, rue Joseph Bara, and it was there, in 1917, that he provided the artist with a space to paint.) The provenance notes that, like *Nu blond*, it was obtained by Carco directly from Zborowski; there was no prior owner. Could the *Nu blond* or the *Nu couché* be the one that Zborowski gifted to Carco?

In *L'Ami des peintres* (1944), Carco says that he purchased *Nu blond* for 75 francs and later sold it to the art dealer Jos Hessel for 250,000 FF.[48] (Jos was the registered art "expert" for the 1925 auction.) If it was acquired by Carco right after Madame Weill's December 1917 Modigliani exhibit, 75 francs from that period would correspond to $14 in 1917 dollars (or $318 in 2024 U.S. dollars). When *Nu blond* was sold at the 1939 auction, 250,000 FF would have equaled $6,625 U.S. (which in 2024 dollars would be roughly $147,907). Since Carco attributes his ownership of the painting to a purchase of 75 FF, perhaps it's more likely that *Nu couché* is the painting that Zborowski first bestowed upon him. (But it's also possible that Carco reimbursed Zbo with the seventy-five francs after first receiving *Nu blond* as a gift.)

The Secret Modigliani website hosts an image of another *Nu couché* (also from 1917 and of about the same size), alternatively titled *Reclining Nude with Joined Hands*[49] (Ceroni N° 202). The provenance indicates that, first, it was in the possession of Modigliani's dealer Paul Guillaume (who briefly managed Modi beginning around 1915), after which it supposedly entered the Carco Collection.

---

[47] Later recorded as 66.5 x 101.1 cm., then reduced to 65.4 x 99.4 after restoration, according to Kenneth Wayne.

[48] *L'Ami des peintres*, Geneva: Éditions du Milieu du Monde, 1944, p. 43.

[49] See SecretModigliani.com/1917-w-13.html.

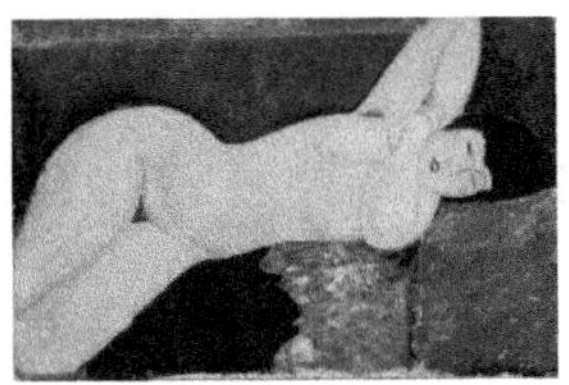

Although the online provenance states that it was included in the 1925 Hôtel Drouot sale, the auction brochure doesn't provide a listing for a second Modigliani nude of this size.[50]

Since the 1925 catalog lists only one large painting with a female subject, and since that *Nu couché* is illustrated in the catalog by photographic reproduction, one wonders if this other *Nu couché* (*Reclining Nude with Joined Hands*) was added to the auction after the brochure was printed, or if the attribution is simply a mistake. In the latter case, the identical title (*Nu couché*) may have led to this error.

The *Reclining Nude with Joined Hands* is currently housed in the Pinacoteca Agnelli Museum, in Turin. Adding to the mystery, the museum's online provenance indicates a missing link in the chain of possession: it begins with Modigliani's ownership in 1917, then shows a gap, after which the painting was in the hands of Paul Guillaume "until 1930."[51] But there is no mention of Carco.

[50] The provenance states that it's 65 x 100 cm., but it also says that, in a 1958 exhibit, it measured 73 x 116 cm., suggesting that the dimensions were either incorrectly recorded or subsequently altered.
[51] See pinacoteca-agnelli.it/collezione/nu-couche-1917.

A Copy of the Modigliani Listings from the 1925 Catalog:

MODIGLIANI

56. Portrait de l'artiste par lui-même.
Très beau dessin original .... 25 x 36
"Certains dessins de Lautrec peuvent seuls rivaliser avec cette maîtrise si distinguée, si hautainement impertinente! Et encore, Modigliani est-il plus synthétique, plus raffiné, plus précieux."[52]
GUSTAVE COQUIOT, *Les Indépendants.*

57. Femme assise.
Très beau dessin original ayant servi à l'illustration du poème : *Les Nymphes,* de Roger Frène et reproduit dans le volume. Signé .... 23 x 33

58. Femme couchée.
Très beau dessin original .... 26 x 42

59. Femme debout.
Très beau dessin original .... 29 x 48

60. Portrait de femme.
Très beau dessin original. Signé .... 25 x 42

61. Nu.
Très beau dessin original. Signé .... 22 x 30

[52] "Only certain drawings by Lautrec can rival a mastery so distinguished, so haughtily impertinent! And yet, Modigliani is more synthetic, more refined, more precious."

62. Portrait d'homme.

Peinture .... 81 x 100

63. Le Modèle.

Peinture. A été reproduite dans le catalogue de
l'exposition Modigliani, à la Galerie Montaigne.
Signée en haut, à droite .... 50 x 81

64. Nu couchée.

Peinture. Reproduite (planche XIX) dans le volume de
FRANCIS CARCO : *Le Nu dans la Peinture moderne*. Signée
en haut, à droite .... 65 x 100

The first six lots are the drawings; the last three are the paintings previously discussed (reproduced below, in larger format). According to Gee, although the buyer of the self-portrait (*Portrait de l'artiste par lui-même*) is listed as "Charraud," this was "probably Pierre Chareau and his wife Dolly" (Louise Dorothee Dyte, aka "Dollie"). One of the most important French interior designers and architects of the early twentieth century, Pierre designed the Maison de Verre: the first house in France that was composed of steel and glass.

Pierre and Dollie (who was also a designer) displayed an impressive collection of modern art in their home, including work by Braque, Klee, Léger, Jacques Lipschitz, Mondrian, and Picasso. They also owned one of Modigliani's caryatids from 1914, which they placed in their garden. (Currently housed at MOMA, it was loaned to the 1939 World's Fair in New York.) Besides acquiring this self-portrait, the Chareaus also purchased the drawings of lot N° 59 (*Femme debout*) and N° 60 (*Portrait de femme*).

The catalog states that the drawing titled *Femme assise* ("Seated Woman"; lot N° 57), served as an illustration for *Les Nymphes*: a verse collection by Roger Frène (one of Carco's friends, who dedicated the book to him). Issued in a limited edition of 130 numbered copies, it reproduces five Modigliani drawings: one on the title page and four inset. Only two feature seated nudes. Therefore, one of these two (illustrated below) corresponds to the *Femme assise* of the 1925 auction.

Gee chronicles many of the other buyers (galleries, dealers, and collectors) who placed winning bids at Carco's auction, as well the artwork they acquired, the estimated sales price, and the final purchase price (displayed as, for example, 1100 / 3200):[53]

Bernheim-Jeune: Founded in 1863 by Alexandre Bernheim (1839 – 1915) and operated with his sons Josse and Gaston. One of the oldest Parisian art galleries, still in existence today.

Paul Éluard (né Eugène Grindel; 1895 – 1952): a founder of the Surrealist movement. Known as the Poet of Freedom, he clandestinely distributed his anti-Nazi poems during the Occupation.

Felix Fénéon (1861 – 1944): art critic and director of Bernheim-Jeune (1906 – 1925), he coined the term Neo-Impressionism.

H. A. Fiquet: art dealer who operated the Galerie Fiquet (formerly known as Nunes and Fiquet).

Jos Hessel: dealer who managed Josse and Gaston Bernheim's gallery (who were his cousins). He later established his own gallery, initially located on Avenue de l'Opéra and then on rue la Boétie. ("The Carco sale was the first occasion that Jos Hessel worked with [auctioneer] Bellier as expert. Hessel was a well-known and influential dealer; from now on he and Bellier

---

[53] Gee cautions us that the records remain incomplete: not all transactions were recorded, and some collectors obtained artwork through purchases made by agents.

worked together regularly." Gee, p. 27.) Both Vuillard and Bonnard composed portraits of Hessel.

Horovsky: "Possibly one of the misspellings of **Zborowski**" (Gee, app., p. 97).

Madame Menginou: A buyer who purchased Utrillo's *Eglise de Clichy* (lot N° 91) for 17,200 FF. A reproduction of this painting appears in Carco's booklet, *Les Peintres Français Nouveaux N°. 8: Utrillo.*

Josef Müller (1887 – 1977): Swiss art collector and curator at the Solothurn Art Museum (1943 – 1967), where a large part of his collection is currently housed.

Jane Renouardt (née Victorine Renouard; 1890 – 1972): silent film star, first director of the Théâtre Daunou, and a friend of Vuillard's, who painted her portrait. She later attributed her love of modern painting to her participation at this auction: "It was in 1925, at the Carco auction that I was struck. My first acquisition was a portrait of a woman by Modigliani." (G. J. Gros, "Les Grands Collectionneurs: Jane Renouardt," *L'Art Vivant*, 1 May 1928, p. 930.) Her other winning bids were for Utrillo's *Le Cours Marigny à Vincennes* (10000 / 16500) and *Place de l'Eglise et l'Eglise de Couchey* (4500 / 15055). The latter painting was hung in her office at the Théâtre Daunou, along with the Modigliani.

Rousseau: This was not the celebrated painter Henri Rousseau, since "Le Douanier" died in September 1910. Gee remarks that he was "thought to be a dealer." (App., p. 101.)

While examining the 1925 catalog scanned by the Institut national d'histoire de l'art, I made an exciting discovery: faintly inscribed penciled notations that appear in the left-hand margin beside the listings are actually numbers corresponding to the estimated sales price followed by the final purchase price of each item (noted in French francs). We can safely make this assertion because identical sets of numbers are found in Gee's text. But while Gee only registers the price of the oil paintings, the notations in the catalog also appear beside the Modigliani drawings. The prices for the drawings are as follows:

– Lot 56. **Portrait de l'artiste par lui-même. (200 / 650.)** Purchased by Pierre and Dollie Chareau.

– Lot 57. **Femme assise. (200 / 350.)** Illustration for Roger Frène's *Les Nymphes*.

– Lot 58. **Femme couchée. (200 / 480.)**

– Lot 59. **Femme debout. (400 / 1480.)** Purchased by Pierre and Dollie Chareau.

– Lot 60. **Portrait de femme. (200 / 650.)** Purchased by Pierre and Dollie Chareau.

– Lot 61. **Nu. (100 / 300.)**

When peeling back the onionskins of Carco's biography, other layers of cultural history often come to light. Inaugurated on 1 June 1852, the Hôtel Drouot, which hosted Carco's sales, was a preeminent auction house located at 6, rue Rossini. Its most prominent auctioneer was Alphonse Bellier (1886 – 1980), a former notary and the son of a baker. Carco did much to launch his career as salesman of modern art.

Bellier is now being investigated for his role in the sale of art, jewelry, and furniture that was pilfered by the Nazis from the

Jewish population and auctioned at the Hôtel Drouot. During the Occupation, as part of a well-organized network, Hôtel Drouot served as a useful conduit for the laundering of such stolen goods, some of which were even advertised in the press. The auctions featured enforced sales as well as artwork that was removed from the ateliers of certain artists. Between 1941 and 1944 Bellier helped to organized over 250 sales for the Hôtel Drouot, some of which contained this illicitly obtained booty.

Although it's still regarded as one of the top auction venues in Paris, Hôtel Drouot has continued to be plagued by scandal: in particular, for its role in auctioning Eskimo, Native American, and pre-Columbian sacred ceremonial artifacts and relics. Between 2013 and 2014 hundreds of such items rightfully belonging to the Hopi and Navajo Nation were sold, despite a letter of protest from Jane Hartley, the American Ambassador to France. In the United States, legislation enacted in 1990 to forbid such sales has empowered tribes to recover relics from museum collections, but the law doesn't protect artifacts in sales held abroad.[54]

[54] "Controversy over auction of Native American masks in France," *Radio France Internationale*, 30 November 2013, www.rfi.fr; and Pascale Mollard-Chenebenoit, "Native Americans try to block French auction of sacred artifacts," *Agence France-Presse*, 14 December 2014, afp.com.

This is the first of two seated nudes featured in Roger Frène's *Les Nymphes*, which appears after the title page. The simple elegance of the composition is classic Modigliani: a balance of forces resulting in serene motionlessness. With just a handful of lines, the presence of the model is drawn forth in a manner suggesting both rhythm and stasis.

Modigliani's lean, economical style, combining elements of classicism and modernity, is easy to recognize in this exquisite drawing. The fifth and final illustration in *Les Nymphes*, it's the also most successful. It was later featured on the cover of André Warnod's *Les berceaux de la jeune peinture*.

Portrait d'homme, 1914. Later titled *Portrait of Diego Rivera*. (Auction lot N°
62; Ceroni N° 41.)

Le Modèle, 1916. (Lot N° 63; Ceroni N° 111.)

(To be viewed sideways.) *Nu couché*, 1917. Later titled *Reclining Nude with Coral Necklace*. (Lot Nº 64; Ceroni Nº 185.)

(To be viewed sideways.) *Nu couché*, 1917. Later titled *Reclining Nude with Joined Hands* (Ceroni N° 202). The provenance indicates that it was first in the possession of Modigliani's dealer Paul Guillaume, after which it may have entered the Carco Collection.

Nu blond, 1917. Later titled *Standing Nude*; *Blonde Nude with the Dropped Chemise*; and *La Môme Haricot Rouge*. (Lot N° 158 in the 1939 auction; Ceroni N° 193.)

"Auction of the Jacques Cannone collection, Hôtel Drouot,
5 June 1942. Under the hammer of auctioneer Maître Alphonse Bellier."

Bellier's other grievous mortal sin was to preside over the enforced liquidation of Daniel-Henry Kahnweiler's art collection in 1923. A respected dealer who, "by 1914 ... had Braque, Léger, Gris, as well as Picasso under contract," Kahnweiler (1884 – 1979) was a true visionary who had the misfortune of being a German Jewish expat in Paris when WWI was heating up. While he was exiled in Switzerland in 1914, his holdings were confiscated by the French state as "enemy property" to be auctioned off, and Kahnweiler was declared an "alien."

Bellier conducted the auction in a shameful, shabby manner that revealed what a provincial ignoramus he truly was. John Richardson describes the fiasco by first quoting from Robert Desnos' article in *Paris-Journal*: "The preview was a scandal. Paintings were stacked any old way; drawings were rolled up or folded in boxes, some were sealed in cardboard tubes so that it was impossible to see them, others had been stuck in hampers or concealed behind the rostrum. Everything was in an indescribably filthy mess." Richardson adds: "The sale itself was no less of a scandal ... Bellier, who should have known better, made silly jokes about the cubist gems he was selling – 'silly jokes that drew attention to his lack of intellect.' His crassness encouraged the porters to outdo him…. they showed paintings upside down, crumpled the drawings, trashed the papiers collés and sand paintings, and failed to display things to the buyers. Lot numbers were struck onto the surfaces of paintings, many of them with signs of recent splattering and in one case the unmistakable imprint of a shoe." Richardson eulogizes Kahnweiler as "unquestionably the most intelligent, farsighted, and scrupulous dealer of his generation." John Richardson, *A Life of Picasso III: The Triumphant Years*, New York: Knopf, 2007, pp. 107, 224-225.

Photo of the celebrated actress Jane Renouardt. Her collection (including work by Bonnard, Degas, Vuillard, Toulouse-Lautrec, Renoir, Utrillo, Foujita, Modigliani, de Segonzac, and Pascin) was displayed in her Art Deco villa in Saint-Cloud, designed by Louis Süe and André Mare.

Selection of Works Cited in the Intro and Notes:

Books:

Beadle, Charles, *Dark Refuge. Edited with Annotations and an Afterword by Rob Couteau*, New York: Dominantstar, 2023.

Jean-Jacques Bedu, *Francis Carco: Au coeur de la bohème*, Éditions du Rocher, Monaco, 2001.

Céline, Louis-Ferdinand, *Journey to the End of the Night*, Ralph Manheim, trans., New York: New Directions, 1983. (Originally published as *Voyage au bout de la nuit*, Paris: Denoël et Steele, 1932.)

Cohen-Solal, Annie, *Picasso the Foreigner: An Artist in France, 1900-1973*, New York: Farrar, Straus, and Giroux, 2023.

Colt, Henri, *Becoming Modigliani*, Laguna Beach, CA: Rake Press, 2024.

Coughlan, Robert, *The Wine of Genius. A Life of Maurice Utrillo*, New York: Harper & Brothers, 1951.

Day, George, *Pleasure guide to Paris for bachelors*, London: Nilsson and Co., 1903.

Douglas, Charles, *Artist Quarter: Reminiscences of Montmartre and Montparnasse in the first two decades of the twentieth century*, London: Pallas Athene, 2021. ("Charles Douglas" is the portmanteau pseudonym of Charles Beadle and Douglas Goldring.)

FitzGerald, Michael C., *Making Modernism*, Berkeley: University of California Press, 1996.

Frène, Roger, *Les Nymphes*, Paris: Ronald Davis and Cie, 1921.

Gee, Malcolm, *Dealers, Critics, and Collectors of Modern Painting: Aspects of the Parisian Art Market between 1910 and 1930*, New York: Garland, 1981.

Grana, Cesar, *On Bohemia: The Code of the Self-Exiled*, New Brunswick, NJ: Taylor & Francis, 2017.

Hewitt, Nicholas, *Montmartre: A Cultural History*, Liverpool, UK: Liverpool University Press, 2017.
– *The Life of Céline: A Critical Biography*, Hoboken, NY: Wiley-Blackwell, 1991.

Jacob, Max, *The Dice Cup*, Christopher Pilling and David Kennedy, trans., London: Atlas Press, 2000.

Koda, Harold and Andrew Bolton, *Poiret*, New York: The Metropolitan Museum of Art, 2007.

Mac Orlan, Pierre, *A Handbook for the Perfect Adventurer*, Napoleon Jeffries, trans., Cambridge, MA: Wakefield Press, 2013.

Marevna, *Life with the Painters of La Ruche*, New York: Macmillan Publishing Company, 1974.

Nevill, Ralph, *Days and Nights in Montmartre and the Latin Quarter*, New York: George H. Doran Co., 1927.

Olivier, Fernande, *Picasso and His Friends*, Jane Miller, trans., New York: Appleton-Century, 1965.

Richardson, John, *A Life of Picasso Volume II 1907 – 1917: The Painter of Modern Life*, UK: Random House, 2011.
– *A Life of Picasso III: The Triumphant Years*, New York: Knopf, 2007

Shattuck, Roger, *The Banquet Years*, New York: Vintage, 1968.

Spotts, Frederic, *The Shameful Peace: How French Artists and Intellectuals Survived the Nazi Occupation*, London: Yale University Press, 2008.

Street, Julian, *Paris à la Carte* (Second, revised edition), New York: John Lane Co., 1912.

Warnod, André, *Les bals de Paris*, Paris: Les Éditions Georges Crès & Cie, 1922.

Warren, Rosanna, *Max Jacob: A Life in Art and Letters*, UK: W.W. Norton, 2020.

Wayne, Kenneth, *Modigliani and the Artists of Montparnasse*, New York: Harry N. Abrams, Inc., 2002.

Weill, Berthe, *Pow! Right in the Eye! Thirty Years behind the Scenes of Modern French Painting*, University of Chicago Press, 2022.

Weiner, Seymour S., *Francis Carco*, New York: Columbia University Press, 1952.

Journals and Periodicals:

Basha, Elyas, et al., "Suicidal Ideation and Its Associated Factors among Patients with Major Depressive Disorder at Amanuel Mental Specialized Hospital," *Neuropsychiatric Disease and Treatment*, 21 May 2021, pp. 1571-1577, dovepress.com.

Cai, Hong, et al., "Prevalence of Suicidality in Major Depressive Disorder," *Frontiers in Psychiatry*, 16 September 2021, frontiersin.org.

Crawford, Virginia M., "Jerome and Jean Tharaud," *Studies: An Irish Quarterly Review*, vol. 15, no. 58, 1926, pp. 204–216.

Elsevier, "Corporal Punishment Affects Brain Activity, Anxiety, and Depression," *Science Daily*, 16 November 2022, sciencedaily.com.

Madis, Alex, *A la Taverne du Panthéon* ("At the Panthéon Tavern"), *Revue Des Deux Mondes*, 1956, pp. 510-519; jstor.org/stable/44595972.

Prial, Frank J., "Heyday of Paris's Le Boeuf, Cradle of Modernism, Re-created at Gallery," *New York Times*, 15 July 1981, Section C, p. 17.

Rector, Patricia, "Ernest Boyd, a Semi-detached Intellectual. A Thesis Presented to the Faculty of the Department of English, University of Houston," January 1957.

Vitz, Evelyn Birge, "Symbolic 'Contamination' in the Testament of François Villon," *MLN* vol. 86, no. 4 (1971), pp. 481-483, jstor.org/stable/2907647.

Selected Books and Essays by Carco:

1913 – *Charles-Henry Hirsch*, Paris: E. Sansot and Cie.

1914 – *Jésus-la-Caille*, Paris: Mercure de France. (*Frenzy*, Lowell Bair, trans., New York: Berkley Publishing, 1960.)

1916 – *Les Innocents*, Paris: La Renaissance du Livre. (*Depravity*, Lowell Bair, trans., New York: Berkley Publishing, 1957.)

1919 – "Modigliani," *L'Éventail*, Geneva: Librairie Artistique Kundig (15 July 1919).

1919 – *Scènes de la vie de Montmartre*, Paris: Éditions Arthème Fayard, 1919.

1921 – *Francis Carco Raconté par Lui-Même*, Paris: Éditions Sansot.

1921 – *Les Peintres Français Nouveaux N°. 8: Utrillo*, Paris: Gallimard.

1921 – *Rien Q'une Femme*, Paris: Éditions Arthème Fayard. (*Only a Woman*, Ralph Manheim, trans., New York: Berkley Publishing, 1953.)

1922 – *L'Homme traqué*, Paris: Albin-Michel.

1924 – *La Nu dans la peinture moderne*, Paris: Les éditions G. Crès et Cie.

1925 – *Perversité*, Paris: J. Ferenczi. (*Perversity*, Jean Rhys, trans. [falsely attributed to Ford Madox Ford], Chicago: Pascal Covici, 1928.)

1926 – *Le roman de François Villon*, Paris: Plon-Nourrit.

1927 – *De Montmartre au Quartier Latin*, Paris: Albin-Michel.

1927 – *Rue Pigalle*, Paris: Bernard Grasset.

1938 – *Montmartre à vingt ans*, Paris: Albin-Michel.

1940 – *Bohème d'artiste*. Paris: Albin-Michel.

1944 – *L'Ami des peintres*, Geneva: Éditions du Milieu du Monde.

1946 – *Vertès*, Rosamond Frost, trans., New York: Athenaeum
Publishing Co., 1946.

Utrillo, *Le Cours Marigny à Vincennes*, oil on board, 36.5 x 51 cm. Purchased
at Carco's auction by Jane Renouardt for 16,500 FF. Vuillard's portrait of
Jane (1927) was sold at Christie's in November 2021 for $2,670,000.

A Note on the Translation

Madeleine Boyd (née Reynier; 1886 – 1972) was a translator and literary agent best known for placing *Look Homeward, Angel* and *Of Time and the River* for Thomas Wolfe. A native Parisian, she was the wife Ernest Boyd (1887 – 1946), who worked on the staff of the *Irish Times* and was considered an expert in French literature.

Literary historian Alan Churchill characterizes Ernest Boyd as a "transplanted Irishman who emerges as one of the most staggeringly erudite figures ever to take a bow on a literary stage. Ernest Boyd seemed familiar with every known language, and obscure dialects as well. Not only did he appear to have read every book published but every magazine, pamphlet, brochure, and broadside.... With ladies he was a charmer, among men a cherished carouser. 'A combination of urbanity and humanity,' one smitten lady breathed." Employing his trademark telegraphic style, in a letter composed in 1926 Hemingway simply remarks: "Ernest Boyd was grand."

They married in 1913, while Madeleine was studying at Trinity College, Dublin. After Ernest entered the British consular service as Vice Consul he was posted to Baltimore, where the couple socialized with their friend H. L. Mencken. Ernest's satirical portraits of the American literary scene were published in Mencken's highly influential *America Mercury* magazine; Ernest was also co-founder of *The American Spectator* and author of a book about Mencken. (The Georgetown University Library houses the H. L. Mencken – Ernest A. and Madeleine E. Boyd Collection, which consists of 19 letters from H. L. Mencken to Ernest and Madeleine Boyd.) Following false accusations of being a Sinn Féin supporter, in 1920 Ernest resigned from the consular service and the Boyds moved to New York. While living there, Madeleine edited a Modern

Library edition of *The Memoirs of Casanova* (1929), which features an Introduction by Ernest.

At the end of 1928, while Madeleine was building a career as a literary agent, one of Ernest's friends asked him to read a hefty manuscript titled "O, Lost," composed by an unknown scribbler named Thomas Wolfe. This was Aline Bernstein, an intimate companion of the author and the woman who should be considered as the true discoverer of Wolfe's genius. Ernest agreed to help but, uninterested in fiction, advised Aline to pass it along to his wife. Aline hesitated but finally acquiesced once she heard that Mencken thought highly of Madeleine. In turn, Madeleine agreed to read it with the proviso that, if she felt it was publishable, she would serve as agent. The Bernsteins' chauffer later delivered the manuscript: an ironic detail in the story, given the author's alarming state of poverty.

Madeleine let a couple of weeks go by before examining the imposingly sized parcel. But once she sat down with the novel, she grew so absorbed that she soon lost track of the time – pausing at 3 a.m. to exclaim: "A genius! I have discovered a genius!" The book would later be published by Scribner's as *Look Homeward, Angel* (1929).

Upon their first encounter, agent and author took an immediate dislike to one another. Boyd regarded Wolfe as unkempt and told him so; Wolfe concluded that Boyd was "a fat Frenchwoman, hardboiled and out for the guilders." A later event unequivocally supports the author's suspicion. "By the fall of 1931," while seated alone in a cheap restaurant and celebrating his thirty-first birthday, "Wolfe was at one of the lowest points of his life.... His money was running out.... He had no bank account and no savings. Just when he most needed money, he discovered that Madeleine Boyd was cheating him."[55] After a German publisher had arranged to issue a

[55] David Herbert Donald, *Look Homeward. A Life of Thomas Wolfe*, Cambridge, MA: Harvard University Press, 2003, pp. 174, 260.

translation of his novel, Boyd cashed Wolfe's advance check and pocketed the proceeds without showing him the contract. But she was caught red-handed by both Wolfe and his editor, the legendary Maxwell Perkins of Scribner's. Bear in mind this was during the Great Depression, making it even more difficult for the author to sustain himself. Yet, for some inexplicable reason, Perkins convinced Wolfe not to prosecute Boyd for embezzlement.

An equally disturbing event illustrates just how "hardboiled" Boyd could be. In 1939 Henry, Holt and Company published *Life Makes Advances*, Madeleine's autobiographical novel, which the *New York Times* calls an "infinitely detailed account of a French girl's life and adventures in Ireland, France, England and America." Under the headline "Madeleine Boyd's Debut," a review in the *Philadelphia Inquirer* opens: "Reversing the rule, Madeleine Boyd announces that all the characters of her first novel ... are known individuals. Beyond that she has used the names of well-advertised persons. They may not relish the connection." The review adds that both her husband and Mencken appear in the narrative, respectively as "Michael Brandon" (according to the reviewer, portrayed as "sallow, sickly, and brilliant") and as "Henry Mencken." An otherwise sympathetic review in Kentucky's *Lexington Herald* teasingly cautions: "It's as bad for a woman to kiss and tell as a man." Indeed, what the *Times* euphemistically refers to as "infinitely detailed" material could easily have served as grounds for libel, defamation, and invasion of privacy:

> In 1939 Boyd's estranged wife, Madeleine, published her only novel, a distressingly frank account of the most intimate aspects of her life with the critic. In it [Ernest] Boyd is represented as a physical coward and weakling, an unsatisfactory lover, and a selfish hypochondriacal egomaniac. While his talents are

noted, they are used to show his wife responsible for what little he actually did accomplish with them. Nor does she omit to detail dozens of near and actual instances of Boyd's cuckoldry at the hands of men described as his superior in such matters. With a plain woman's fatuousness and a Huguenot's predilection to dramatize sinfulness, she saw a venal approach in every handshake and a proposition in every glance. At the same time she indulged herself in an irresistible fantasy of self-sacrifice whenever her own interests in relation to those of her husband occupied her thought.[56]

Had Carco known of all this, the author of *Perversité* might have regarded poor Mr. Boyd as a stand-in for his ridiculed protagonist Emile. Not surprisingly, the Boyds later divorced, but they each remained in New York. Mrs. Boyd died in her home at 242 East 50th Street on 5 May 1972, at the age of eighty-six.

Madeleine's translation of Carco's *De Montmartre au Quartier Latin* (Paris: Albin-Michel, 1927) was published in New York by Henry Holt in 1928. The following year a UK edition was issued in London, by Grant Richards and Humphrey Toulmin, at the Cayme Press. Her other translations from the French include Raymonde Machard's *A Child Is Born* (1926); Paul Morand's *The Living Buddha* (1928); Rachilde's *Monsieur Venus* (1929); Madame Titayna's *Mademoiselle Against The World* (1931); Lucien Pemjean's *Captain d'Artagnan* (1933); and Baroness de Vaughan's *A Commoner Married a King* (1937).

Every effort has been made to ensure that this newly revised, annotated edition is a faithful reproduction of her original

---

[56] Patricia Rector, "Ernest Boyd, a Semi-detached Intellectual. A Thesis Presented to the Faculty of the Department of English, University of Houston," January 1957, p. 109.

work. Corrections in spelling and punctuation have been included without notations, but textual changes involving anything more complex, such inserting missing or censored passages or correcting translation errors, are indicated by brackets.

Maurice Utrillo, *La Rue de Venise*, 73 x 50 cm. Purchased by Josef Müller for 11,000 francs in Carco's 1925 auction, lot N° 87.

Suzanne Valadon, *Femme nue*, 1929, oil on canvas, 81.2 x 64.7 cm. (Later titled *Nude Sitting on the Edge of a Bed*.) This painting was used as a frontispiece illustration for Carco's *L'Ami des peintres* (1944), where it is identified as being part of the Carco Collection.

The Last Bohemia

Jules Pascin, *The Foolish Virgins*, circa 1909, oil and graphite on canvas, 46.4 x 54.9 cm. Metropolitan Museum of Art; Bequest of Scofield Thayer, 1982.

I

Of course it is far, very far, farther than one might think, perhaps, from Montmartre to the Latin Quarter, but one of my generation who wishes to gather his memories will find them nowhere so plentiful and so varied as in these vicinities.

Because about 1910 we all lived either in Montmartre or near the Boul'Mich'.[57] Happy times! They still conjure up verses such as I used to write in the rue Racine, in a small room which the concierge agreed to keep in order for me, against a chance of gambling away at lotto any money she might receive for her services. At that time I knew no one in Paris but this concierge, a good woman ruined by her passion for lotto. Thanks to her, I had a chance to earn my dinner by giving French lessons to the gentleman on the second floor who was studying for some examination at the Préfecture de la Seine. He passed the examination and the dinners lost their providential regularity. Then, they assumed an importance equal to their uncertainty. Even when I was lucky they were more like picnic lunches than real meals, as sparing and sketchy as the free lunches served in the big bars on the Left Bank. My good-for-nothing companions were hardly better off than I was. They waited for the hungry hours of the early morning to enter rooming houses and steal the still-warm rolls and milk left outside the apartments on each floor. Some of us had big appetites and had to go all the way to the top. Ah, what good legs it took to escape being caught! I ran as fast as my friends and came downstairs faster than I went up. As I look back upon it now, it seems like a good sport. At any rate it kept us from getting fat.

Let us be thankful for that practice, which enabled us to combine flights of stairs and flights of fancy with the exigencies

[57] Le Boul'Mich' = the boulevard Saint-Michel.

of a poet's stomach! For we were poets. Poets in verse and poets in prose. Who is not a poet at that age, when the memory of François Villon places a halo around the head of modern Bohemia? There was another halo around its head as well, the one which we could see at dawn, crowning with a pallid light the roofs of the tall buildings, as they stood outlined against the still-dark sky. We were not so proud of our haloes! And yet how pleasant and touching it is to remember and to evoke later for oneself, *et pour quelques amis,*[58] the kind of ecstasy born of all the fatigues and limitless joys of our early twenties.

Today from the room where I write these lines, I can see across the Seine the quays where we roomed: the Pont-Neuf which we crossed as we came back from Les Halles or from Montmartre, and the beginning of the rue Dauphine. Through the branches, across the glassy waters, the scene seems like a mirage. Now nobody walks past the sleeping houses. It is a scene strange to me, and I look in vain for any survivals of my past; nothing I see recalls it to me.[59] Heavens! What a lot of water has run under the bridge since our youth! How many faded dawns, how many days, weeks, seasons have followed those dawns, those days, weeks, seasons!

> *Le fleuve est pareil a ma peine,*
> *Il s'écoule et ne tarit pas*

---

[58] "And for a few friends": the reference to François Villon (circa 1431 – after 1463) is more than incidental. In 1926 Carco published *Le Roman de François Villon*, a "fictionalized" biography of this great French poet.

[59] Boyd's translation of this sentence is a bit awkward. Carco's original reads: *"C'est un tableau étrange, et j'ai beau m'appliquer à regarder de la fenêtre si quelque chose de mon passé y survit, rien ne m'en donne l'immédiate sensation,"* which might be rendered as "It's a strange scene, and no matter how much I try to look out the window to see if something from my past survives there, nothing gives me the immediate sensation of it." Carco's syntax is often complex and difficult to unravel.

Apollinaire used to sing[60] ...

But Apollinaire is dead. Jean Pellerin is dead. André du Fresnois, who lived on the quay of the Grand Augustins, is dead; and Claudien has left the Quarter. As for the carefree companions who lived on stolen rolls and milk, they might not even recognize me if I met them. Where can they be? Where? But who has ever been able to answer such a question? Villon asked it in vain, one sad evening, of all the echoes in the town. Poor Villon! Where, indeed, is he?

> *Villon, qu'on chercherait céans,*
> *N'es plus là ni Verlaine,*[61]

nor so many others who roamed where we roamed, in the taverns, the bars, the beer shops, on the deserted Pont Neuf, along those narrow streets that zigzagged like lizards between

[60] Quoting from "Marie" by Guillaume Apollinaire (né Wilhelm Kostrowicki; (1880 – 1918), the innovative French poet and art critic of Polish ancestry. An intimate of Picasso, Apollinaire was the first to employ the term "Cubism" in a positive sense. The poem honors Apollinaire's companion Marie Laurencin (1883 – 1956) and was published in the collection "Alcools" in 1913: "The river resembles my sorrow, / it flows but never dries up."

[61] "Villon, who one would seek here, / Is no longer here, nor Verlaine." Carco is quoting from his own poem about Villon, *"Villon, qu'on chercherait,"* published in *La Bohème et mon coeur - Petits airs* (1912). Jean Pellerin (1885 – 1921): French poet and founder of the Fantaisiste school, who met Carco during his military service in Grenoble. He died from tuberculosis, contracted during the war. Carco assembled and edited a posthumous collection of Pellerin's poetry, entitled *Le Bouquet inutile* ("The Useless Bouquet"; 1923). André du Fresnois (né André Casinelli; 1886 – 1914): French theater critic, poet, and royalist activist, killed during combat at Courbesseaux on 25 August 1914; his body was never retrieved. Claudien (né Robert de La Vaissière; 1880 – 1937): another member of *Les poètes fantaisistes*, along with Paul-Jean Toulet, Jean-Marc Bernard, Léon Vérane, Francis Carco, Tristan Derème, and Philippe Chabaneix. Moments after sending Carco a telegram of congratulations for having been elected to the Académie Goncourt, Claudien was run over and killed by a truck in Paris.

the dark houses. I stir only ashes with my recollections – very fragile ashes which are lifted on the night wind and shaped like disembodied spirits – ghosts ...

And yet however far it may be from Montmartre to the Latin Quarter, the same ghosts are there, everywhere, alive and smiling and quick to touch me with the heady bitterness that rises from the past. But for them, I should not have been tempted to write this book. Should I have needed to set down here, like a guide, the record of our follies and of the places we used to haunt? Mostly we would meet around Frédéric's table[62] or with Hubert the Magnanimous,[63] circulating from one to another to smoke a cigarette, chat, thumb over some books and keep alive our friendships. It needs nothing more than this to make life full of charm. We desired nothing better; it seemed so simple to live, to have friends and to work. Time might separate us, or chance, but a letter, a book, a note in the newspapers, or an article mentioning our names was sufficient to hold us together then, for we were traveling the same road. And if, occasionally, one of us thought of the future, he found there a place for the rest.

[62] Frédéric Gérard, aka Frédé, ran the legendary Lapin Agile during its heyday. According to Charles Beadle, who interviewed Frédé's daughter Helen, "Frédé, after he had studied at the Collège des Arts et Métiers, began life as a draughtsman, doing portraits and sketches at cafés and fairs." Charles Douglas, *Artist Quarter*, p. 25. ("Charles Douglas" is a portmanteau pseudonym of Charles Beadle and Douglas Goldring.) See also Beadle's novel, *Dark Refuge*, which contains fictionalized portraits of friends and acquaintances such as Max Jacob, Modigliani, Zborowski, Jeanne Hébuterne, and Beatrice Hastings (the one-time lover of Katherine Mansfield, whose affair is fictionalized in Carco's novel, *Les Innocents*). Charles Beadle, *Dark Refuge. Edited with Annotations by Rob Couteau*, New York: Dominantstar, 2022.

[63] Hubert was the proprietor of the Caveau de la Bolée, located at 25, rue l'Hirondelle. Carco was amused by Hubert's bizarre proverbs, such as: "Uncooked veal and raw chickens make hunchbacked cemeteries" (*Veau mal cuit et poulets crus font les cimetières bossus*).

Alas! See what remains: memories, and some empty places. We would not dare to sit now at Frédéric's table ... what would be the use? The young men who have succeeded us are all there. May it be long before they find more sorrow than pleasure in counting over their friends!

Maurice Utrillo, *Eglise de Leynes*, 15 x 24 cm. This drawing is also reproduced in Carco's early tribute to the painter, *Les Peintres Français Nouveaux N°. 8: Utrillo* (1921). Originally part of his art collection, it went on the auction block in 1925. His fourteen Utrillo lots included a drawing, a pastel, six lithographs, and six oil paintings. Carco's auction featured more work by Utrillo than by any other artist.

II

The first time I met with Utrillo[64] it was not in the street, or in one of those bars where everyone else seems to have met him. That legend has had its day, but, as it was based upon his continuous and unconcealed drunkenness, Utrillo's admirers place more emphasis upon the legend than upon their pretended love for his painting and will never have done with it. Yet there is no painter who can evoke as somberly as he [can] the height of Montmartre nor who is comparable to him in tragic bitterness of vision, compactness of color, detail, atmosphere and direct but tormented language which moves us as soon as we hear it. No, it was not in the street, staggering and in rags, that Utrillo first appeared to me. I met him, one winter's night, on the Butte, after innumerable negotiations with M. G. (who is currently known in Montmartre as *le père G.*), because M. G. had taken charge of him and was trying to stop his debauchery.[65]

The room contained a bed, a chair, a mirror and an easel and

[64] Maurice Utrillo (1883 – 1955): French painter and son of the artist Suzanne Valadon, whose modernist masterpieces immortalize the urban landscape of Montmartre. Utrillo suffered from alcoholism and mental illness throughout his life but achieved great renown during his later years.

[65] "Le père G" (also referred to here as "M. G.": César Gay, a former police sergeant who, upon retirement, opened the Casse-Croûte, located at 1, rue Paul Féval. Gay rented Utrillo a room above the café, where he often painted; the finished work would then be displayed and sold in the café downstairs. Gay was remembered for his patient handling of Utrillo. "Rising more than three hundred feet above the plain," the Butte is a hill in Montmartre, once planted with vineyards, "where the streets fork off from an open square and interlace the upper slopes" and where "artists had established themselves in dozens of little courtyard studios." Robert Coughlan, *The Wine of Genius. A Life of Maurice Utrillo*, Harper and Brothers, 1951, pp. 1, 7.

looked out upon the rue du Mont-Cenis. It was lighted by a poor unshaded lamp.

"Monsieur Maurice!" called *Père G.*

He introduced me. Utrillo peered out at us from behind his easel, upon which he was covering a piece of cardboard with lines drawn with a ruler.

"It is a gentleman who has come to see you," explained his landlord, manager and pupil. M. G. combined all his functions with an air of the greatest gravity and conviction.

He repeated:

"It is a gentleman ..."

"Yes," said Utrillo.

M. G. pointed to a chair:

"Sit down, sir," he said and as Utrillo did not offer to begin a conversation with the intruder I was, the man simpered:

"It is very nice of you to pay a visit to our Monsieur Maurice. If you only knew how hard he works! He has been so good since he came here, he has not wanted to go out at all. You would hardly believe it. In my opinion he even works too hard. It makes him thirsty to work so hard ... the oil, the zinc white, nothing makes one so thirsty."

"Yes, yes," approved Utrillo.

He had put down his pencil and his ruler and a timorous smile of combined mockery and resignation was fixed upon his face like a nervous twist. Such a smile! I shall remember it all my life. His face looked like a wax mask brightened by his sweet, tender eyes. Judged by his eyes it was a child's or a hermit's face, but this was contradicted by the bitterness of the line of his mouth. No, it was hardly a smile. There was in it too much restraint, it was too mechanical, too fanatical, it showed too much dissimulation and hidden weakness.

"Well?" asked M. G., coming up to the easel, which he pointed out to me with the same gesture he had used when offering me a chair. "May we have just one look at your painting, Monsieur Maurice?"

Utrillo drew aside. His expression became so mobile and anxious that I thought he was going to speak, but he kept silent and continued smiling. He was quite indifferent. We might have "just one look," as his host had asked. What did he care? His work did not belong to him. It belonged to M. G. because of some agreement or other they had made, and M. could have been less formal in asking the painter's consent.

However, he kept watching us from the distance and the lamp cast shadows upon his forehead, his sunken yellow cheeks and his black eyes full of a brewing storm. It threw into relief the bumps on his high intelligent forehead up to his dark and oily hair and I noticed that it grew very wide toward the temples; it showed clearly the firm arch of his eyebrows, accentuated the straight line of his nose and cast light upon his chin and the double line of his lips, though they were hidden by a dark drooping mustache. It showed plainly his sunken cheeks as far as his ears, and behind them the disappearing line of his neck. What a brutally realistic and significant picture, full of intense distress and misdirected enthusiasm! I could not keep my eyes from him. And it was no ordinary portrait I saw, but a full-length one, from the old slippers on his feet, his trousers tied around his waist by some twine, his collarless shirt, his coat covered with spots, to his hair which he kept brushed back without the aid of a comb.[66]

While looking at him so closely, I was rather astonished to find that he was, in every way, exactly as I had thought from his paintings. An aura of exaltation, pain, submission, hostility, distrust, naturalness and sensitive, ironical confusion surrounded him and emanated from him. It could not be

---

[66] Note how Carco turns the tables and, in a consummately painterly fashion, conjures a "portrait" of Utrillo. In both his poetry and prose Carco's painterly eye assumes a prominent role, occasionally even endangering the dramatic effects and tensions necessary to maintain a reader's interest.

expressed in words. M. G. could shout with admiration and praise the talent of so great a painter, but I was now less interested in his talent than in his personality. For me he was only one of those men who, whatever they may do, continually need to be helped and are less to be admired for what they accomplish than for their fight against that other inner self which possesses and relentlessly betrays them.

M. G. was describing complacently the life Utrillo was leading and the ceaseless care he took of his astonishing boarder. Words flowed out of his mouth like lukewarm water, monotonously and endlessly. Which Utrillo was he talking about? To hear him name the one who stood in front of us, I would have sworn that M. G. was thinking about the other and that he was very much afraid that the other would sometime take the place of the unassuming M. Maurice whom he was praising. And my own preoccupation was not with M. Maurice either ... M. Maurice? It sounded incongruous to hear that Christian name applied to Utrillo. How could such a somber and strong name as Utrillo be applied to the same man who answered to the unctuous "M. Maurice" of the much-too-glib M. G.? I could not become accustomed to it.

Moreover, it seemed to me that Monsieur G. was avoiding the name Utrillo when he spoke of the painter and that the latter was waiting for an opportunity to react to the sound of that name.

Several times this occurred to me and yet I could not believe it possible, because in the end I had to admit that the pact between Utrillo and his host had been based upon their friendship and was not one of those abominable bargains by which the honorable M. G. was keeping the artist locked up to make up for what he spent. Nowadays, thank God, no one is ever kept a prisoner against his will! Besides, had not M. G. shown me his own work before introducing me to Utrillo? There was evident in it the disconcerting influence of the painter of Montmartre. Leprous walls, livid skies, cold and mournful perspectives of suburbs, it seemed as if M. G. had neglected nothing in trying to equal his master, or at any rate, to deserve his encouragement. On the back of his canvases, one could read in Utrillo's large handwriting: *Good, Fair* or *My compliments to my best pupil G.* Those notes meant a great deal to the pupil and it was evident that he was very proud of them.

"Only," he pointed to me, "sometimes I add a snow effect. It is very funny and not at all difficult. What do you think of it?"

How did I know? I had come to M. G. to see a painter and I had found two, but not the one I was looking for. Where was he? Here was only a very extraordinary M. Maurice, who said nothing, and another gentleman who spoke all the time. In the end I was at a loss. I must go. I had started to go. I opened the door. M. G. followed me.

"Well?" he asked. "Will you come back soon to pay us another visit?"

"Yes, certainly," I answered him.

"Monsieur Maurice will be pleased!"

"I am sure he will."

The kind man looked at me without saying a word.

"You see," he said, while seeing me out, "you must not be astonished about Monsieur Maurice's manners. He is always like that the first time, and please call him simply: Monsieur Maurice. It is better. Because Monsieur Maurice reminds him of the time when he was small and easy to lead. I know him so well, you see! And if I wanted him to leave at once and never come back, I would only have to call him Utrillo. You have no idea – at the sound of the name Utrillo, he would go out for a drink ... and what a disaster that would be! We would have to begin all over again ..."

III

Max Jacob[67] was more discreet; he lived at 9, rue Ravignan, in a kind of greenhouse in a court, where the sole ornament, the signs of the zodiac drawn with green and pink chalk, spread over the walls and offered a delightful rebus to his comrades.

I had met him at Édouard Gazanion's,[68] the poet who was my host at the time and who carried hospitality so far that he never left Paris without marking on each piece of his furniture with chalk the order in which I could sell it and distress him least. Max's kindness, his distinguished manners, his readiness to help others and his clever talk inclined the people in the house to put up with him. If, for example, some poor woman in the neighborhood who knew his reputation came to ask him to bring back her son to the house – he would put on a small bowler hat – which he only wore on such occasions – and hurry off. He always managed to bring the runaway back to his mother. Sometimes, a neighbor would come surreptitiously and, not afraid of being in the way, ask him to read the cards for

[67] Max Jacob (1876 – 1944): innovative French poet, painter, occultist, and long-time companion of Picasso, who portrayed Max as a monk in his two oil paintings of the *Three Musicians* (completed in 1921). Despite having converted to Christianity Max was arrested by the Gestapo for the "crime" of being Jewish on 24 February 1944. Jean Cocteau attempted to secure his release but failed. On 5 March he died at the Drancy internment camp, two days before being shipped to Auschwitz. His brother and sister were arrested, deported, and killed in Auschwitz.

[68] Édouard Gazanion (1880 – 1956): poet of Montparnasse and author of *Chansons pour celle qui n'est pas venue* ("Songs for she who did not come"), Paris: Vers et Prose, 1910, whom Fernande Olivier describes as "a sort of *poète maudit*, [who] would burden us with his dreams, his griefs and his marital and literary frustrations." See Fernande Olivier, *Picasso and His Friends*, Jane Miller, trans., New York: Appleton-Century, 1965, p. 77. Fernande adds that Carco was Gazanion's "most intimate" friend.

her. Max would leave his work and do so. The small coin he found later under the pages of a manuscript he would give to "his" poor in the street.

What a charming and precious friend Max was to me! He often walked about Paris with me at night talking about the poets. I remember a story published in a review which began with these words: "As they had taken the wrong road, they had to begin the funeral all over again." His fantasy changed everything; it was natural and spontaneous; he played cleverly with the most watertight reasoning to overthrow it and to build with the pieces small tales where one could see as in colored glass balls a thousand glistening reflections. Thanks to him, I really learned what life is or ought to be for the artist and that there is nothing of which one ought ever to tire. Wasn't he curious about everything? Wasn't he always ready to listen to what the passers-by were saying, to their reflections and their most intimate thoughts? He read people's faces and could see through them at once; then from this quick divination he would draw very apt conclusions and improvise marvelous stories. He was never at a loss. Sometimes it was "the question of servant girls in Mexico"; sometimes "Fantomas," or the birth of *Orphism*. One evening, Frédéric, at the Lapin Agile, asked him to write a line in his guest book. Max took the pen and wrote the following poem:

[*9 heures du soir*]

> *Trouver la rime à Frédéric ,*
> *Voilà le hic !*
> *J'aime mieux attendre d'être ivre*
> *Pour m'inscrire à bord de ton livre !*

[*2 heures du matin*]

A bord ! Piano A. Bord.
Livre de bord.
Paris, la mer qui pense, apporte
Ce soir au coin de ta porte,
O tavernier du quai des Brumes,
Sa gerbe d'écume.[69]

The agility of his mind, which his friends perhaps helped him

[69] "9 P.M. / Finding a rhyme for Frédéric, / That's the hitch! / I prefer to wait until I'm drunk / To inscribe my name on the edge of your book! / 2 A.M. / On board! Piano A. Bord. / Ship's log! / Paris, the sea that ponders, brings / Tonight, to the corner of your door, / O tavern keeper of the quai des Brumes, / Its sheaf of foam." (My translation.) "A translation cannot hope to capture Jacob's clever puns, verbal and imagistic associations: 'à bord' means on board … A. Bord is also the name of a French piano firm. By playing on these associations, and stressing drunkenness, Jacob arrives at the image of the sea and its drunken motion." Cesar Grana, *On Bohemia: The Code of the Self-Exiled*, New Brunswick, NJ: Taylor and Francis, 2017, p. 384. Max is also playing with the expression, "to get on board your book." The fulcrum point of the poem rests on the fact that Frédé's guest book served as a ship's log: a list of all the passengers on a madcap voyage into the avant-garde, with the Lapin's façade akin to the cutting-edge prow of a ship. "The Lapin Agile has also been thought of as a quayside sailors' rest from which one would set out on the seas of adventure, and also as a refuge from the perils of society…. Frédé kept a 'livre du bord,' in which transients and crew sketched and wrote their momentary impressions." Seymour S. Weiner, *Francis Carco*, p. 224, n. 5. For Nicholas Hewitt, the poem resonates with "the notion of the Lapin Agile as a vessel on the stormy seas of Montmartre," the latter akin to one "of the great sea ports" replete with "crime, drinking, and prostitution." And he quotes from Carco's Utrillo biography: "Did we not all have the sensation of living on some ship in Montmartre?" (Hewitt, *Montmartre*, p, 132-133.) Later in this memoir, when the focus shifts to the Latin Quarter, Carco again indulges in this maritime metaphor: "More than in Montmartre, the illusion of a maritime town, with its low pubs, its buildings at the corners with high prows, its poor population, its fog, its houses of prostitution, pursued us at each step. The sharp groaning of the ships' whistles that the wind sometimes brought and the soft breeze full of a sickening smell coming from the Seine made the illusion very real."

to cultivate, is shown very plainly in this small poem, and also his way of using one word successively in all its meanings and aspects. That was how unthinkingly he belonged to the cubistic movement which Picasso and he rendered fashionable about 1900, to the astonishment of the crowd.

But what did Cubism matter to him? He played with it as he did with everything else and was not greatly in earnest. He left to Apollinaire the task of discussing it, on the terrace of the Café de Flore, with that good-natured seriousness of his which dazzled so many foreigners who were slow to understand, but were convinced before they understood. For him it was a game he enjoyed playing as soon as he tried it and he pushed it to the limits of absurdity until his fantasy mastered him. And what did Max Jacob not invent to amaze people? He told the famous story of the lozenge which Picasso showed him one Sunday, asserting it was the portrait of a peevish mistress. That lozenge amused Max immensely and with the idea of complicating matters he provoked the discovery of the cube. I am not inventing anything. Max told me that himself, and more interesting is the fact that he made a hundred stories out of it, because he was a chatterbox.

It seemed to be his greatest pleasure to lead well-intentioned men astray, so that afterward he might teach them to rise above their pettier natures and know themselves. But who gave heed to his lessons? None ever followed Max any further than the astonishment into which he plunged them, and they were only angry with him for that. But Max did not care. Rich only in his fantasy, he had for himself humbler disciples who listened to him, made use of his words and got out of them what they could – humble people, small people. His imagination was his only wealth. Indeed, how many times have I seen Max, as he was dressing to go out, put on an old pair of too-wide trousers which he had inherited from his father and tie on a stiff shirtfront a very narrow black tie which he could only have found in his father's wardrobe in Quimper. He used to laugh at himself. His small round mirror, which he gave me one day in return for one in which he could see better, dated from ancient times. Maclet[70] would corroborate my story. He shared Max's lodgings, slept on a chair and frequently appealed to him to write letters to convince the [connoisseurs] who were considering buying his paintings.

There was always at least one painter at Max's, for he loved the arts and himself drew the people he watched in the streets. The gouaches and watercolors which he painted helped him to make a living, and are much sought after today, and rightly so.[71] Salmon[72], who made an inventory of Max's palette, mentions "some so-called Chinese pencils worth a sou a piece"; a Conte pencil presented at the Lapin Agile, by a fifteen-year-old painter, full of generosity and enthusiasm; a carpenter's blue pencil; charcoal "very much better than the usual charcoal sold to painters" and some pastels in a few ocher and pink tints, all shades of blues and a beautiful light green. Max even went so far as to buy a green pencil, rather soft, of the kind called "Raphael." He also owns a brush, white lead in a tube and a bottle of Chinese ink, pleasing to the eye with its label covered with undecipherable signs and its yellow silk ribbon dangling like that on a package of cigars. Speaking of cigars, I must not forget the cigar ashes, left by the artist and his guests, which was carefully left in a china bowl.

"Also, on the little snoring devil – the stove on which he used

---

[70] Jules Maclet (1881 – 1962): French Impressionist known for his paintings of Montmartre.

[71] "Their charm derives from his love of the grays and blacks of the Paris atmosphere. Between him and this city there existed those 'communications' whose relationship only great artists discover." Francis Carco, *Vertès*, 1946, p. 78.

[72] André Salmon (1881 – 1969): poet, memoirist, hashish enthusiast, friend of Picasso, and one of the first French critics to write favorably about Cubism, along with Apollinaire.

to dry the watercolors – some coffee was always boiling, kept hot as long as the lamp lasted. Max Jacob needed it for his backgrounds."[73]

How he loved manipulating his paraphernalia and painting his friends when they came to see him! I have my portrait done in ink on a parchment envelope. But how could he stand Maclet after Picasso? Max was not finicky. Of course he was devoted to Pablo Picasso, he had made him known and established a name for him at the price of a thousand visits to dealers and he had worked for him, as he did for everybody – and later for Maclet. Poor Maclet painted at night by the light of a candle, after Max had cleared off the table upon which he painted all day, and began writing the *Terrain Bouchaballe*.[74] A splendid comradeship existed between the painter and the poet. They shared their earnings, which will not surprise any of Max's old friends who have dined at his expense more than once, in a bistro in the rue Cavallotti.[75]

I also shared the amiability of the restaurant owner who gave

[73] Carco's 1925 auction featured six pieces by Max Jacob, including a 11 x 20 cm. drawing entitled *Petite prostituée de Londres*.

[74] *Terrain Bouchaballe*: Max published both a play (1910) and a novel (1923) with this same title. Set in Quimper, his place of birth, these wry, comic works feature a severe social critique of the narrow-minded hypocrisy of a small provincial town. "He was at his best when he told us stories about Quimper, where he'd spent his childhood and which he still loved. Quimper and his stories about it would unleash an inexhaustible flow of humor and invention. He had a talent for seeing the ridiculous side of almost anything, and it was this that fed his tireless imagination." Fernande Olivier, *Picasso and His Friends*, p. 59.

[75] Fernande Olivier identifies this as "Vernin's restaurant on rue Cavallotti." (The café-restaurant Chez Vernin was located at 8, rue Cavallotti.) The other eatery they frequented was "Azon's restaurant on rue de Ravignan, opposite the house where Max Jacob lived." Ibid., p. 101. This was Chez Père Azon, at 12, rue de Ravignan, an establishment where the proprietor offered credit and even accepted artwork in lieu of payment. It was also at Azon's that Picasso ingested hashish pills with Max Jacob and Apollinaire, and, later that evening, shouted that he had discovered photography.

credit to Max. I even recall one winter's night when Max came to my house after I had gone supperless to bed, made me get up and took me with him. I was exceedingly hungry, and we had only a twenty-sou piece between us. This allowed us afterward to take the bus to the Gare Saint-Lazare, where Max had to go to bid farewell to his brother, the explorer, who was going back to Brittany.

We devoured what was given us, but the dog belonging to the establishment sat on his hind legs and looking at us so pitifully that unthinkingly I took the slate on which Max's expenses had accumulated, poured some sauce on it and held it out to the dog. He licked it clean and thus wiped out my friend's debts, which goes to prove that a good action is never without its reward.

Max Jacob's portrait of Francis Carco

IV

We did not feel the want of money so very badly then, for we could always find something to eat at Frédé's, the Lapin Agile, and a drink in exchange for a song, which we did not begin till our glasses had been refilled. Frédé was not stupid and he loved artists of all kinds, so that one met at his place poets, painters, and writers. The amiable ladies who shared our destinies at that time were not hard to please. They always answered when asked what they wanted to drink:

"The cheapest there is!"

They all knew and admired Max, and would follow us to his house to ask his advice on some problem or other, which he would solve very cleverly. Sometimes, when blessing one of those unions which lasted as long as they generally last in Montmartre, Max Jacob would accompany his blessing with one of his drawings which, according to the love he bore the lady in question, was signed with a J., large or small, sometimes very small. Max's affection could be measured by the size of that J. But only a few of us knew this and we kept his secret.

Only one of us, an actor named Ollin[76] who had some talent,

[76] The actor Marcel Olin, a friend of Picasso, Salmon, and Juan Gris, who was killed by an exploding shell during trench warfare on 4 July 1916. (Although Carco spells his name with a double "L," in most other accounts he appears as Marcel Olin.) According to Max Jacob biographer Rosanna Warren (who describes Olin as a "hot-tempered," "tall, domineering man"), "Jacob wrote his old friend Sylvette Fillacier to commiserate about Carco's deformed picture of Marcel Olin, her dead husband. 'Marcel was the first to defend and protect me, no one spoke ill of me in his presence,' Jacob recalled. 'He cared for me when I was sick and helped me when and how he could. Carco's book is full of lies and horrors.'" See Warren, *Max Jacob: A Life in Art and Letters*, UK: W.W. Norton, 2020, pp. xvii-xviii, 11, 104, 137. Although Carco's portrait of Max as "Monsieur Crabe" in his novel, *Scenes from the Life of Montmartre*, is, at times, far from complimentary, the same cannot

would enlighten the ignorant on that point and take a malign pleasure in making trouble. Ollin was one of Max's evil geniuses. He encouraged him to drink, tormented him, talked of the Boulevard, and, to be different, pretended he believed only in success. Not one of us had seen him act, as we hardly ever left the Butte; but his reputation had preceded him at the different places where we met him at night. He was supposed to have acted in Marseille with de Max[77] in the *Houppelande* and

be said here; and one wonders if Jacob was indeed protesting too much. (Carco even pays Max the ultimate compliment: "His imagination was his only wealth.") In any case, biographical information on the actor remains scarce. Fernande Olivier remarked upon his "charmless stupidity" and remembered Olin as "a huge, violent and unpleasant, though amusing, man, who was always trying to scrounge money out of somebody." She also recalls, in another context, that "Max saw himself as perpetually persecuted … even by those who loved him best." (Olivier, *Picasso and His Friends*, pp. 34, 39, 154.) Picasso's masterful biographer John Richardson would later characterize Olin as "a celebrated actor" and "Max Jacob's *'ennemi intime'* … a bellicose pacifist and anarchist, who would die in battle in 1916." (Richardson, *A Life of Picasso Volume II 1907 – 1917: The Painter of Modern Life*, UK: Random House, 2011, pp. 5, 147.) A biographical note that appears in an edition of Max Jacob's poetry collection, *The Dice Cup*, reads: "Sylvette Fillacier (1895 – 1960): an actress at the Théâtre des Arts, wife of actor and poet Marcel Olin, but only for two years as he was killed in July 1916. She later married Pierre Lazareff. Jacob looked on her as a sort of godmother, and in fact asked her to be his, but the clergy deemed her unsuitable." Max Jacob, *The Dice Cup*, Christopher Pilling and David Kennedy, trans., London: Atlas Press, 2000, p. 74. Jacob's fickle temper is also recorded by the artist Marevna, who says that Max was often "cursing his friends and railing at his enemies." She also poses an interesting question regarding Max's desire to convert. "Jacob led a dissolute life; this caused him untold torment, and he was haunted by an intense fear of hell. He became a convert to Catholicism …" See Marevna, *Life with the Painters of La Ruche*, New York: Macmillan Publishing Company, 1974, pp. 68-69.

[77] Édouard Alexandre de Max (né Eduard-Alexandru Max Romalo; 1869 – 1924): celebrated Romanian fin de siècle theater actor, who frequently appeared on stage with Sarah Bernhardt. According to the Puccini Museum,

that was enough to give him prestige with us. But Ollin was not only an actor and could be very entertaining when he allowed a free reign to his fantasy.

For several weeks at the beginning of winter this tall and amusing young man spent all his afternoons in the big shops under the pretext of buying an overcoat. He gave his address to the cashier and those of us who had no roofs over our heads and shared the actor's garret were regularly awakened by a knock at the door and a voice saying:

"The Louvre!" Or "The Samaritaine! ... The Bon Marché! ... Pygmalion!"

"I can't open," Ollin would answer very gravely. "Leave it downstairs with the concierge."

And when he asked downstairs if there were any parcels for him:

"Monsieur Ollin," the *pipelette*[78] would answer, "what do you expect? They are not such fools!"

But Ollin never gave up and would try again every day, explaining to us in all good faith:

"If you want to dress for nothing, you have only to be lucky enough to have the coat brought by a stupid delivery boy. Wait ... I am damned if it won't work one of these days. But Ollin went without an overcoat all that winter.

Generally his companion was the songwriter Gaston Couté, whom one could always see at the Lapin Agile lying dead drunk upon a bench. Couté, the author of *La chanson d'un gâs qu'a mal tourné*, "Songs of a boy who took the wrong turning," was to end in a hospital, but that time he came willingly with

"It is likely that Puccini had seen in Paris, in May 1912, the drama *La houppelande* by Didier Gold (1874 – 1931), from which he drew up the first panel of The Triptych" (a collection of three one-act operas). See PucciniMuseum.org.

[78] Gossipmonger.

us.[79] Owen looked after him as if he were his mother, and if we had no money to pay, Couté recited his verses and squared matters.

One morning in a bar in the rue Lepic frequented by streetwalkers and gunmen, Couté, who had already drunk too much, asked Max to take his place. At that time, Max, full of his approaching conversion to Catholicism, spoke of the Virgin Mary and the ladies and gentlemen in question were quite bewildered. We were getting uneasy about what would come of it, when one of those ladies, quite tired after her work, entered the bar. Max at once tried to catechize her. He walked up to her and began to praise the delights of religion, giving Ollin the time of his life. The woman listened to him with open mouth. But her friend, a very tall Negro, came in and, before any of us had time to interfere, took Max Jacob's hands between his huge paws and broke his thumbs. This painful adventure, which Ollin told all over Montmartre with great glee, enlightened us as to his character and we soon stopped going around with the actor, who shortly afterward went on tour.

Max's other evil genius remained, a much cleverer one than Ollin, the mathematician Princet.[80]

[79] Gaston Couté (1880 – 1911): poet and *chansonnier* originally from Beaugency, France, who occasionally composed in *patois*. An avid absinthe drinker, he contracted tuberculosis and died of pulmonary congestion in the Lariboisière Hospital. "How often would Couté, with his crowd, drink until he collapsed. Then when the glasses were all empty they would shake him back to life sufficiently to get him on his feet and recite a new poem, which paid for another round." Charles Douglas, *Artist Quarter*, p. 30. A collection of his poems and songs titled *La chanson d'un gâs qu'a mal tourné* (which could also be translated as "The song of a guy who turned out badly") was published posthumously in Paris, in 1928. Regarded as an anarchist, at the time of his death he was scheduled to appear before the French criminal court for publishing a revolutionary antimilitary song.

[80] Maurice Princet (1875 – 1973): French mathematician who was also employed as an actuary. A friend of artists and writers such as Apollinaire, Duchamp, Jacob, and Picasso. Known for his theories of non-Euclidean

We respected him, for he earned a princely living as a consulting counsel in a big business and was always well-dressed. When he sat at Frédé's table he looked like a slightly tired gentleman, sad and given to persiflage. His conversation had the effect of exasperating Max and inspired him with irresistibly sharp remarks. Princet, however, was not easily upset and with his insinuating logic he could convince even Max and rob him of his success.

So there were all sorts of people in our group during those happy days when Picasso, to strike a great blow, declared: "When you paint a landscape, it first must look like a plate." Then something happened which was to be full of consequences for Cubism. Max's brother, whom we called the explorer, came back from the colonies and brought with him his portrait, which I believe had been done at Dakar by a Negro. The likeness, very much neglected for the sake of size, struck all the painters at once and they noted that the gold buttons of his coat were not represented where they ought to have been, but as a halo around his face. Surprising discovery! Thus was the disassociation of objects discovered, accepted and acquired. It must have been a stepping stone to Picasso's first researches, for he asserted a short time afterward: "If you paint a portrait, you must put the legs beside it on the canvas."

geometry and the notion of a "fourth dimension," Princet was regarded as the "mathematician of Cubism." The painter Maurice de Vlaminck once wrote: "I witnessed the birth of Cubism, its growth, its decline. Picasso was the obstetrician, Guillaume Apollinaire the midwife, Princet the godfather." But John Richardson notes that despite claims that Princet "supposedly provided Cubism with a mathematical and theoretical rationale," "Picasso and Braque furiously denied this." Richardson, *A Life of Picasso Volume II 1907 – 1917*, p. 5. Indeed, Princet's influence had a more direct impact on the Cubists aligned with Gleizes, Metzinger, and the Duchamp brothers, who openly acknowledged their allegiance to his quasi-metaphysical notions.

And everybody applauded.

Roger Allard[81] was to write: "M. Picasso's career is a masterpiece – one of the rare masterpieces of our time. So much patience combined with so much decision, such minute application hidden under an attitude of nonchalance, such calculated audacity, such prudence masked with an air of lightness, artistic genius regulated to the utmost yet free in its artificiality, all these qualities were combined in a singularly pleasing personality. Everybody knows the edifying anecdote told by the authors of moral schoolbooks, in which M. Lafitte picks up a pin in a banker's corridor and the banker, greatly impressed by this action, gives him the position he had just refused him. M. Picasso always knew how to pick up the pin at the right time, even if he had to take it from a dangerous or too long drawn-out game."

There is a typical story about Picasso which is worth telling. Vlaminck, the untamable, had just discovered in a Bougival bistro a Negro statue and he had acquired it by treating everybody in the place with white wine. Vlaminck at that time was always with Derain, with whose aid he founded the famous [École de Chatou].[82] Vlaminck brought his statue to Derain, placed it in the middle of the studio, looked at it and said:

"Almost as beautiful as the Venus de Milo, don't you think?"

"It is as beautiful," said Derain emphatically.

The two friends looked at each other.

---

[81] Roger Allard (1885 – 1961): French poet, essayist, and art critic who composed a collection of poetry, *Les Élégies Martiales*, while recovering from a wound during WWI.

[82] The French painters Maurice de Vlaminck (1876 – 1958) and André Derain (1880 – 1954): principal figures in the Fauve movement, along with Henri Matisse. At that time Chatou was a small village on the banks of the Seine, slightly to the west of Paris. In 1900 Vlaminck and Derain shared a studio on île de Chatou. The École de Chatou painting style, with its vivid colors and energetic brushwork, is now recognized as a forerunner of Fauvism.

"Shall we go to Picasso? Vlaminck proposed. They went, bearing their piece of wood, and Vlaminck repeated:

"Almost as beautiful as the Venus de Milo! Yes ... almost ... and perhaps! ..."

"As beautiful," Derain repeated.

Picasso thought for some time and at last, deciding he could go no further than they, whose opinions were very daring for the times, he asserted:

"It is more beautiful!"

I hope Picasso will forgive me, but this little story is most instructive. The person who told it to me will not deny it when he finds it here. As Adolphe Basler[83] notes in his work on *Painting – A New Religion*: "Picasso then started despoiling the Negro as he despoiled the Egyptian, the Phoenician and as he would later despoil the Pompeian decorator, the Coptic carpet designer and all the artistic people of the earth."

And yet it was only necessary to see the inventor of Cubism at the Lapin, where the walls were ornamented with one of the paintings of his Blue period, to be convinced of the extraordinary radiance which hovered around him. He had stopped coming every evening when I first went there. And yet the conversation was all about him and it was easy to know when he was there from the animation which his paradoxes always provoked. The Negroes, made fashionable by him, by Luc-Albert Moreau,[84] and by Vlaminck, who had already

---

[83] Adolphe Basler (1876 – 1951): Franco-Polish art historian, critic, and collector who was portrayed in paintings and drawings by contemporary artists such as Moïse Kisling (in 1914) and Modigliani (in 1916). Carco is quoting from his *La Peinture. Religion nouvelle*, Paris: Bibliothèque des marges, Paris: Librairie de France, 1926.

[84] Luc-Albert Moreau (1882 – 1948): French painter and printmaker who originally studied Asian and African languages and graduated from the École des Langues Orientales in Paris, in 1906. Moreau exhibited at the Salon d'Automne in 1908 and at the Salon des Indépendants in 1909. In the 1920s he created sixty lithographs on the subject of boxing.

retired to far away Montparnasse, were already taking their rank as classics, and it is undoubtedly to them that our generation owes its freedom, for the most part, from aimless fantasy, sarcasm and facetiousness.

Of course Pierre Mac Orlan,[85] a young man who differed greatly in his conversation and manners from the ordinary clients of Frédé, used to frequent the Lapin. He was listened to with respect. He sat at the head of the table, and no one, when he began the chorus of the *Legion* or the *Bataillonnaires* would have dared to interrupt him. Compared to his, my songs were only banal repetitions of music hall airs, but one evening, chance bringing me to the Lapin, he heard and liked them and made me sit beside him.

That evening is still engraved on my memory. I had never been inside that Montmartre cabaret before and did not know a soul there. All I knew of that magnificent place was what I had read when still in the provinces, in a little review, *La Nouvelle Plume*, which had praised its charm and offered a free drink there in return for a subscription. A photograph of the Lapin on the back of the review had astonished me greatly. I had cut it out together with the coupon for the free drink and for five years I had been carrying them in an old notebook which I had always with me. Would I pay for my glass with the ticket? I had made up my mind to do so, but Mac Orlan decided otherwise and I was added henceforth to the clients of the famous cabaret

[85] Pierre Mac Orlan (né Pierre Dumarchey; 1882 – 1970): French novelist, illustrator, playwright, and *chansonnier*, who often performed at the Lapin Agile. A key figure among the modernists of bohemian Paris, his work is largely focused on the disillusionment of the post-WWI generation. Marcel Carné's film *Quai des Brumes* (1938) was based on Mac Orlan's novel of the same name, and many of his songs were recorded by popular singers such as Juliette Gréco and Germaine Montero. The Bibliothèque Nationale lists seventeen pseudonyms for him, including "Sadie Blackeyes" and "Pierre Du Bourdel."

of whom Frédé never asked a sou![86]

Thus ties of friendship are established when luck is on your side and suddenly confronts you with the one man who can make them lasting and attractive. Pierre Mac Orlan lived by doing the most discouraging literary jobs, and by composing songs which he sold in the Faubourg Saint-Denis for what the songwriters would give him, and by drawing for some newspapers. He made very little money, even for that time, but was establishing a reputation under his nom de plume of Mac Orlan, and the *Journal* was publishing his tales.

Those tales sparkled with humor and were in keeping with the very Scotch name of their author. Was it the result of a bet, a joke? I think rather that, in adopting the nom de plume of Mac Orlan, this attractive young man gave free rein to his tastes. He loved all sports and when I knew him was on the U.A.I. team as back and was very proud of a magnificent blue-and-red sweater, the colors of the Union. He had spent two years at a seaport and his experiences there were sufficient excuse for him to dress as an athlete or even as a cowboy. If you understand that such was our only taskmaster; that we were enthusiastic about bohemia, adventure, Negroes, Cubism, and traveler's tales and that we had a certain presentiment of the events which were later to upset the world, you will understand Pierre Mac Orlan in spite of his poses.

They were not extravagant for the good reason that the low cafés of a great commercial port teach decency. In those bars Pierre Mac Orlan had met seamen of all colors, their officers and those specimens of the four human races who live picturesquely in such places. He had modeled himself upon them, borrowing their practical morality and trying, with an energy one could read upon his face, to be ready for any eventuality. To us, he was a man and life had taught him, as it had taught Kipling's

[86] Seymour S. Weiner reports that the Lapin, where he was "soon taken into the inner circle," was Carco's "favorite hangout." *Francis Carco*, pp. 60-61.

soldier who even when in irons does not lament his fate but declares bravely:

I paid my price for findin' out[87]

Like the hero of the road to Mandalay, for whom he did not hide his sympathy, Pierre Mac Orlan had paid, but to his experiences, however rough they had been, he brought gaiety and a lightheartedness which reestablished his mental balance.

He had started as a painter about 1900 and had exhibited some canvases at the Sagot Gallery which, happily for the admirers of the great novelist he has become, did not attract any attention. Pierre did not even earn enough money for food for his painting and he had to try something else. For a long time Montmartre was to him only a corner of the wide world, to which he came back between two unsuccessful business ventures. He would stay a week and then his adventurous spirit would urge him to seek another field. He tried his fortune in Florence, where he lived more than two years, in Bruges, Antwerp, Sluis, and Amsterdam. He was a master of many trades and did many things, from reading proofs at a printer's in Rouen to guarding a villa through the winter in a small half-dead town abroad. He always accepted what was offered him, was always poor and always tried cheerfully not to remain so. Alas, how deceiving life is to such a very young man as he, who, unable to live by his brush, thought he could live by writing verses! Because Mac Orlan was a poet. Poet and

---

[87] From "For to Admire," by Rudyard Kipling: "Oh, I 'ave come upon the books, / An' frequent broke a barrick rule, / An' stood beside an' watched myself / Be'avin' like a bloomin' fool. / I paid my price for findin' out, / Nor never grutched the price I paid, / But sat in Clink without my boots, / Admirin' 'ow the world was made." The poem was published in the popular *Pall Mall Magazine* in February 1894. Kipling's poem "Mandalay," sometimes referred to as "The Road to Mandalay," was published in the *Scots Observer* on 21 June 1890.

sportsman, shooting inedible seabirds on the sand dunes of Belgium and mastering himself, battling with fate and standing up to it. None of his poems remain, and yet they were inspired by the rhythm, the spontaneity, the intensive vibration which we saw later in *L'Inflation sentimentale*.[88]

The best of Mac Orlan may be there, in the perverted taste of the men of his generation for the most delightful uneasiness and a bitter enjoyment of it. But at the time of which I am writing[89]

[88] Pierre Mac Orlan, *L'inflation Sentimentale*, Paris: La Renaissance du Livre, 1923.

[89] Carco's original text does not contain the phrase "But at the time of which I am writing …" Besides inventing this sentence, Madeleine Boyd omits what precedes it, undoubtedly because no British or American publisher in the 1920s would have allowed for its inclusion. This is a literal translation of the censored passage (which follows the first mention of "*L'Inflation sentimentale*"):

> … this intense vibration, which we were later to encounter in *L'Inflation sentimentale* and which we can judge by this evocation of Montparnasse:

> We see coming from America,
> Eyes still barely opened
> To public perversity,
> The blonde girls of Mortimer.
> But on their too new mucous membranes,
> They are looking for some love
> The very intimate ecstasy for
> Finally establishing its proof,
> Eyes ringed at daybreak.

> The best of Mac Orlan is there, perhaps, in this perverted taste of the men of his generation for the sweetest worries and their bitter jubilation. But other girls, like Mortimer's blonde girls, attracted him to Antwerp in the Shippers-Wartier, among the last vestiges of the Rut-Dyk sung by Georges Eekhoud.

Carco's original French text reads as follows:

he was drawn to Antwerp in the Shippers-Wartier, to hear the last vestiges of the Rut-Dyk sung by Georges Eekhoud.[90] I can see Mac Orlan, standing in waterfront bars, already feeling his way. If, like Salmon in Russia, during a certain period, he was only a very minor poet, there was no doubt that the ardent and unconscious desire to express his own individuality and to use a new language made him capable of understanding his youthful joys and sorrows. His rough life was urging him on, tormenting him and forcing him to find himself when he came back to Paris, at the end of his resources. Necessity drove him to assume responsibilities. Speaking of that subject, I recall that once at Max Jacob's in the rue Ravignan, we remarked that only when a poet is abandoned by the whole world and battered by

… cette intense vibration, que nous devions plus tard rencontrer dans *L'Inflation sentimentale* et dont on peut juger par cette evocation de Montparnasse:

On y voit venir d'Amérique,
Les yeux encore à peine ouverts
Sur la perversité publique,
Les blondes girls de Mortimer.
Mais sur leurs muqueuses trop neuves,
Elles attendent de l'amour
La très intime extase pour
En établir enfin la preuve,
Les yeux cernés au point du jour.

Le meilleur de Mac Orlan est là, peut-être, dans ce goût perverti des hommes de sa génération pour les plus suaves inquiétudes et leur amère jubilation. Mais d'autres filles alors que les blondes girls de Mortimer l'attiraient à Anvers dans le Shippers-Wartier, parmi les derniers vestiges du Rut-Dyk chantés par Georges Eekhoud.

[90] Georges Eekhoud (1854 – 1927): Belgian novelist whose early work received praise from Huysmans and Zola.

the bitterest or the tenderest of disillusionment, does he know why he was born and what fate has in store for him.[91]

At that time we all suffered from a deep and incurable disillusionment, but as recompense we had our friendships and experiences, premature and incomplete perhaps, but bought at their full value. I can't help coming back to that subject. All of us paid with our best years for the sad knowledge of life and only the stronger amongst us have been able to stand it.

To understand how the men of my generation used to fight against taking themselves too seriously one must have heard Mac Orlan tell stories, on returning from his long journeys. For instance, on winter nights, in Holland, he would go on board one of the boats anchored along the quays, at the invitation of some captain or other. In the cabin a bottle of whiskey would be placed between the two men and each in turn would take a long drink. At the second or third bottle, Pierre's host, who until then had not uttered a word, would suddenly become very loquacious, but as nine times out of ten he did not know French, he would simply utter proper names, then look at Pierre triumphantly, wait a moment, shake his head, utter a cry, until Mac Orlan would answer him, whereupon they would shake hands very affectionately.

" Napoleon!" The seaman would say with a very Swedish or American accent. "Napoleon, ah!"

"Ah! Yes!"

"Yes! Yes!"

There would be a moment of silence, or more exactly preparation, then they would smile at each other and Mac Orlan would go on:

[91] Cf. this passage from Carco's novel, *Scènes de la vie de Montmartre* (1919). Referring to Monsieur Crabe (Max Jacob), a character named Coquelet is given this eloquent line: "He remembered that Monsieur Crabe had said to him one day that a man must have been alone in the winter upon a high road, and stripped of all earthly possessions to find that manner of expression which shall go to the hearts of men."

"Of course, Napoleon ... But Tierra del Fuego, well, little brother, what about it? Tierra del Fuego? ...

"Oh! Yes ..."

"And Pondichéry ... Very good!"

"I know," the seaman would assert ... "Yes, Pondichéry ... Very good!"

And so on till the early morning.

From those extraordinary encounters, with proper names the only means of communication between the two drinkers, Mac Orlan has probably acquired the neat and quick style which is admired in his books; and their great power of evocation.

No superfluous talk. Words, facts, a few sincere statements, is that not enough for people of his kind? Mac Orlan never wasted time in speeches. At Frédé's table as he sat smoking his clay pipe he always listened more than he talked, but no matter how brief and desultory the observations he contributed to the conversation, they were always significant!

Pierre Mac Orlan

V

His first friends had been Guillaume Apollinaire, Salmon, Max Jacob and then Warnod,[92] nicknamed *petite père Dédé*, and Roland Dorgelès.[93] Both the latter and Mac Orlan drew. Warnod sketched the little streetwalkers and the girls of the brasseries and Dorgelès drew immense plans, for he intended to become an architect. Does that not partly explain the subject of the *Reveil des Morts*?[94] It is worth looking up. But Dorgelès had long hair and wore a cloak with a most magnificent and romantic effect. Warnod also adopted that queer fashion. He looked so well, indeed, that his models used to pursue him everywhere he went.

Dorgelès, who preferred the papers and the big restaurants to our stories and meager repasts, and who only climbed to the Lapin to fight against the ready-made admirations everybody

[92] André Warnod (1885 – 1960): art critic, illustrator, and chronicler of Montmartre and Montparnasse in works of fiction and nonfiction (e.g., *Le Vieux Montmartre*; 1913). Along with Carco, he was one of the first to write about Utrillo in books such as *Les Peintres de Montmartre, Gavarni, Toulouse-Lautrec, Utrillo* (1928).

[93] Roland Dorgelès (1885 – 1973): novelist and member of the Académie Goncourt; most remembered for his award-winning *Les croix de bois* (1919), a study of World War I, later made into a film by Raymond Bernard (*Wooden Crosses*; 1932). Dorgelès claimed to have coined the phrase *drôle de guerre* (phony war). During WWII he attempted to arrange a republication of *Les croix de bois*, but when he refused to remove the word *boche* from the narrative he was refused a publication license by the German official responsible for overseeing censorship, Gerhard Heller. Dorgelès was a correspondent for the right-wing journal, *Gringoire*, but resigned "in September 1941 because of its collaborationism and anti-Semitism. Nevertheless, he remained both nationalist and a Pétainist …" Nicholas Hewitt, *Montmartre*, pp. 177, 220. He later fled to Marseille.

[94] *Le Réveil des Morts* ("The Awakening of the Dead"), Paris: Albin Michel, 1923.

entertained there, is certainly the one of us who has changed least. Although he has repudiated his clothes and has cut his hair, his enthusiasm and his generous heart and spirit have still the same intensity which they had then and he retains the same surprising verve. He was always ready to fight windmills, even those which were the ornaments of the Butte and only turned to the wind of paradoxes. He spent his forces trying to convince the most indifferent among us. Who in Montmartre does not remember the adventure of Frédé's donkey? Dorgelès, on a bet, had sworn to make the beast famous. It also happened that on a certain occasion he had wagered with the painters who were annoyed by his enthusiasms that he would exhibit in the *Indépendants*[95] the most original and revolutionary canvas of the exhibition. His challenge was taken up and Dorgelès racked his brains. Accompanied by Warnod, *petit père Dédé*, he arrived one day at Frédé's with a sheriff at his heels whom he at once asked to draw up an affidavit. The poor man of law was frightened – to impress him Dorgelès had put in his buttonhole the enormous rosette of an officer of Public Instruction – for he did not understand what the joke was all about. The donkey was brought. A brush was tied to his tail and he was given something to eat.

"Please, don't do any harm to my Lolo," Frédé kept saying. "You see, he is a good donkey ... He has no guile ..."

"All right ..." Dorgelès replied ... "You'll see!"

The brush full of color, *petit père Dédé* brought a big canvas, and as the good animal showed his contentment by swishing his tail, the brush began its work.

"Whereas ... " was writing the sheriff, very much astonished to be taking part in such an affair ... "Whereas, a brush having been affixed to the caudal extremity of the said donkey, Messrs. Dorgelès and Warnod in the presence of Mr. Frédéric, owner,

<hr>

[95] *Salon des Indépendants*: annual art exhibit first established on 29 July 1884.

etc...."

"It is stunning," the last would say.

The brush was doing its work and, slowly but surely, a nameless motley was covering the surface which was to be presented for the admiration of the snobs. The picture was taking shape. To tell the truth, it was not a work carefully thought out, but by dint of emptying many tubes, one could see occasionally very curious effects, rare values and relations, and all sorts of intentions.

"Well, isn't it extraordinary," Dorgelès would exclaim. "Lolo is lucky. His first daub will bring a lot of money."

"And we'll drink it all, you can count on that," Warnod would assert to Frédé, who was scratching his head.

"Gentleman," interrupted the sheriff, whom this artistic and zoological affidavit had completely bewildered, "what is the name of this work?"

"Of course ..." said Dorgelès.

"Write down: *Still life*, proposed Frédéric.

No ... No ... cried Roland, "wait: still life, do you think?"

He gave his accomplice a dig with his elbow and asked:

"What do you think?"

Petit père Dédé was not sure.

"We could," he began, "call it ..."

"Silence!" Dorgelès, wrapped in meditation, was tapping his forehead and had at last found an idea."Sheriff, write this down."

He dictated:

"Title: Et le soleil couche sur l'Adriatique," then he signed it in big letters: *Joachim Raphael 'Aliboron*.

At the *Indépendants* the success of this canvas went much further than they had dared to hope. In the exhibition rooms, the [aficionados] only asked for the donkey's picture and crowded close around it to see it better. And they all laughed and shouted so much admiration that the most remarkable paintings of that year were neglected for the benefit of Lolo. Dorgelès won his bet easily.[96]

Such jokes were in fashion at that time and Dorgelès, if he had not succeeded, would have found another. He had inventiveness, audacity and a great need to rid himself of his superfluous energy. Wasn't it he who installed in the Louvre, in the Gallery of Antiquities, a bust that he had picked up at the studio of a sculptor friend, telling him that all Paris would soon be talking of it? The episode created a great scandal, for the bust was left among the perfect examples of statuary till Dorgelès himself and its creator went to claim it. Every minute he would have an idea for astonishing the idiots and he would carry it out at once. Sometimes he would discuss medicine when writing about an exhibition of painting, sometimes, urged by his unconventional mind, he would put up in the Paris streets barriers and signs in big letters: *Street Closed*, with lanterns which he would light at night, thus upsetting the traffic. Nothing frightens him. He made certain photographers quite rich. When he could not get a sheriff to witness his amazing adventures, he used photographs to illustrate his articles and bear witness to their amusing authenticity.

Since he came from the Artois, as did Mac Orlan, he carried a joke to the bitter end. From the years he had spent at the École des Beaux-Arts he had gained habits, which are still in good repute in the studios of the rue Bonaparte but scandalize the bourgeois. But he had this in his favor, he was always inventing new jokes and would draw the wisest conclusions from them, so that everybody was obliged to laugh, and yet, he tells himself that his efforts at the school, far from being rewarded, brought

---

[96] Based on Carco's account Dorgelès might be regarded as a proto-Dadaist prankster, but as a conservative traditionalist his acts were symptomatic of a hostility and antagonism toward modernism and the avant-garde (especially toward Picasso). In any case, his acute sense of humor might not be appreciated by many of today's humorless conceptual artists.

down upon him the director's wrath.

"That, a leg?" Jean-Paul shouted as he watched him working hard ... "No, my boy ... It is anything else you can think of, but not a leg. Upon my word, young fellow, you draw like a blind man."

"Really!" said Dorgelès politely.

"Yes, really."

Dorgelès did not protest. He was satisfied to smile happily behind the director's back and from that day on never put his foot inside the place.

I don't know who was blind, the pupil or the master, or whether or not the master has repented since, because the chief quality of the author of *Les Croix de Bois* consists precisely in his eye for things and for people and his acute observation. Dorgelès never interprets falsely the spectacle of life. He sees first, before he starts to write, before he even chooses his words. Whatever he is writing about, his keen perception is so direct that it arrests and startles you from the first line. He is a blind man one can envy! But to display this gift, since his common sense is allied to a sense of humor, Dorgelès prefers to use satire and farce. We are indebted to him and to Gus Bofa[97] for the astonishing "Petite Semaine" which he edited for the *Sourire*, and for a hundred extremely amusing articles and beautiful bits of reporting. Without Bofa's advice, Pierre Mac Orlan, who was then drawing for the papers, might never have thought of expanding his captions into tales, for he was a poet and wanted

---

[97] Gus Bofa (né Charles Blanchot; 1883 – 1968): illustrator whose artwork was often featured in satirical newspapers and novels. He also designed the cover of *Les Mystères de la Morgue*, a book coauthored by Francis Carco and Pierre Mac Orlan. Nicholas Hewitt regards Bofa as "probably the greatest influence on French caricature during the interwar years, both through the example of his own work and his role as an intermediary and impresario." Hewitt, *Montmartre*, p. 185. Bofa is also remembered for his keen non-verbal book reviews, consisting of a single image that captures the essence of a text.

to remain one. We do not regret the change. Mac Orlan as a humorist has widened his appeal; he made a mixture which has all the savor of cocktails and at the same time their well-balanced strength. But Mac Orlan was not the only one who changed for the better through a friend's advice; his friend also has improved and the only proof needed is the following verse written by Roland Dorgelès, which he sent me instead of saying goodbye:

> *Marseille, poison pénétrant ...*
> *Sur le vieux port passe, sans presse,*
> *Le tram du boul'vard Vauban.*
> *Les cagoles de ta jeunesse*
> *Montent-elles toujours pour trois francs*
> *Et ce Blan, chez qui l'on danse, est-ce*
> *Au Prado qu'il a ses gonzesses*
> *Ou Cimetière Saint-Vincent ?*[98]

The allusions of this charming poem may be obscure to those who have never frequented the Lapin, but they go straight to my heart and recall to me the happy times when, in spite of our common poverty, I sang at Frédé's as best I could this Marseille song:

> *De la rue des Saules*
> *Au boul'vard Vauban,*
> *Toutes les cagoles*
> *Vont danser chez Blan !*[99]

[98] "Marseille, penetrating poison ... / On the old port passes, unhurried, / The Boul'vard Vauban tram. / The *cagoles* of your youth / Always climb up for three francs / And this Blan, with whom we dance, is it / At the Prado that he has his chicks / Or at Saint-Vincent cemetery?" The term *cagoles* refers to a vulgar, provocative, boisterous, or garishly made up woman from southern France, loosely translated as "bimbo" or "slut."

Yes, I am right: Dorgelès was a poet, in his way. Impulsive, generous, excitable, erratic, enthusiastic. If he did not admit it to anyone, even denied it, his life and his temperament gave him a way. He adored red waistcoats, the Boers, the cabarets where we lived, luck, great men, and although he absorbed a great many incredible ideas, his real nature would always burst forth. What did it matter then if his "copy" was for newspapers only! He was to take it elsewhere after the war and give us his unrivaled book, *Les Croix de Bois*.

If I should try to describe him as he was before the war, youthful and ardent, I would conjure him up in the red shirt and the linen trousers he wore when in the country. He looked like a real bandit. People pointed him out. And since he earned a lot from his newspaper work, the amount of money he spent was amazing. One Sunday we went to see him near Paris with Warnod and Marc Brésil[100] and the four of us walked from Fourqueux to Saint-Germain to take the train. Someone proposed that we should drink a glass in a café. It was late and we could not choose. We entered a very unattractive place where, as the owner preferred to close up rather than to serve us, a rather lively discussion and ensued, which brought the police. Charming evening! Dorgelès shirt contributed in making it memorable. Ten minutes later, indeed, we were all at the police station, and we spent the night in the lockup.

The story ran thus through the town, "The police have

[99] "From rue des Saules / To Boul'vard Vauban, / All the *cagoles* / Will dance chez Blan!"

[100] John Richardson reports that Brésil was the "handsome son of a well-known journalist and brother of the musical comedy actress Marguerite Brésil." According to the painter Serge Férat, Brésil was "a young writer who is ... remarkably unintelligent." See Richardson, *A Life of Picasso, Volume II 1907-1917*, p. 204.

arrested a gang of bandits, the chief was dressed all in red and had a large sum of money on his person. He had not had time to divide it with his accomplices ..."

Warnod was engaged to be married, so he missed the splendid luncheon we were tendered the next day. The gentlemanly police released us only with great regret, after having investigated us carefully.

It was to one of his charming friends, Mademoiselle Rara, who had such tiny feet that one of them would go into a beer glass, that I owed my introduction to the attractive André Warnod. During his period of military service Mademoiselle Rara did not leave me for a moment, because she said we were so much alike that no one could call her unfaithful. My resemblance to *petit père Dédé* saved appearances until the day when he reappeared in Montmartre. Rara introduced us to each other and sealed our great friendship forever.

Happy times, when the days passed uselessly and ended by our meeting at dear Frédé's:

La misère aussi faisait rage.[101]

We bore our poverty lightly, without uneasiness or care of any kind since each of us, impelled by fate, was answering his own call. There were Asselin, Girieud, Mario Meunier, Alfred Lombard, Warnod, Brésil, Dorgelès, Mac Orlan, Gazanion, Max Jacob, Manolo,[102] Princet, Durio, Chas Laborde, Utrillo, Couté, Picasso, Vaillant, Ollin, La Vaissière, Marie Laurencin, Falké, Julien Callé, Markous,[103] Daragnès, Pichot,[104] Jean Pellerin,

[101] "Misery was also raging."

[102] Manolo (né Manuel Martinez Hugué; 1872 – 1945): Catalan sculptor and close friend of Pablo Picasso.

[103] Louis Marcoussis (né Ludwik Markus; circa 1878/83 – 1941) Polish painter and engraver, who studied in Paris at the Académie Julian and exhibited at the Salon d'Automne in 1905. He changed his name to Marcoussis (the name of a French village) at the suggestion of Apollinaire.

Bannerot[105] ...

We only thought about life and living; the poorest lived with the others and paid their shares in songs. We were always together. No one was missing and it is because I remember the names of those who never again will sit down at the Lapin's long table that I wrote the following verses full of their dear presence:

> *Tout le jour je vous ai cherchés,*
> *Comme au temps de notre jeunesse*
> *Dans les cafés... Ce temps renaisse*
> *Et nos amours et nos péchés ! ...*
> *Je vous ai cherchés en moi-même*
> *Comme un disparu, ceux qu'il aime,*
> *Les appelle et se tient caché.*[106]

I remember Jean Pellerin especially. I brought him to Montmartre and he was the most faithful and tactful of friends. I see him still, with his dark felt hat, his thin silhouettes, his warm, sincere glance. Everyone loved him. He was the last comer to our band and his poems impressed us by their rhythm, made us value and esteem him. We recited them sometimes, when he was not there, as we do today, with the

An associate of Braque, Degas, and Picasso, he aligned himself with the Cubist movement around 1911. He later collaborated with Joan Miro and taught him engraving techniques.

[104] Ramon Pichot Gironès (1871 – 1925): Catalan and Spanish artist and friend of Picasso, who portrayed Pichot in the painting, "Three Dancers."

[105] Georges Bannerot (1891 – 1917): French poet and brother of the poet Hélène Bannerot.

[106] "All day long, I looked for you, / As in the time of our youth, / In the cafés ... This time is reborn / And our loves and our sins! ... / I looked for you in myself / Like one who has disappeared, calling / Those he loves, who remain hidden."

difference, alas, that if then Jean Pellerin was absent for a night or two, now he will be absent during all the nights and days we still have to go.

Carco with Père Frédé, inside the Lapin Agile.
Photo by Michel Brodsky.

VI

I must speak now of a curious person sometimes seen at Frédé's who, through pure love of mischief, I suspect helped in the birth of the novel of adventure as conceived by Mac Orlan.[107] He was a cool, polite young man who knew Asselin[108] and who did some painting himself. He was said to be captain of a freighter, and indeed he appeared only occasionally at the Lapin, supposedly between trips all over the world, and he always tried to dampen our enthusiasms about other countries.

"In Tahiti, for example," he asserted when one of us spoke excitedly of Gauguin, "it is always raining and the women are dressed in oil cloth."

We would argue with him, but he made his assertions so confidently that we ended by believing him. He knew what he was talking about for he had been there. When Max Jacob tried to trip him up by saying:

"There is an alarm clock on the top of each mountain in Switzerland."

"It is quite possible," would reply this quiet well-mannered man.

"And do you know to what extent cleanliness is carried in Holland?" Mac Orlan would ask. "I assure you that, in certain towns, it is not rare to meet smokers coming out of the saloons

---

[107] According to Mac Orlan, "It must be established as a law that adventure in itself does not exist. Adventure is in the mind of the one who pursues it, and no sooner is he able to touch it with his finger then it vanishes, to reappear much further off in another form, at the limits of the imagination." See Pierre Mac Orlan, *A Handbook for the Perfect Adventurer*, Napoleon Jeffries, trans., Cambridge, MA: Wakefield Press, 2013.

[108] Maurice Asselin (1882 – 1947): French painter, printmaker, book illustrator, and friend of Pierre Mac Orlan.

to empty their pipes beyond the town limits, so as not to spoil it's cleanliness."

"Why not?"

His "Why not" took our breath away by its perfectly phlegmatic indifference and the superior tone in which it was uttered.

But after all, why not? The man was right. Since in Tahiti Gauguin's flower girls were only a myth, anything was possible. One could give free reign to one's imagination; it was only necessary to keep within certain limits. Frédé's cabaret with its low ceiling and the unsteadiness which came to us from drinking and telling stories became a kind of drunken boat upon which we were sailing without either compass or map. On some nights the illusion was perfect.

> *Nous étions deux, nous étions trois,*
> *Nous étions trois marins de Groix...*
> *Il vente !*
> *C'est le vent de la mer qui nous tourmente.*[109]

The whole crew of us would sing.

The wind was strong indeed, but the gay companions clinging to the table were not the kind of friends which the wind carries away! On the contrary they clung strongly to each other through heavy weather, folly and adversity.

Had Georges Delaw[110] not discovered at the very door of the Lapin, in the small Saint-Vincent cemetery, the tomb of Admiral

---

[109] "We were two, we were three, / We were three sailors from Groix ... / It's windy! / It's the sea breeze that torments us."

[110] Georges Delaw (né Henri Georges Delaw; 1871 – 1938): illustrator, cartoonist, interior designer, and memoirist. A native of Sedan, France, Delaw moved to Montmartre in 1893, hunkering down in the Hôtel du Poirier, located next to the future site of the infamous Bateau-Lavoir. Delaw later frequented the Lapin Agile and rubbed shoulders with both Carco and Mac Orlan. He built a successful career as an illustrator and was especially

de Bougainville?[111] The melancholy lines on the tomb inspired him and strengthened our convictions and when Girieud[112] the painter, at the foot of the rue des Saules, hired a fleet of taxis in which we could all pile and start a pleasure tour of the less savory quarters of Paris, we could all have sworn in good faith that our vessel was in port and that we had just landed.

On our way back the man who had revealed Tahiti's secrets to us and who never worried would invite us to his place. He lived in the rue Lamarck in an empty apartment where we squatted on the floor and passed bottles of Tafia from one to the other. Big flat steamer trunks, a sextant, binoculars and canvases piled up in the corners, a hammock and a medicine chest were all his furniture. He also had sailor's clothes hanging on the wall. And at once marvelous tales would begin – he filled

gifted in his work with children's books. After serving in WWI at the Battle of Verdun, he resumed his artistic career and provided illustrations for authors such as Anatole France, Jules Renard, and Charles Perrault. Delaw is credited with helping to develop the comic-strip medium, having worked with the construction of sequential imagery.

[111] Louis-Antoine, Comte de Bougainville (1729 – 1811): the fourteenth navigator to circumnavigate the globe and the first French navigator to do so. Disembarking from Nantes in November 1766, he arrived in Tahiti in 1768, where he visited the island of Otaheite. During the expedition a valet on board who went by the name of "Jean Baret" was discovered to be a woman named Jeanne Barret. Barret thus became the first woman to circumnavigate the globe. Bougainville also participated in the Seven Years' War and the American Revolutionary War.

[112] Pierre Paul Girieud (1876 – 1948): French painter who exhibited in the 1913 Armory Show, aka the International Exhibition of Modern Art, which opened in Manhattan's 69th Regiment Armory and then traveled to Chicago and Boston. Girieud lived near the place du Tertre in Montmartre and was a regular at the Lapin Agile. His style combined elements of Fauvism and German Expressionism. Born in Paris but raised in Provence, Girieud once declared: "I would like to paint like a fig tree produces figs; it does not care whether there are rotten ones or some eaten by the birds, it fulfills its function as best it can. I would like to be a good fig tree!"

us up with them as he walked up and down among us as on his bridge.

The more his revelations were outside the realm of common sense, the more we were inclined to believe them, until one day he disappeared completely and we learned that, although once upon a time perhaps he had traveled, he had been living for a long time on his property in Touraine and that he was only a rich and ordinary farmer whose innocent mania was to take himself seriously as a sailor.

But what did it matter after all; he had given us the impulse. A love of the sea combined with the love we all had for the unknown kept us from changing and urged us on. Brittany, where some of us spent the summer painting, seemed the promised land. Asselin, Vaillant,[113] and Mac Orlan brought back from Brigneau-en-Moëlan and Pont-Aven such colorful impressions that we swore only by them, and we bought boats in frames and heavy canvas trousers. Naturally we were longing for the adventures of pirates and of the Brothers of the Coast.[114]

Jacques Vaillant, who was certainly the most enterprising of our crowd, ended by abandoning Montmartre to run up a fantastic bill at La mère Baron, and to enjoy life in every way without bothering to do anything. What a gay young man he

[113] Jacques Vaillant (1879 – 1934): French painter from Saint-Fargeau-Ponthierry, who portrayed Mac Orlan in a drawing entitled *Pierre Mac Orlan à l'accordéon*. Vaillant was also a friend of Maurice Asselin and a habitué of the Bateau-Lavoir. In her memoir *Picasso et ses amis* Olivier describes a "shindig" at his flat: "When the painter, Jacques Vaillant, came to live in the house there was some kind of shindy and uproar there every night. He was sociable, hardworking, in a perpetual state of excitement, singing, shouting, breaking things; with his peculiar laugh becoming a sort of grating shriek whenever he got drunk, which he did every single evening." Fernande Olivier, *Picasso and his Friends*, pp. 73-74.

[114] Brethren of the Coast: a group of mostly English and French pirates that terrorized ships in the Atlantic and the Caribbean Sea during the seventeenth and eighteenth centuries.

was, a great drinker and a perfect friend ... He only abandoned Brigneau when he signed up in August 1914 to go from the territorials to a regiment at the front, where he became second-lieutenant and won magnificent citations.

I remember meeting him on the Butte during the war when we were on leave. We dined in the place du Tertre and the news which came to us from the front was not very reassuring. Vaillant, when he was spoken to by an anxious and sorrowful comrade, left us hastily. He put on his uniform and then took us to a hotel where we spent the night drinking and dancing in spite of the regulations and the canon thundering in our defense. In the morning he shook hands without any fuss, put his packs in a taxi and, although he was entitled to five days more of good living away from the lines, left to rejoin his regiment which had been decimated at the Chemin des Dames. He shouted to us:

"I shall come back!"

Adventure with those men was not only a word and it was under such circumstances that this could be seen most clearly. Pierre Mac Orlan's heroes resemble them; they have a joyful air and playful manners, quick minds, and whatever has been said of them, a trueness to life which is always recognizable because of their virile determination. There is in Mac Orlan's work an unmistakable energy and his character is revealed in a way which justifies his work. Even when miserably poor he let no one know of it and never complained. He lived courageously. Without saying a word to anyone, he slept one whole winter on a pile of newspapers in his small room because he had sold his last sticks of furniture. Is that worthy of mention? I tell it only because even if Pierre does spend his days comfortably now in his modest apartment in the rue de Ranelagh, it would be doing him an injustice to call him a bourgeois.

At his table and among his books, his pictures and his musical instruments, some very important guests meet his friends.

Sometimes a sailor of the Legion passing through Paris will open his door, and his presence in that peaceful and studious atmosphere puts everything in a revealing light. After dinner Mac Orlan plays his phonograph, or better still, when urged by the deep and obscure attachment which draws both of us toward the lower strata of humanity, he takes up his accordion and, fingering its mother-of-pearl keys, plays a rhythmic and quick air of Java.

Once he owned a hunting horn which his neighbors could not endure. He does not play it now in Paris and anyone who wants to judge Mac Orlan and his hunting horn must take the train for Saint-Cyr-sur-Morin.

*

That village, which the Battle of the Marne was to draw out of its sleep, has a story for us. It became to the clients of the Lapin synonymous with the reaction of the country lovers against Brittany, and was the annual rendezvous of those painters who were disgusted at not meeting pirates at Brigneau and who preferred to give them up once and for all or to seek them in other places.

Frédé owned in Saint-Cyr a tiny house where he sometimes spent the warm months of the year. Astride his donkey, the same Lolo made famous by Roland Dorgelès, he rode through the fields in his pointed hat, surrounded by his dogs and his sheep. Did he give his address to anyone? I do not know. But at any rate people in Montmartre began to talk about Saint-Cyr around 1911. Julien Callé[115] – of whom I shall speak later in this

[115] Julien Callé (1880 – 1945): author of the novels *La Nuit du Bar des Clowns* (Paris: Librarie de France, 1926) and *Sainte-Guillotine* (Paris: Éditions du Tambourin, 1930; with a Preface by Mac Orlan). Speaking of how Carco had seen an ad for the Lapin Agile in a provincial newspaper, Nicholas Hewitt writes: "One unusual example of this connection with the provinces was the founding by Julien Callé of the Auberge de l'OEuf Dur et du Commerce in

chapter, for he is well worth it – Georges Delaw, Marcoussis and Zyg Brunner[116] were the first to revolutionize the countryside and to accustom the inhabitants to anything. They gathered fruit by shooting at it with guns; in the night they filled the river with dried herrings into which live fish had been sewn, thus making the herrings seem alive and swimming; they went to bathe, quite naked, on their bicycles, and when a theatre at a fair gave performances they took the places of the actors and greatly complicated the action.

With Zyg Brunner and George Delaw I acted an unactable part in *Roger la Honte*.[117] I caught the *garde-champêtre*, the policeman of the village, behind nut trees peering at the painters bathing with their young models. So I asked the good man why he did not fine them.

"Why should I? If I did they would never come back."

The natives of that charming country place were as clever as the *garde-champêtre*. They let the Parisians do as they pleased so that they might fleece them better and laugh at them and tell stories about them, later on, during the long winter evenings. We lived in the hotel. I don't know who was paying. Gazanion was there, and Girieud and Coccinelle with his lovely voice,

the village of Saint-Cyr-sur-Morin, southeast of Paris in the region of Meaux. Callé, like many Montmartre bohemians, worked as a civil servant, specifically as a clerk in the law courts, but was also a talented humorist and writer. He rapidly established this traditional country inn, discovered initially by George Delaw, as a weekend and holiday venue for his fellow bohemians, which had considerable success until the First World War." Hewitt, *Montmartre*, p. 134.

[116] Zygismund Brunner (1878 – 1961): Polish draftsman and caricaturist who illustrated children's books such as *Grimm's Fairy Tales* and Anatole France's *Abeille*, as well as erotic novels, such as Carco's *Les Innocents*.

[117] *Roger la Honte*: a melodramatic novel by Jules Mary (1851 – 1922), published in 1886 and set during the Franco-Prussian War.

and Sauvayre.[118] The others had rented houses beyond the church or lived like Mac Orlan in a neighboring village.

In that beautiful country life was easy, fresh and restful and we did not know what to do to expend our energy and spoil our health. And yet in the end Mac Orlan settled there and he still can be seen shooting partridges, followed by his dog Friquette.

Once Mac Orlan had an adventure of which the peasants still tell with astonishment. One day when watching in the fields he shot an extraordinary bird. When he looked at it, he scratched his forehead. What was it? He had never seen one like it. A huge beak, a silly air, webbed feet, and smoke-gray feathers. Pierre hesitated a long time, then threw it in his hunting pouch and in the evening consulted his neighbor. The neighbor could not make head or tail of it. He inquired in the village if anyone had any idea what kind of bird it was, but no one could help him.

"A strange bird!" people said.

Books and encyclopedias were consulted, but in vain, and Mac Orlan, quite rightly intrigued, took the train for Paris. Well, such a mysterious bird had never been seen in Paris either and when the sportsman came back to Saint-Cyr, after many long consultations with naturalists of all kinds, he was obliged to calm public opinion by declaring that he had by chance killed an authentic *chevalier bécassin*, a very rare bird indeed.

The name of that bird is attached to Pierre Mac Orlan's reputation in Saint-Cyr, and the inhabitants are not very far from believing that he is a sorcerer. Luckily for him, Julian Callé gave these good people something new to talk about. He was clerk of the court somewhere in Alsace and came every year to

[118] Maurice Sauvayre (né Marius Sauvayre; 1889 – 1968): French illustrator who contributed satirical drawings and cartoons to various periodicals; he also pursued a career in landscape painting.

be present at the Bal des Quat'z'Arts.[119] He did better still –
through his efforts an inn was opened which he called the
Auberge de l'OEuf Dur et du Commerce. The prospectus was as
followed:

Société des Grands Hôtels borgnes

English Spoken   ——————   Se habla español
Man spricht nicht deutsch   Si parla italiano

AUBERGE DE L'ŒUF DUR ET DU COMMERCE

Julien CALLÉ, Successeur général

à SAINT-CYR-SUR-MORIN (Seine-et-Marne)

(sur la ligne de la FERTÉ-SOUS-JOUARRE à MONTMIRAIL)

A 1 h. 1/2 de la Gare de l'Est.   A 40 jours de chameau d'Alger.

Établissement fondé par Napoléon en 1814 — Reconnu d'utilité
publique en 1918 — Honoré de souscriptions en 1919 par la Munici-
palité de Saint-Cyr-sur-Morin; les Sociétés locales; l'A. des Étudi-
ants; la Commune libre de Montmartre; le Mercure de France;
l'Orphéon Cyclocubiste de l'École des Beaux-Arts; la Compagnie
du Gaz en poudre; les Bateaux Parisiens, etc., etc.

PRIX TRÈS MODÉRÉS

RABAIS pour SÉJOUR durant la SAISON DES BAINS

1 seule Table - 1 seul Cœur - 18 Marmites

These are unusually good references but strangely enough the
Auberge de l'OEuf Dur et du Commerce is famous now and
frequented by so many good clients that Callé can live on its
profits.

This curious gentleman has always had a genius for
organization and the idea was not so stupid as it seems.

Once in the rue du Mont-Cenis, in his small shanty which
looked out upon the courtyard of Jenny, the working-girl's

[119] A notorious saturnalia first held in 1892, the art students' ball was
celebrated annually, usually at the Salle Wagram (near the Etoile), the
Moulin Rouge, or the Parc des Expositions Porte de Versailles. "The Bal des
Quat'z'Arts … has always been noted for the modest amount of clothing
worn by ladies taking part in it, a number of whom, generally models, are
fond of giving impersonations of Eve." Ralph Nevill, *Days and Nights in
Montmartre and the Latin Quarter*, New York: George Doran, 1927, p. 309.

well-known house, he treated his friends superbly and offered them parties which lasted for days. He closed the shutters, nailed bags over each window, and placed the wardrobe on its side. It then became a bar and, with all the lamps lighted, he poured out all kinds of liquid incessantly. It was here that I once saw Mac Orlan, as he sat on the back of a chair, empty bottle after bottle and still manage to keep his balance all night. Those who could go on no longer slept upstairs, all in the same room, or else were pushed discreetly under the furniture so that the others might continue to amuse themselves. Dunoyer de Segonzac[120] sometimes took part in the revels and the happy *petit père Dédé* would tell about them in *Comoedia* and describe their splendors and glories. I also went several times accompanied by the poet Édouard Gazanion with whom I boarded, but tragedies followed. One morning when we had returned to the house, while undressing Édouard awoke his wife and drew her attention to him by a sad discovery:

"Think of it, it is really very annoying, I have lost my suspenders."

Why did he not think of borrowing mine!

*

Callé, when I first knew him, had no fixed idea as to what he wanted to do, or rather he was embarking upon the career which chance offered him. We still can read his tales in the papers. Would he have succeeded as a writer? Possibly, because at that time no one could tell what the future had in store for us. As for myself, without the help of Charles Henry Hirsch,[121] who

[120] André Dunoyer de Segonzac (1884 –1974): French painter, graphic artist, and member of the Section d'Or art collective. His etchings were used to illustrate Roland Dorgelès' *Les Croix de Bois*.

[121] Charles-Henry Hirsch (1870 – 1948): Parisian novelist whose stories were turned into screenplays in the 1920s and '30s. Hirsch was also the subject of Carco's biography, *Charles-Henry Hirsch*, Paris: E. Sansot and Cie, 1913.

begged me to give up Montmartre for a more regular life, I would rather have kept a café than do anything else, and today I would not be any worse off. Life has her unfathomable designs, she leads us according to her own sweet pleasure, and if I had not, for example, followed the good advice that Maeterlinck[122] once gave me about how to work, I should never have written any other verses than the following:

Prends l'omnibus, crains le métro,
On ne se soigne jamais trop ...[123]

which, thank God, represents all my Montmartre production during those happy years.

"The only thing to do," asserted Maeterlinck, "is to shut yourself in for three hours every day. Even if you can't work, stay in your room for that length of time."

It is an excellent method, but at that time, when I tried it I fell asleep, because we were literally drunk with sleepiness. Our nights, after the Lapin had closed, ended at Manière's,[124] in the rue Caulaincourt, or in the low bars of the rue Lepic with men hardly fitted to understand us. It was in those bars that I met Jésus la Caille and his young friends and, at the bottom of the

[122] Maurice Maeterlinck (1862 – 1949): Belgian playwright, poet, and essayist, who was awarded the Nobel Prize in Literature in 1911.
[123] "Take the tram, take care on the metro, / One can never be too careful."
[124] Chez Manière, located at 65, rue Caulaincourt, on the northern incline of the Butte, between avenue Junot and rue Lamarck. The Manière was one of the principal cultural focal points of the interwar years, serving as a bohemian meeting place for illustrators such as Gus Bofa, Chas Laborde, and Francisque Poulbot; artists such as Jules Pascin and the Czech painter François Kupka; writers such as Marcel Aymé, Louis-Ferdinand Céline, Roland Dorgelès, Anatole France, Pierre Mac Orlan, and Georges Simenon; and the mathematician Maurice Princet. In Céline's *Féerie pour une autre foi* the Restaurant Manière is re-created as "Beaunière," in keeping with Celine's playful juxtaposition of concrete reality with a journey "entirely imaginary." Nicholas Hewitt, *Montmartre*, pp. 44, 113, 124, 180-185, 262.

rue Tholozé, discovered the oven of a certain bread-making shop, which gave me later the idea of writing *L'Homme traqué*.[125]

Until dawn, which we tried not to see through the panes, for the first who was imprudent enough to see it paid a last round, we talked – about poets, or the Boulevard, or the adventure novel, or Cubism ... Everything was matter for discussion to us and we were all so ingenuous that, for example, we did not realize that Cubism was essentially Jewish in its origins[126] and destined by its development less to enrich us plastically than mentally or, if you like it better, to be of less aid in the triumph of art than to an exchange of ideas and theories where art took second place.

"It has rather the same relation to art," someone said one morning, "as a check has to money."

"Yes," someone else replied, "but it is like a check without funds."

And the idea was not so bad.

But how could we help laughing at the unexpected and sometimes very pretentious formulas of the new school – for

[125] One of the main protagonists of Carco's *Jésus-la-Caille* (1914). His novel *L'Homme traqué* (1922) was awarded the Grand Prix du roman by the Académie française. They were each adapted to the cinema. Robert Bibel directed *L'Homme traqué* in 1947; André Pergament directed *M'sieur la Caille* in 1955, starring Jeanne Moreau.

[126] These comments reflect not only the anti-Semitism that was prevalent in France during this period (from which Carco would distance himself in the decades ahead) but also the typical French fear and abhorrence of "foreigners." As previously mentioned, even Picasso was denied naturalization just before WWII – when he was already a world-renowned artist – which could have led to deportation back to Franco's Spain. During WWI rumors circulated that Cubist paintings and Cubist-inspired ads were "encoded" with information vital to the Germans. In her memoir Marevna reports: "Soon the terms 'Bolshevism' and 'Cubism' were virtually synonymous in the public mind." (Marevna, *Life with the Painters of La Ruche*, p. 114.) During the Nazi Occupation Carco went into exile in Nice, then escaped into Switzerland with his Jewish wife, Éliane Négrin.

instance when Picasso, after doing a study on one of the quays of packing cases of all sorts which were being unloaded, called it: *Portrait of My Father*. One could even read on the cases the ordinary inscriptions: TOP, BOTTOM, KEEP DRY, and numbers, and tags.

"Now if you saw your father arriving in Paris with such a mug," said either Princet or Max Jacob to Picasso ... "Well? What would you really think?"

But that did not stop other painters from exhibiting very seriously the following year at the Salon des Indépendants innumerable "portraits of my father" with inscriptions of the same kind, numbers and, sad but true, an eye here, a nose there, some teeth and a piece of an ear somewhere else.

Picasso, *Portrait of Berthe Weill*, 1920,
Conté pencil and charcoal on paper, 62 x 47 cm.

VII

Meanwhile right at the top of the rue Ravignan[127] at friend Emile's[128] in a bistro where they liked paintings, as all the bistros on the Butte do, Marcoussis had begun to decorate the walls of the back room which many people used as a rendezvous. These decorations, done with care, seemed excellent to us and the story goes that, one evening Utrillo, who had heard about them, came to see them, and that he said nothing, but counted the cubes.

The rue Ravignon however deserved to be consecrated to Cubism because Cubism was born a few yards away from friend Emile's on the place Emile-Goudeau. Picasso, Max Jacob and Salmon lived on that square at number 13, in a wooden building which still stands and which looks like one of the boats on the Seine used by washerwomen.[129] Studios look out on the square or damp gardens, and a succession of indefinite

[127] In her translation Madeleine Boyd changes the rue "Ravignan" to rue "Davignan" for no apparent reason. Although there was once a rue d'Avignon – also spelled rue Davignon – in the old sixth arrondissement, it disappeared in 1853 during new construction.

[128] What Boyd translates here as "friend Emile's" was the café L'Ami Emile, a meeting place for the Cubists. (See footnote below.)

[129] The Bateau-Lavoir (literally, the "washing boat," taking its nickname from a supposed resemblance to the washing barges docked in the Seine) was located at 13, rue Ravignan, at place Emile Goudeau. (Originally known as place Ravignan, but renamed after the novelist Emile Goudeau, in 1911.) Everything except for the building's facade was destroyed by fire in 1970, but it was reconstructed in 1978. The Bateau-Lavoir was the "refuge of assorted painters, sculptors, writers, humorists, actors, washerwomen, dressmakers, and barrow-boys." Fernande Olivier, *Picasso and His Friends*, p. 26. Charles Beadle says that Mac Orlan, Roland Dorgelès, André Salmon, Van Dongen, Braque, Vlaminck, and Derain were all living there "at the same time as Picasso," while "A few yards away lived Max Jacob, Guillaume Apollinaire, and Zuloaga." See Charles Douglas, *Artist Quarter*, pp. 39-40.

cubbyholes open on a long passage. Everywhere is an atmosphere of poverty, abandonment, austere and complete lack of resources, but it is there, nevertheless, that admirers of the gentle custom officer Rousseau[130] offered him a great banquet, at which, for a reason still unexplained, he did not arrive until the next day.

The place Emile-Goudeau is a narrow triangle, on a very steep slope, which on one side boasts of the celebrated building already mentioned, and on the other of the Hôtel Poirier, where I found La Vaissière. We had been instructors together at the college in Agen. We had been expelled because of our wild behavior and a great affection united us. At that time the Viscount Robert de la Vaissière was publishing in the small reviews lovely prose poems which he signed with the name Claudien. When I met him he was beating the owner of the hotel with his cane, shouting in a high-pitched voice as was his custom. I separated the gentlemen and asked them the reason for their disagreement, and I was not surprised to hear that the host was objecting to the innumerable young ladies [that] the

[130] The celebrated self-taught painter Henri Rousseau (1844 – 1910), aka Le Douanier ("the customs officer"). The passage refers to a party that Picasso organized for Rousseau, which is beautifully described by Fernande Olivier in her memoir, *Picasso and his Friends*, in a chapter titled "The Rousseau Banquet." A great admirer of Rousseau's work, Picasso was also amused by Rousseau's megalomania. Hence, by anointing him as the guest of honor they were also, as Fernande says, "pulling the *douanier's* leg." The event, which Picasso paid for and hosted at his studio, also featured a large banner hanging over Rousseau's "throne" (a chair set on a packing case) that read: "Honor to Rousseau." Picasso's exquisite collection of Rousseau's artwork is housed at the Musée Picasso, in Paris. When he later reflected upon the event, Picasso was quoted as saying: "Rousseau is not an accident. He represents the perfection of a certain order of thought." And he regarded Rousseau's *Portrait of Mlle. M* (which Picasso had purchased for five francs, in a junk shop) as "one of the most truthful of all French psychological portraits." Roger Shattuck, *The Banquet Years*, New York: Vintage, 1968, pp. 66-67. For Picasso, it was a painting's truth that shaped its beauty, just as a certain form of beauty embodies a unique truth.

poet was receiving every night. The affair was settled in some way or other, but from that day on I had one more friend in Montmartre and a very dear one.

Anyone who has not met Claudien can have no very clear idea of the kind of person he has always been. His red beard, his cane and his clothes are all distinctive. He has a great air. Impertinent, dignified, and imposing. But at that time, poverty – like ours – was extreme and what astonished me was that there was nothing abject about it. On the contrary, Claudien wore clothes which an old friend secured for him and since they did not quite fit, he looked different with each suit that he put on. Claudien did not much care and was always the first to laugh at his transformations, which used to amuse us greatly. Goodness knows what the author of *Labyrinthes* lived on that time. Every year had as many addresses as costumes, and they hardly fitted him any better. Sometimes it was in a garret – one would have thought – to shelter the tenderest idyll, that he would receive me grandly, sometimes in an empty apartment, or in a room of a none-too-respectable hotel, or at the poet Gazanion's where I had had lodgings too. Everywhere he was the same, interesting to listen to and to study, calm and Olympian. The only thing he wanted to do was to do nothing. In the street, among the hurrying and agitated passers-by he walked slowly, smoking a big cigar, or else he sat in a café where he pulled from his pocket a small bottle of ether and calmly poured its contents into his drink. Kirsch with ether was his favorite. He had revealed its charm to me in Agen in the small cafés which the other clients, holding their noses, would leave at once. His rare and choice taste, his great knowledge, his conversation, which was always original, made him very attractive, and under a perfectly snobbish exterior he was the most faithful and tactful of friends. How many nights have we spent together walking about the lowest quarters of Paris! He would deliberately enter the most ignoble and dangerous dens, go in among drunkards and prostitutes, lean his elbow on the bar and order:

"One *vieux marc!*"

Once when we were attacked under the Canal Saint-Martin and not unexpectedly, he refused to let himself be searched:

"Here," he said, as if he had been giving charity to a beggar, "here are two francs for you."

Later in the evening he took out his wallet in a bar and I saw three hundred-franc notes.

Whatever he attempted his supercilious and quiet manner was always against him at first sight, and among his friends, his picturesque misadventures had become a byword.

At the Bon Bock[131] one evening when he was dining and chatting, a disagreeable remark uttered loudly by one of the clients of that quiet restaurant struck his ear. La Vaissière rose, fixed is monocle and then leisurely walked over to the table where, he thought, someone had dared to mock him. Being very shortsighted he made a mistake. He slapped the wrong person twice and he happened to be a fencing master! A dual was inevitable. La Vaissière prepared for it and all of Marc Brésil's cleverness and tact were necessary to make him give up the idea.

Another evening in the place Saint-Georges, La Vaissière, as he was on his way home, was very much annoyed by the big gold letters of an antique dealer's sign. He stopped, read slowly the name of the well-known Jew, and then, led by his demon, climbed up a balcony, took an enormous *W* out of the name and put it under his arm.

Soon he had quite a collection of those big *W*'s, because every time the antique dealer replaced the missing letter, La Vaissière stole it. In the end, the dealer complained to the authorities and

[131] Brasserie du Bon Bock, frequented by Toulouse Lautrec, Apollinaire, and Picasso, located at the foot of Sacré-Coeur at 2, rue Dancourt. First established in 1879 and now the oldest restaurant in Montmartre.

the police found out the secret of this uncanny disappearance. They arrested the delinquent and took him to the police station where he had much explaining to do.

He never gave rein to his fancy without getting into trouble, but he always faced the music and kept calm through everything.

When he was an instructor, to the great despair of the head of the College of Agen, the school was very parsimonious about light. La Vaissière was not at all disturbed. He would go to the suburbs, take down a lighted street lamp and come back, very seriously, with his lamp in his hand. He wore nothing in the summertime and sat on the mantelpiece of his room explaining that the marble kept him cool.

He was unequaled in the jokes of all kinds which he perpetuated and when he was caught he defended himself in such perfect and pure French that no one could blame him.

The spectacle of Paris at night took him haphazardly from Belleville to Vaugirard, from the Bastille to the fortifications of Auteuil. He was always walking and talking tirelessly of poetry and mathematics. His secret taste, his passion for the degradation and corruption of a large city, took him to places where men, gnawed by their vices, teem and ferment in a state of horrible distress; it was with a perfect knowledge of the most unapproachable dens that he composed his short poems, filled with such an acute torment.

What did it matter where he lived? He wrote to me, or else, if some night I forgot to keep an appointment with him, he broke the pane of a fire-alarm box, telephoned my address and, as the fireman besieged the building where I lived, I would remember my appointment. Such were his simplest antics. He did not boast of them, he was always master of himself, always dignified and impervious to everything. His moves were made under the cover of darkness and when he gave me the address of a new lodging place I wrote it down on a page of my notebook kept specially for this purpose.

The only place in Montmartre that he would not go was the old Hôtel du Tertre, where we have all lived. Maybe it was too high up for his laziness, or maybe it was too full of joyful remembrances for his secret humor, uneasy and self-centered. The Viscount Robert de la Vaissière has always hated Montmartre. If he lived there years ago it was because he was following his star but we shall see later in this book that another setting suited him better.

Pierre Benoît,[132] the first time he went up to the place du Tertre, found out why it was so called. According to him it was because of the famous Captain Dutertre, who died in Africa, and whose glorification in the bistro Au Clairon de Sidi Brahim, situated on that square, is thus explained. Depaquit[133] lived once upon a time at the Hôtel du Tertre. He was called *le bon Jules*; he was well-mannered, very discreet, very clever and naturally astute to such an extent that after we had had to give it up, he could continue to drink on credit at the famous Clairon de Sidi Brahim, run at that time by old father Spielmann.[134] He

---

[132] Pierre Benoît (1886 – 1962): French novelist, screenwriter, and member of the Académie française. Benoît is best known for his 1919 fantasy novel, *L'Atlantide*, which was published in English the following year, under the title *Atlantida*, and serialized in *Adventure* magazine. *L'Atlantide* was also adapted into numerous TV and cinema productions, including the film *Siren of Atlantis* (1949), starring María Montez. During WWII Benoît joined "Groupe Collaboration," a pro-Nazi arts organization. He was arrested as a collaborator in 1944, and his work was subsequently blacklisted.

[133] Jules Depaquit (1869 – 1924): French illustrator, poet, and lithographer, who designed publicity posters for the Moulin Rouge and Moulin de la Galette. According to Robert Rey, Depaquit "invented almost the whole aesthetic of present-day humorous drawing, as well as that of the modern poster." Nicholas Hewitt, *Montmartre*, p. 171, quoting from one of Rey's essays.

[134] Also known as Au Clairon des Chasseurs à pied, located at 3, place du Tertre. The Hôtel-Restaurant Bouscarat was at 2, place du Tertre, at the

had a great deal of childish maliciousness and his repartee was often so good that it was disarming.

One morning, when a creditor knocked at his door and threatened to smash everything, Depaquit answered:

"Monsieur Depaquit has gone out."

"I recognize you," the creditor shouted, "I recognize your voice ... Come on ... Open!"

Le bon Jules obeyed.

"Well," said the creditor, you see that you are lying!"

"I am not," answered Depaquit. "Monsieur has gone out ... has been gone now for more than an hour ..."

"So?"

"I swear."

The creditor was half convinced, but suddenly thinking better of it, he pointed to the shoes of his debtor, and growled:

"Monsieur Depaquit, why are you so obstinate? Look ... here ... Your shoes are still there, you have not put them on yet!"

"I?"

"Yes, certainly, you."

corner of rue du Mont-Cenis. "The Place du Tertre contained many cafés and bistrots, particularly the Bouscarat, which was a major meeting place for artists at lunchtime and Spielmann's Au Clairon a pied bataillon des chasseurs, while L'Ami Emile, at the bottom of the rue Ravignan, was much patronized by the Cubists from the Bateau-Lavoir ..." Nicholas Hewitt, *Montmartre*, p. 117. In *Artist Quarter*, Douglas Goldring and Charles Beadle report that Spielmann's "consisted of a tiny bar and one longish dining room. The walls were decorated with scenes from the Butte by some unknown artists, painted, no doubt, in exchange for numerous meal tickets, but from an artistic point of view of no interest." Spielmann's was previously known as "Au Clairon de Sébastopol, for the proprietor had been a bugler at Sébastopol – a fact of which he was excessively proud." Charles Douglas, *Artist Quarter*, pp. 78, 80.

Then *le bon* Jules pushed the creditor out saying as he shut his door: "When I go out in the morning I always wear my slippers."

Chaim Soutine, *La Femme en rouge*, oil on canvas, 91.4 x 65.1 cm. According to Sotheby's it was "presumably acquired by Carco just after its completion circa 1924, later to be auctioned at his 1925 sale at Drouot and sold to Zborowski." However, Malcolm Gee (a more reliable source) identifies the buyer as the surrealist poet and friend of Picasso, Paul Eluard, who purchased it for 2000 FF. It would later be acquired by the Tate Gallery, the Guggenheim Museum, and then the Musée de l'Orangerie. During its last auction at Sotheby's the final bid was for $10,970,600.

VIII

A hundred stories could be told about Depaquit. He was a very well-behaved man, puny, almost [invisible],[135] with no flamboyant fantasy about him, and always so much in the clouds that he seemed to live in a perpetual *quiproquo*.[136] His big nose, which he was the first to ridicule when he made a self-portrait, his round and surprised eyes gave him the appearance of one of those strange night birds which light blinds and renders unfit for motion. And indeed, the bon Jules carried the resemblance so far, that, when he walked in the streets he crept along furtively, close to the walls. When he came into a bistro, he always seemed to have been pushed in sideways and he looked suspicious, frightened and uneasy. At the Lapin the seat he preferred was not in the big room, but in the corner of a narrow alcove, near the fire, where one had to move chairs, tables, furniture, linen, customers' coats, a thousand objects, in order to see him. Only there did he feel sheltered from the curious. He loved dark places; he would grovel in them delightedly and, by moments, when everyone had absolutely forgotten him, he would talk to himself or recite verses. Depaquit's voice! His grating voice, with a register too high or too low, remains in my ears like the wounded cries of village weathercocks in the winter. He himself knew it, because if he was a poet, he sang only about the petty annoyances of life, its mediocre dramas, its obscure despairs and its unwanted idealism. I said that one could hear him sometimes during our noisy nights. The term was wrong, one perceived – rather than one heard – Jules' voice and it was no more than a rusty

---

135 Carco's original reads "presque effacé," meaning "almost invisible" rather than Boyd's "almost neutral."
136 "Quiproquo": a misunderstanding.

groaning which, suddenly, would float out from a corner and would recite in a comical tone:

> *Ah ! quel triste sort*
> *A le hareng saur;*[137]

or, else, about the street organ:

> *C'est la musique incomprise*
> *Qui fait vomir et qui grise*
> *Et qui tue …*
> *A la fin, on s'y habitue.*[138]

It was necessary to get accustomed to him, otherwise no relation with him was possible. He had to be taken as he was, grumpy, sleepy, or when he had been drinking, mocking and disillusioned. Strange young man! He was loved by everyone for his childish maliciousness, his common sense, his humor, his very fine and sharp wit. Had he not given to his poems the only title that fitted them! When asked:

"What do you call your poems?"

He would answer: "*Les moments perdus !*"[139]

And he would add:

"So lost indeed, that no editor wants them."

And yet those verses, which he would recite for one or two friends, were beginning to be known on the Butte. Everybody remembered fragments of them, but Depaquit could not endure

[137] "Ah! What a sad fate / has the pickled herring." "Le Hareng saur" is derived from a nonsense verse by the French poet-inventor Charles Cros (1842 – 1888), a friend of both Verlaine and Rimbaud. Cros's proposed method for recording sound waves anticipated Thomas Edison's photograph by eight months.

[138] "It's misunderstood music / that makes you get drunk and vomit / and that kills … / In the end, you get used to it."

[139] "The lost moments."

to have them recited in his presence and if anyone did, he would be annoyed and go away hurt. Under his mocking exterior he was irritable and disconcerting. He had to be known and to be managed, and then there was no one as amiable or as gay.

Unintentionally, he was, we told each other, the author of a magnificent alexandrine, full of effects, of nuances, intentions, meat, balance, and sometimes after a lot of managing we would induce him to recite it so we could admire it. Now this magnificent line was buried in the twaddle of an absurd tragedy, so that we must have had a great longing to hear it, and much leisure, when good old Jules coughed and began. The story was about a king away at the crusades, who was deceived by the queen with her nephew, regardless of the scandal. Scene followed scene, all the rhymes rhymed, all the expected catastrophes happened. Jules went on. At last, in the third act, the king came back. He hastened to his beloved spouse, anxious to press her to his heart, but he came upon Gontran in her arms and withdrew, disheartened. The author would choose his moment. He showed us the unhappy crusader pulling his goatee, shaking his head, and then slowly crossing the stage, uttering in a dignified manner:

> *"Tiens ! Tiens ! Tiens ! Tiens ! Tiens ! Tiens !*
> *Tiens ! Tiens ! Tiens ! Tiens ! Tiens ! Tiens !*[140]

And the audience was delighted.

*

---

[140] "Tiens ! Tiens !" has a variety of meanings, including: "Look!," "Well, well!," or "Tsk, tsk!"

Those jokes were not cruel but they were enough to amuse us, because we were so young at that time that very little sufficed to do so.

But we laughed more with Depaquit than at him. His adventures had always something extraordinary which he used in order to divert us the more.

Alphonse Allais[141] having asked him one day to lunch, good old Jules – he told me this tale many times – put on his Sunday best, took his big umbrella and went to the humorist's house. At that time Depaquit was not celebrated and his dreadful shyness, far from facilitating his going about, regularly brought him a thousand annoyances.

"Whom do you want?" The concierge shouted at him.

"Monsieur Allais."

"Yes, he is here. What do you want?"

"I must see him," Depaquit asserted.

"All right, take the service stairs in the courtyard," grumbled this Cerberus who did not like good old Jules' embarrassed air. "Can't you understand?"

Depaquit hastened to obey. He climbed up the stairs, knocked politely at the door of the apartment, waited till it was opened and then, giving his name and surname, entered:

---

[141] Alphonse Allais (1854 – 1905): French humorist, journalist, and editor of the *Chat Noir*. As early as 1883 Allais exhibited monochromatic paintings, such as *Première communion de jeunes filles chlorotiques par un temps de neige* ("First Communion of Anemic Young Girls in the Snowy Weather"), consisting of single sheet of white paper. In 1897 he created his *Funeral March for the Obsequies of a Great Deaf Man*, a silent musical composition consisting of twenty-four blank measures. Allais' works are often considered to be precedents of the Dada movement. Regarding his role as an original member of the Hydropathes group of the 1870s, Roger Shattuck sketches him as "chief *fumiste* (perpetrator of tall tales and hoaxes) and short-story writer, with the mixed talents of Poe and Mark Twain." Roger Shattuck, *The Banquet Years*, p. 22.

"Sit there," said the cook. "I shall tell Monsieur, but between ourselves, you are not lucky, my good man, you have come at the wrong moment."

"Why?"

"Because the master is giving a big luncheon today; he won't see you."

"Really."

"Well," said the cook, "have patience, we'll see."

Depaquit sat in a corner and waited for more than an hour. He did not dare to ask the servants to announce him, because seeing them nervous and agitated, "Monsieur's guest hadn't turned up," an unreasonable terror was taking hold of him. Good old Jules sat quietly in his corner and saw very appetizing dishes pass under his nose. He smiled, doing his best to be brave under trying circumstances. He tried to look dignified when, as she sat down to her meal, the cook asked him to join her. As you can guess, Depaquit accepted at once. He ate heartily, lighted his pipe and when Madam Allais came in, and asked him rather brusquely who he was and what he was doing there, Depaquit answered tactfully: "I was waiting ... You see? I did not want to disturb anyone ..."

*

The most dreadful misadventures happened to him all his life and curiously enough, instead of growing tired of them, he began to like them and collect them. They were, so to speak, foreordained for him, perhaps because:

Par un décret des puissances suprêmes,[142]

they could not happen to anybody else, perhaps because, as he was continually looking for them, he was entitled to them. At

[142] "By a decree of the supreme powers."

the Lapin, as at Marie la Bonne Hôtesse,[143] he was exactly the same shadowy human being, rather silent, ghostlike, fluid. His gray hair, his clothes always too big and the air he had of moving constantly in a dream, made him a perfect butt. Beside him Utrillo showed off better on account of his manners. He would frequently disappear for long periods and when by chance one of us would try to find him, it was in vain.

To compensate for Depaquit's absence, M. Maurice, covered with paint, ragged, gesticulating, would make a lot of noise. When he was present at our meetings, it meant that he had escaped his 'jailer and then instantly everything was changed. Utrillo, on those nights, very pale, a dark look in his eyes, would empty bottle after bottle of red wine with surprising rapidity. Then the great painter would begin his stunts. He would approach our tables, hover around, stare at us, and then seize a glass or a bottle and run away. All of us would run after him shouting, but too late, for he would escape to the street, only to come back and knock till the door was opened. Alas, drinking was his vice. He showed as much stubbornness in bringing confusion wherever he went as our friend Jules showed in trying to be forgotten.

The cabaret owners, who all knew him, never missed an opportunity. Some even had tubes, pencils, canvases and brushes for M. Maurice, and they encouraged his drinking

[143] Marie Vizier, also known as la Bonne Hôtesse, ran La Belle Gabrielle, a café cabaret located at 12, rue Saint-Vincent, at the intersection of rue du Mont-Cenis. Vizier leased the property from César Gay, whose Casse-Croûte was close by, at the corner of rue du Mont-Cenis and rue Paul Féval (where Utrillo lived and exhibited his work). Vizier was a friend of Utrillo and often acted as his protector as well as his tormentor (she was said to beat him "mercilessly"). Yet Utrillo looked back upon La Belle Gabrielle as the place where "I lived the happiest moments of my life." Utrillo completed several portraits of the café, including an oil painting on board titled *Belle Gabrielle et rue Saint-Vincent sous la neige, Montmartre*, circa 1946. It depicts the café's emerald-green façade, shimmering beside Utrillo's trademark Payne's gray building facades and snow-covered lanes.

because his Montmartre studies were already worth about fifty francs apiece. At Marie's, the most beautiful Utrillo's could still be seen at the beginning of the war. They were hung side by side, most of them without frames and nailed crazily up and down the walls. No one paid any attention to them. There were also canvases by the mother of Maurice Utrillo, Suzanne Valadon[144] – Maurice Utrillo always signed himself Utrillo V. through filial love – some Tiret-Bognets,[145] some Depaquits, at the Belle Gabrielle, because the bills were paid in that hospitable house by painting, stories or songs, depending upon whether one was a painter or a poet. Marie was not stingy. She kept open house for all who came as long as they were artists, and only thought of getting paid later.

In the rue du Mont-Cenis, between the angle of the stairs and the narrow passage of the rue Saint-Vincent, her restaurant, its curtain always drawn since 1914, was very attractive. The food was excellent, thanks to Marie, who did the cooking herself, and chose the wines as well. The good hostess deserved her nickname. She had no coquetry, but I really believe that under her easygoing exterior she was very shrewd and had a keen critical sense. Otherwise why should she have seen in her neighbor, Utrillo's landlord, Père G., who lived at the bottom of the stairs, a dangerous rival? No one knew at that time what paintings by Utrillo would eventually be worth, and while Utrillo lived with Père G., Marie thought about the canvases he had and felt she was badly treated. Heavens! What scenes there were between M. Maurice, Père G. and the very quick-tempered Marie. What disputes, but M. G. had the guardianship of Utrillo by contract and did not worry.

---

[144] Suzanne Valadon (née Marie-Clementine Valadon; 1865 – 1938): French post-Impressionist painter, mother of Utrillo, and former model for Renoir and Toulouse-Lautrec, who was mentored by Degas. Valadon was first female painter to be admitted to the Société Nationale des Beaux-Arts.
[145] Georges Tiret-Bognet (1855 – 1935): French painter and book illustrator.

That very fat and unctuous man was no idiot. If he had agreed to prevent his strange lodger from leading a drunken existence in Montmartre he was paid with his lodger's works. I bought my first Utrillo's from him. M. G. sold them to me for a hundred francs and treated me to a drink besides, because he also had a café, as is fitting, and he carried on both callings. Every wine merchant on the Butte is a picture dealer to some extent. The two businesses go hand in hand and perhaps we would never have had a painter of the strength and greatness of Utrillo without the obscure Père G., his *pinard* and his fantastic alcohol.

*

Let us come back to Depaquit. He always listened peacefully to the foolish sayings of others, shook his head and never took sides, being always on the defensive. He had other fish to fry, because his carelessness brought him creditors every morning who, not understanding jokes, claimed money from him and worried him. The Dufayel shop, amongst others, annoyed Jules a great deal. Invariably he answered that since he had rented furniture from Monsieur Dufayel,[146] he would only deal with Monsieur Dufayel himself, and that if Monsieur himself would come to collect, he would be paid at once. He lived, or rather borrowed, a little everywhere, he never gave his address, and when once he remained in bed more than a week at Bouscarat's, it appeared so strange to us that we all went to see him.

[146] Georges Dufayel (1855 – 1916): Parisian retailer who operated the flamboyantly designed Dufayel Department Store at 26, rue de Clignancourt, which featured a 180-foot dome crowned with a searchlight. Dufayel was one of the first proponents of buying on credit via the installment plan and through the use of catalogs. To help attract clientele his store hosted concerts, lectures, films, and dramatic performances, held in a theatre that seated 3,000.

"I have a temperature," he explained to us, a little embarrassed. "I cough, I don't feel at all well."

"Really?"

Depaquit scratched his nose, and then as we did not seem inclined to believe him, for he looked exceedingly healthy, he began:

"A week ago, I got my money from the *Journal* and I wanted to show off."

"What?"

"Yes."

"You?"

"Well," said Depaquit, "I picked up a girl ... We dined on the boulevards ... we came back here ..."

"And then?"

"Then ... She left me in the morning ... yes ... and ... since then ... no more money ... I have looked everywhere ... Nothing ... not a sou ... It sounds stupid ... So while waiting, I stay in bed. Bouscarat[147] brings me food ... I work."

"And your money," said one of us, "where was it?"

"In my purse."

"And your purse?"

"In my pocket," answered Depaquit.

We were obliged to admit that Jules had been robbed and we were sympathizing with him, when suddenly the friend who had asked him questions, went on:

"Where are your trousers, Depaquit? Did you look? ... Did you search well?"

"Oh," moaned Depaquit, "my trousers ..."

---

[147] According to Modigliani biographer Pierre Sichel, Bouscarat was a "tough landlord" (in 1907 he evicted Modigliani for nonpayment of rent), who owned the "Hôtel-Restaurant Bouscarat," located at 2, place du Tertre, at the corner of rue du Mont-Cenis (also known as the "Hôtel du Tertre," "Auberge de la Marine," "Auberge Bouscarat," and "Maison Bouscarat"). Other tenants in the hotel included Carco, Max Jacob, Mac Orlan, and Erik Satie.

But an idea came to him. He jumped out of bed, lifted the mattress and suddenly cried joyfully:

"Here they are," he cried, here they are … and in the pocket, no, can it be?"

"The purse?"

"And the money," said Depaquit … "Look … really, it is so stupid of me, so idiotic … and I, who thought she had even taken my clothes. La! la! la! how lucky for me that you came … otherwise, I would have remained in bed till Doomsday!"

*

With Georges Delaw, *"imaginer de la reine,"*[148] Depaquit ended by creating in Montmartre a kind of reaction against the adventure craze and the corsairs dear to Pierre Mac Orlan. Delaw, who was conscientious and a hardened addict of dry land, hated adventure. He owned, in the rue du Mont-Cenis, a small house furnished with old furniture from the Ardennes, and a clock with a sonorous pendulum. Its windows were decorated with short curtains of blue or pink and white squares. Some [tobacco] pipes [stored in a stand] and some big and light tempera paintings brightened the walls. He frequented the Lapin a lot, but his group was subconsciously hostile to us. The prose poems, the drawings, the sayings of this charming artist, everything made him different from us, even his dog and his hobnailed boots, indicative of the life he led.

Already, without preaching to us to renounce the extravagant ambitions which warmed our souls, another lover of the country, of the same kind as Delaw and Jules Depaquit, had just

[148] The original French text reads *"Imaginer de la reine,"* a highly ambiguous phrase that literally translates as "imagine of the queen." The Boyd translation replaces this with *imagier de la reine*: "The queen's picture maker." (*Imagier* implies creating visual images.)

been able to fulfill his dreams. His name was Capy.[149] Capy, the humorist, more in love with the suburbs than with the real country, had invested in a shanty near Saint-Ouen and had made it into a bistro. A sign painted by him pointed his house out to the curious. On the door was another with the inscription: *A l'ancien Conscrit*.[150] And within was a room furnished with a bar, small tables, high stools, mirrors and bottles of all kinds, among which Capy, a napkin over his arm, waited. In the little village where everybody knew the humorist, not one of the inhabitants felt tempted to enter. They mistrusted him. But, one day, a traveler who wanted to lunch quickly passed by that strange inn, sat down and called the waiter:

"Here I am," grumbled Capy.

He himself served his customer, brought him choice wines, coffee, cigars, then some cognac and as the other, in a very good humor, asked for the bill:

"Allow me," said Capy in a murmur, "please don't mention it, you are in my house, sir."

"Well?"

"Well, … nothing … you don't owe me anything. I am only too happy to have had you to lunch."

"Well, I'll be damned! … You... Are you joking?"

"Goodbye," said Capy.

The customer could not make it out. He looked stupidly at his host, then fearful that he might be the victim of a joke, he took to his heels and ran away as fast as his legs could carry him.

There is a great difference between this pleasing story and those of Jack London's buccaneers and I rather suspect Capy of having invented it so that he could laugh at us. What does it matter? Those who loved the land wanted to make us disgusted

---

[149] Marcel Capy (1865 – 1941): French cartoonist of the Belle Époque who illustrated books by Alphonse Daudet and Georges Courteline.

[150] *A l'ancien Conscrit*: "To the former conscript."

with desert islands and phantom ships and every means seemed justified to them. If they opposed vagabondage to adventure, they never went further than teasing us and they did not mind drinking a toast with us. In the two camps, a clay pipe made everybody agree that it was best to take life joyously.

And there was room for us all in Montmartre and each one of us could lead freely the existence he chose. For some of us, this happy place with its view of Saint-Ouen and Saint-Denis and their thick clouds of smoke looked without doubt like a tragic port exposed to the wind of the open sea. For others, it was a tiny village with its narrow streets, its silent and sleepy shops, and I must say that, more than once, if I had been obliged to decide between the lovers of the land and the lovers of the sea, I should have been very embarrassed, as I sometimes saw the sea in the far-off distance, and sometimes those mute spaces which one sees only in the open country and which surround one on every side.

IX

Alas! with time, how many illusions have I left behind! When I think of them, and when I see Montmartre, not as it was then, but as it is now, with its high buildings and its *guinguettes*[151] full of foreigners, I feel as if I had lived a dream, and I don't know where I am. And yet, there is Frédéric on his threshold, the Hôtel du Tertre, the Coucou,[152] the Belle Gabrielle, and the small church whose bell tolled devotedly every evening. Here behind the wall of the old Calvary graveyard are the big trees, whose leaves in autumn covered the illustrious slabs and fell into our glasses. Here are the innumerable lights of Paris and the same wind which makes them twinkle as before, when we look at them. Nothing has moved or changed its appearance, nothing, except our years and our loves, which though dead may be renewed temporarily, only to disappear at once.

Mon beau navire

[151] Saloons that often featured dance gardens, located by the riverside in the suburbs of Paris, where they were exempt from state taxes (and thus could offer cheaper commodities). From the term *guinguet*: an inexpensive green wine served in such taverns.

[152] "The rather inaccessible position occupied by the Restaurant du Coucou has saved it, so far, to the coterie of artists, actors, journalists, and literary folk who, with their friends, make up its clientele. It perches like a bird's nest on the steep hillside which surrounds the Sacré Coeur. In front of the picturesque, dilapidated old building which is the restaurant proper, lies a tiny square, the name of which I shall not give — for if you have not the energy to find it, you don't deserve to know about the Restaurant du Coucou." Julian Street, *Paris à la Carte* (Second, revised edition), New York: John Lane Co., 1912, pp. 52-53. Also known as the Auberge du Coucou, it was located at 7, place du Calvaire. Fernande Olivier says that it was frequented by Picasso, Apollinaire, Jacob, and Braque.

cried Guillaume Apollinaire,

> *ô ma mémoire*
> *Avons-nous assez navigué*
> *Dans une onde mauvaise à boire*
> *Avons-nous assez divagué*
> *De la belle aube au triste soir.*[153]

What can I answer? He is no longer with us,[154] though his invisible presence still lingers in that setting of palings, studios and small gardens where we used to wander together. At the Lapin, when we felt that he was secretly hurt, in spite of his loud laughter and his jokes, did he not leave to his friends the task of evoking him as he really was?

Those who knew him better than I could tell of this and show him with Salmon, Picasso, Max Jacob, talking of pure poetry, food, Negro art, Cubism, Orphism. He loved to teach others, to trouble them, to mystify them, and to laugh afterwards at them and at himself without any malice. No one in Montmartre had his kindness and no matter what he undertook, it brought him sympathy and provoked enchantment. It was royal. It was fairy-like and if I allude to it now, it is because in 1913, I saw much of Guillaume Apollinaire in the cafés on the Left Bank, where he was surrounded by his court.

Long before that date, between those two sections which were so different, the Butte and the Quarter, the fight had opened. Derain, Salmon, Apollinaire, Picasso, Modigliani, only came

[153] "My beautiful ship, oh, my memory / Have we sailed long enough / In a wave unfit to drink / Have we wandered enough / From the beautiful dawn to sad evening." From the poem "La Chanson du Mal Aimé," featured in *Alcools* (1913).

[154] Apollinaire served in the infantry during WWI and sustained a severe head wound. He died two years later, a victim of the 1918 flu pandemic. In Picasso's 1921 paintings of the *Three Musicians* Apollinaire is portrayed as the pierrot, Picasso as the harlequin, and Jacob as the monk.

very rarely to the Lapin. They took their pleasures elsewhere, and I am obliged to admit that without them our evenings were rather dull. Another kind of spirit was in us, a more ordinary, earthly one; other cares also and perhaps a deep-seated uneasiness which sometimes made us count ourselves as if we were afraid our group would disappear into space at the first weakness.

However, at the place du Tertre, at Bouscarat's terrace, Charles Laborde, Daragnès, Asselin, Girieud, Deslignières[155] Warnod, Dorgelès made a joyous company. We dined at the same table then, and when Frédé's cellar drew us, we would join Mac Orlan and our crew was complete. We spent the night thus. Girls and apaches who were fond of poetry made friends at Frédéric's with his ordinary clients. We were treated as comrades by them and they offered us drinks. Those men had tender hearts, "artistic tastes," and when one of their women would pass them up for some one of our group, those gentlemen did not get angry; they would leave us for a while, dance at the Moulin de la Galette and come back with new girls. All were not, luckily, of the same kind, because the place would have lost its charm, but they all loved the easy life one led at the Lapin and its very literary poisons.

And indeed, under the lamps veiled with red silk handkerchiefs, and the low dark ceiling of the big room, where

[155] Charles Laborde (aka Chas Laborde; 1886 – 1941): born in Argentina, prolific French journalist, painter, and graphic designer, who was gassed during WWI while serving at Verdun. Once called the "wittiest man in Paris," Laborde illustrated at least sixty books, including a half dozen by Carco. His dark, foreboding urban portraits have been compared to the sinister realism of George Grosz. In his essay, "Chas Laborde," Mac Orlan regarded his art as the most prescient and "lifelike chronicle … of the turbulent years which preceded the war of 1939," when "the future drama was hidden under everyone's faces." Jean-Gabriel Daragnès (1886 – 1950): French printmaker, painter, illustrator, and book publisher, whose workshop was located in Montmartre. Marcel Deslignières (1847 – 1914): French architect and watercolorist.

Frédéric sang, who did not feel as if drugged with some powerful opiate? No dream or pleasure even approaches that sensation. It was quite another thing. A very special sort of intoxication, mixed with fancies and depression, uncertain and voiceless. It seized us, as in autumn the falling rain stops to fall again, to lull us, to make us inert and half conscious. It really rained on those nights, or else it snowed, while the drunkest lay stretched upon the benches and innocent white mice, friendly yet cautious, trotted along the mantelpiece. How can I describe without a pang, without a feeling akin to the most sorrowful partings, the atmosphere of our long night watches? Part of it came from the surroundings of confused bric-a-brac, from the obscene moldings, from the immense plaster Christ, from Picasso's canvases, Utrillo's, Girieud's. The heavy smoke of the pipes added to it. And Frédéric with his guitar, Mac Orlan dressed as a cowboy, the dampness of the walls, the barking dogs, the hidden despair of us all, our poverty, our youth, wasted time, completed the atmosphere. Am I right? There were some evenings when we were all drunk and some of us were in the depths of despair and great loneliness, but it did not show. Except for Couté,[156] who was put to sleep on the ground, under the tables, since he seemed unable to stand, nothing would have been noticeable. But he shouted often and very loudly when he awoke, or else stood up, upsetting bottles and glasses. To stop the scandal we would sing so loudly that we could not hear each other's voices.

Such things happened often then. No one paid any attention to them. They belonged to the customs of the place and even on some nights shots from outside through the panes brought those pleasurable moments to the height of their intensity. If I speak about those shots, it is only to show that the gentlemen whom Frédé did not wish in his place also wanted to take part

[156] Gaston Couté, author of *Chanson d'un gas qu'a mal tourné*. (See earlier footnote.)

in the festivities, so they shared in them in their own way and their erstwhile girls felt the thrill of it. For them, it was the call of the street, of its hazards, its furious and threatening loves, and for us a supreme excitement. At other times, the men who had decided to punish their women would make a surprise attack upon the Lapin and, brandishing sharp razors, bring the terror with them.

Astonishing hours! These same men who, one winter's night, a little later, surrounded me as I was going home, were huge brutes. Their coats looked as if they were made of sacking and were shaped like Inverness capes, such as those formerly worn by highway robbers, and they carried, tied to their wrists, thick, short sticks. Where did they come from? What faraway quarter? A gay ball at the Butte must have been what attracted them, for they went everywhere ...

Salmon in his *Tendres Canailles* shows them as they were and in the verses he dedicated to them:

> *Partageant mon vin, des filous*
> *M'ont laissé caresser leurs armes,*[157]

he shows what kind of underhand comradeship existed between the poets and the gangsters. But there was also, at Frédéric's, his son, young Victor, for whom the girls who came from the Moulin de la Galette did all kinds of foolish things. Victor turned their heads: they were "turned inside out" by him and many mysterious intrigues complicated matters and awe-inspiring gangs watched the entrances of the Lapin. In the summer of 1911, about midnight, at the time when the Lapin and the *guinches* (dancing halls) close their doors, one could hear Victor being called and threatened. He did not answer, but was behind the counter, peaceful, looking straight ahead, with a smile upon his lips. What happened? I won't tell it all.

[157] "Sharing my wine, the rascals / Allowed me to caress their weapons."

However, a short while after, the newspapers announced that Frédé's son had been killed at the cashier's desk by a man who, while asking change for ten francs, had emptied his revolver into him.

I heard this news in the provinces and at once I felt everything would be different. I thought of Frédé and imagined him alone in his closed house. An immense pity filled me as I thought of him, forsaken, old and discouraged, in the midst of his café's absurd scenery, decked in his operatic bandit's costume. Life has such paradoxes. We were all very sorry for him. This adventure plunged us into the deepest gloom. But, on my return, I saw the Lapin wide open and its customers installed as usual ... Doubtless there was a little less gaiety and lightheartedness than formerly, but one evening Frédé sang, we also sang, and life went back to its queer course which nothing could circumvent.

"There you are," said a friend, "we are still the same as ever and can begin all over again."

Mac Orlan had married; and had left Montmartre and most of his comrades, who were enjoying the welcome given to them by Gus Bofa at the Sourire. He came less often to the Butte and went and more to the boulevards and the newspapers. Roland Dorgelès was seen only in taxis. Warnod went to Comoedia, Charles Laborde ran around Paris looking for the kind of people he draws and deserted the Lapin. That was the end. And as for myself, one day I decided to work and left the rue Caulaincourt for the Latin Quarter. Gradually, through the force of circumstances, we met only rarely at Frédé's, where a younger people had taken our place.

Daragnès, Asselin, Girieud, Deslignières, Depaquit, Delaw, Falké[158] and some others alone stubbornly clung to their old

[158] Pierre Falké (1884 – 1947): Prolific French book illustrator and cartoonist, who specialized in wood engravings. Carco's *Les Vrais de Vrai* ("The Genuine

habits, led the same life and were wise to do so. However, they also abandoned Frédé a little later. One met them at Adèle's, in her wooden shanty, where the cooking was good, at the Billard-en-bois, at Manière's, who today has assembled the last habitués of the Lapin of that time, at Bouscarat's, at old Spielmann's, but although still quite numerous the group was losing its unity. The Billards en Bois[159] was discovered by the designer Gassier, and an old rivalry with Poulbot[160] obliged him to keep it up to the mark. The restaurant's arbors in a shaded garden, its customers, tradesmen and young men and young ladies of the Butte were not objectionable, quite the contrary. And to tell the truth, two beautiful Renoirs painted on the walls

Ones"; Paris: Au Sans Pareil, 1928) was illustrated with six of his etchings. Falké also illustrated texts by Roland Dorgelès and Pierre Mac Orlan.

[159] Aux Billards en Bois: located in Montmartre at the corner of 2, rue des Saules and 18, rue Saint-Rustique, in a building that dates back to the late sixteenth century. According to the restaurant's website, Toulouse-Lautrec once invited Van Gogh to drink absinthe at Les Billards en Bois, and it was there, in the restaurant's garden, that Van Gogh painted *La Guinguette*. "Pissarro, Degas, Sisley, Cézanne, Renoir, Gauguin, Van Gogh, then Toulouse-Lautrec, Suzanne Valadon, and her son Utrillo, as well as writers and poets, came to refresh themselves under the shaded arbors.... Discussing their projects, they played billiards in the garden. This is how Renoir painted his famous canvas, *Le Bal du Moulin de la Galette*, on this very spot in 1876." In the early twentieth century Francisque Poulbot, Henri-Paul Gassier, and Mac Orlan founded l'Association fraternelle des joueurs de billard en bois and played billiards in the garden at a five-meter-long table. The restaurant changed its name to La Bonne Franquette in 1925. It was later featured in several films, including Georges Lacombe's *Montmartre-sur-Seine* (1941), starring Édith Piaf.

[160] Henri-Paul Deyvaux-Gassier (1883 – 1951): French caricaturist and illustrator. Francisque Poulbot (1879 – 1946): French poster designer and illustrator, whose patriotic posters of WWI led to his arrest by the Nazis during WWII.

and a charming canvas by Marie Laurencin[161] helped to keep us faithful to it.

Anyone who has ever known Marie Laurencin without becoming attached to her forever, is a monster, for she certainly is the most charming and most sprightly of friends. Her gaiety, her charm, her talent would move hearts of stone. And besides she had the prestige of having been bitter and sweet to our friend Guillaume and of having inspired his most beautiful poem. When she appeared, with her blonde hair blowing around her face like a halo, her clear eyes, her laughing mouth and her natural amiability, the verses of the *Chanson du Mal* came to our lips and we would say them over to ourselves while Marie sat down at the table, looked at us and asked us sometimes what we were thinking about. Could anyone tell her? No one would have dared.

*

Dear Marie! She knew, she could see that we were not angry with her for having made Guillaume so unhappy. Sometimes she asked about him. Sometimes, astonished by our silence, she would hum a little song and go away, and it appeared impossible for her not to be at least as upset as we were. So many tender memories clung to her that, in spite of everything, she remained the too-much beloved friend of the poet, and our sister in the amazing sufferings of which she was the cause. Why should I not acknowledge it? It seemed as if her presence through a thousand subtleties prepared us, as well as Guillaume, for despair and to welcome it when it came. What

[161] Marie Laurencin (1883 – 1956): French painter, born in Paris, who aligned herself with the early twentieth-century avant-garde. The muse of Apollinaire. Fernande Olivier displays her acute powers of observation when she characterizes Laurencin as "an innocent abroad," who "looked like a little girl, and had a little girl's mixture of naivete and viciousness, a good deal too naive to be true." Olivier, *Picasso and His Friends*, p. 43.

did our Montmartre loves amount to in comparison? Very little, less than nothing, because if we thought about them, a bitter feeling born of disgust and fatigue came over us. Truly, sad love affairs, too mechanical and too obvious. In spite of often borrowing new faces, they were always the same and our mistresses who thought they were making us happy, only succeeded in irritating and tiring us. What was missing? I hardly dare to say it. Perhaps they would have been better if there had been less joy, less compliance and less stupidity. But no matter how the days and nights passed, if one of the girls left us we were so sorry that we had to hide it somehow.

How many times, as I went back to my room at dawn, I suffered from loneliness and lack of courage. I would have given half of my life to get rid of that emptiness within me, that emptiness which made me tolerate in others and commit myself a thousand excesses! I would have gone to the end of the world, even if I had to come back alone, as always. There was in me, in those moments, such a desire to escape from my life that it seemed to me that I acted, thought, and slept in a dream. It was a great torment. I saw my disorder clearly; I judged myself accurately. I pitied myself, but at the same time, my youth triumphed and far from making a decision, I was carried away by my pleasures, and they blinded me.

In the evenings – I remember it quite well – the streets drew me when the bars and the hotels lighted up. I roamed around Montmartre, where, lost in those quarters dear to the heart of Robert de la Vaissière, I intoxicated myself by wandering through the rain looking for the most dismal adventures. In Grenelle, at the Bastille, I stayed several days in disgusting lodgings, drinking, smoking, unable to explain the disgusting taste I had for the company of prostitutes and their friends, the thieves. In their noble company I danced in the bals-musette.[162] I

[162] French dance halls that featured instrumental music played on the accordion.

would forget everything else in the world till the moment when, heartily sick of all that stupid life, I seemed to revert to purer feelings. Then nothing could have held me. I would cross Paris hastily, go back to my house and would feel as sentimental as if I were coming back from a long journey. Everything greeted me with joy and when, in my mail, a *pneumatique* scandalously perfumed would recall to my mind a transient love affair, I was quite sincere in my gladness.

My confidences will have to be excused, but it would be hard to understand without them the following lines:

> *L'heure amère des poètes*
> *Qui se sentent tristement*
> *Portés sur l'aile inquiète*
> *Du désordre et du tourment*[163]

and that bitter hour, so troubled and unsettled, rang on my alarm clock more often than is customary perhaps or good taste to confess to my readers.

Was it my fault? I had to pay that price for my restful hours, and the bad opinion these adventures gave me of myself filled me with delight and pain. Should I have struggled? It was beyond my strength, and the most curious thing is that, while despising myself on that account, I was persuaded that it would be a good enough reason for my absolution. Being in that frame of mind I had very little chance to mend my ways. My lower self decided what tastes I should have, what errors I should make and I laughed at the time lost when some innocent creature tried to awake better feelings in me, and I played up to her. Everything was useful to deceive her; if I gave myself away, I took back all I said it once, even if I regretted it

---

[163] Carco quoting from his poem, "L'heure du poète," featured in *Petits airs* (1920): "The bitter hour of the poets / Who feel sadly / Carried on the restless wing / Of disorder and torment."

afterward and under my matter-of-fact air saw myself as I really was. Of course, I regret none of that period in my life when my real satisfaction came only in doing wrong and in enjoying it. And yet if I suffered I was quickly consoled, and singularly enough, as soon as I had stopped moaning, I started suffering again and did not grudge it.

It has been said of poets that they are always ready to sacrifice their happiness in order to celebrate it better and to find a more humane passion. It is quite possible. Baudelaire and his "voluptuousness of regret" have long fascinated me, but each man has his own nature and has to deal with it. Mine inclined me to the worst excesses and to the lowest pleasures, through sorrow and the want of money. What is the good of theorizing about it? I admired the falseness of women and I was taken in by them. Perhaps one, after telling me she copied my letters in a notebook so that she could reread them as she sat beside her husband,[164] deceived me with him; perhaps another, wishing me well, yielded to me only in tears and discouraged me. They educated me, they taught me how to play their game, and always furnished me reasons to run away from them.

Thus I spent most of those beautiful years in a perpetual uncertainty and I discovered in my friends the same desire to break off any affair when they began to really fall in love. Why should I not have done as they did? Some of them caused melodrama and were delighted, while I, renewing relations with fallen women, at which I should have blushed, struggled with drunkenness, disgust and awful torment. The more I went on and the more my torment increased, the more I felt the prey of my sad habits. However, it was not only the women I loved but, most of all, the black streets, the low cafés, the cold, the fine rain upon the roofs, the bars, the chance meetings, and in the bedrooms an air of sad abandon which tightened my heart. The

[164] A reference to Carco's brief but torrid affair with the author Katherine Mansfield.

tragic winter nights, so dark and so pathetic, fascinated me and gave me such sensations that, perfectly insensible to other attractions than theirs, I intoxicated myself, as with a bitter wine, with my own misfortunes.

Has not Utrillo expressed in his work that secret and cruel obsession which during a certain period of his life pursued him more than any other? It has laid its weight on our teens with a heavy load and has marked the men of my generation with such a mysterious sign that without it they would have no means of recognizing themselves.[165] In Utrillo it can be seen at once, as he has cherished his illness and has dissected it so minutely that he could not deny it. Recall the perspectives, deserted for the most part, of his Paris streets and of the suburbs. There shines upon the walls, upon the houses with closed shutters, upon the brown windows of bistros a fixed light which comes from nowhere, except from those dream regions which no one dares talk about. And what anxiety there is, an anxiety that cannot be captured, what an ambiguous, fleeting, unattainable presence, what a piercing call! It seems that, at the precise minute when he could have helped us, the only human being alive in the world had just turned around the corner of those plaster houses and disappeared forever. Why has he not heard? As I write these lines I'm looking at one of Utrillo's canvases in which these qualities which make his greatness and his strength are magically portrayed. In that picture, the whites and the blues and the pinks blend with such perfection that they overwhelm me. A narrow yard, an open

[165] Cf. Carco's 1921 booklet on Utrillo: "Remember Kipling's painter who, in the steerage of a ship, composed the most abominable vision that a being could have created in the image of his torment. This is the case with Utrillo, and it is a particular trait, I believe, of the sensitivity of the men of our generation, who, constantly tossed around, by the chance of a mediocre existence, have baptized their grotesque delirium with the horrible nickname of 'cockroach,' like our brothers the soldiers." Francis Carco, *Les Peintres Français Nouveaux, N° 8. Maurice Utrillo*, p. 11. (My translation.)

door, some leaves on the roofs. Such calm! One thinks of Verlaine, who sighed:

> *Mon Dieu, mon Dieu, la vie est là*
> *Simple et tranquille !*[166]

and little by little one is struck by the air of that very clean small yard, with the entrance ornamented by an enormous inscription: LAVOIR CHAMPEAU,[167] in big letters; you look at it, you approach it with curiosity, as if, from behind the shutters someone were watching you, and you act as if you had not seen him. But is one sure of anything? Isn't it rather that other self, which every man spends his life crushing down, who before this canvas awakes as if by enchantment? Those places are so familiar to that other self! He knows them. I mean to say, he recognizes them and the emotion that seizes him – at that moment – is one which only a few human beings can feel if they have been weak the first time, only to push temptation away and to fly from it, afraid of giving in.

Shall I be believed? I felt then a fear and an uneasiness which I did not analyze, and in the streets where I roamed very late, I had the impression of being swept into the confused and blind totality of existence which stalks about at night, in secret, haunts desperately, comes and goes ... borne by the wind. I can't express myself better: the next day when I came back in broad daylight, it took a long and hard effort to get hold of myself. I was suffering. I was struggling against someone who had taken hold of me – and finding my ordinary self at last, I was irritated and felt cheated. And indeed, everything was

[166] "My God, my God, life here is / Simple and quiet!" From an untitled poem now referred to as "Le ciel est, par-dessus le toit," composed in 1880 and first published in 1881 by Paul Verlaine (1844 – 1896).
[167] Carco is describing Utrillo's *Champeau washhouse*: an oil painting that portrays a narrow lane, running between two whitewashed buildings, over which hangs an enormous sign: "Lavoir Champeau."

changed – the poet inspired by the night had been turned by me into a copyist without imagination who, even while writing down verses, would forget their meaning, if not their rhythm and their ambiguous and nostalgic fervor.

Sad homecomings! Montmartre was then only an ordinary quarter of Paris, very ordinary, without any character. Creditors rang the bell. The concierge, her receipted bill in her hand, asked for money.

"Rather than get yourself in such a state," this ridiculous person would say, "it might be better ..."

"Yes!"

Max Jacob used to escape with the aid of a compliment. Others, sitting naked at their worktables, would shout to her: "Come in," and say coolly: "You see, everything has been taken away from me!" Ordinarily, it was outside that the disputes took place and we avoided them by running rather than by insisting. On the fifteenth of every quarter, fatal date, couples who appeared united would separate because of the rent, and the milkman, the grocer and the butcher would draw a moral to bore us with. However, it was a moral, the only real one, though perhaps if we had followed it, we would have been disgusted before the right age with the chances of life. I remember what happened to me one morning in the rue Lepic, in a hotel where I was plunged in a deep sleep. I had to give up to the hotel keeper my poems, my clothes, my shoes and, shivering, I soon found myself in a bar on the place Pigalle, without a coat – in spite of winter – and without a hat. How ugly the square seemed that morning, with its fountain and its green buses. Standing in front of the counter, sleepy and cold,

J'admirais comment va le monde[168]

---

[168] "I admired how the world is doing."

but my heart was failing me. "What?" I said to myself. "Is life only a question of paying, paying all the time!"

I thought of my comrades who must have been thinking as I did, and who, discouraged, understanding that Montmartre was no more than any other place the habitat of artists, did not know where to go. The water in the basin, the streets on the slope which led to Paris, invited one to travel, to go away ...

Je sens que les oiseaux sont ivres.[169]

"Ah! not the birds! That's enough!" said I, outraged ... And I went out of the bar at the moment when, throbbing with life, the motor bus "Place Pigalle-Halle-aux-Vins" was starting ... and I jumped inside.

[169] "I sense that the birds are drunk."

X

The contrast between Montmartre and the Latin Quarter can be seen at once on the route followed by the bus Pigalle-aux-Vins. One suddenly discovers other places than the Moulin Rouge, la Galette, the Lapin Agile, even Sacré-Coeur. And greater memories can be evoked.

The pointed and lacy spire of the Sainte-Chapelle, the towers of Notre Dame, the *parvis*,[170] Saint-Julien-le-Pauve, in that winter morning appeared to me in a bluish light and although I had no credit whatsoever on that side of the water, I felt quite reassured. When I first arrived in Paris,[171] I had stayed in the Île Saint-Louis where Charles-Louis Philippe wrote to me, from his little room, that for a poet it was the only place to live. When Charles-Louis Philippe died I went to live on the quai de Bourbon but I didn't stay long there. The place was too calm, too far away, with the river, its sad trees and its old houses. It seemed to me that I was still in the provinces. I was bored there and as I often came back very late at night, the concierge was offended by my conduct and I was unhappy about it. Why should I lie? I had no self-assurance at that time. Paris with its brasseries, its cafés, its carriages, its perpetual and feverish animation frightened me. I did not know many people, and when I sat in the bars and looked at the women, they inspired in me more astonishment than desire and I did not dare go near them. One of them whom I met at the Taverne du Panthéon[172]

[170] Parvis: a large square facing Notre-Dame, which contains the official kilometre zero marker: an eight-pointed bronze star, set in the pavement, that denotes the center of Paris. Road distances to locations throughout France are measured from this radial point.

[171] Carco arrived in Montmartre in January 1910 at the age of twenty-four.

[172] Located at 63, boulevard Saint-Michel (with another entrance at 26, rue Soufflot), facing the Café d'Harcourt. Throughout his memoir Carco refers to

and whom I secretly admired, was very much amused by my shyness. She was a [brunette], very [loose], who smoked luxurious cigarettes with gold tips, and who, far from [sticking to her prices],[173] accepted when the café was closing, anything that was offered. It never occurred to me to take advantage of such a reduction in price and one evening the woman herself spoke to me, explaining that her feet were hurting her and asked me for three francs so that she could take a carriage to go home. I gave them to her. But to my great surprise I saw the charming borrower forget all about her feet, and run as fast as she could to a bakery, where women of her kind went on feasting the whole night.

That incident taught me more about those women than a whole night spent with one would have, because I missed the three francs dreadfully the next day. At that time one could eat three square meals for that sum, and even drink and smoke as well. In the rue de la Montagne-Sainte-Geneviève, where Bernouard[174] and I were learning to set type and to print books, our meals cost twelve sous. Bread, ten centimes; meat, thirty centimes; vegetables, fifteen; hot chocolate, one sou, so that from three francs there was enough left for luxury. But I

this as the Brasserie du Panthéon, Bar du Panthéon, or Taverne du Panthéon: a hangout for many of the characters portrayed here, including Jean Giraudoux, Charles Derennes, Pierre Benoît, Antoine Albalat, and André Billy, all of whom are mentioned in an essay by Alex Madis titled *A la Taverne du Panthéon* ("At the Panthéon Tavern"), *Revue Des Deux Mondes*, 1956, pp. 510-519; jstor.org/stable/44595972.

[173] Boyd euphemistically translates this phrase as "far from being very hard."

[174] François Bernouard (1884 – 1949): French poet, publisher, and playwright. "For a while, Carco worked for François Bernouard as a typesetter, and set by hand his own volume of poems. The edition was never published." Seymour S. Weiner, *Francis Carco*, p. 63.

thought philosophically, one must learn, and I did not trouble myself anymore about it.

I was richer another night. I can see myself crossing the Petit Pont and playing with a small gold coin which was going to give me a week of ease. It was about dawn. A fine winter rain was wetting the pavements and the roadway, the dark shrubs shone along the quay and in a line around the *parvis*, and the gaslights were glowing. No one was abroad at such a time, except a *garde-républicain* who, to keep warm, was stamping his feet in his sentry box and grumbling under his long coat. He saluted me as I passed near him and as I turned around to greet him in return, the coin I held in my hand escaped me and rolled I don't know where.

"Oh, how stupid!"

"What is the matter?" asked the *garde*.

"I had ten francs …"

"Ten francs!"

"Yes," I said, very much upset, "and now it's gone …"

"You must look for it," said the *garde* as he stopped stamping his feet on the bottom of his box. "It can't have rolled very far …"

At that moment, a miserable beggar, on his way to Les Halles, came up. He held the collar of his ragged coat close around his neck:

"What is the matter?" he asked in a raucous voice. "May I help you in any way?"

We explained matters to him, and then I struck a match.

"Wait," mumbled the man. "Come around here. If you move when you look, you won't be able to find anything … There, in the gutter, give us a light."

He was down on his knees, feeling in the dirty water, searching on the ground, his fingers moving along slowly in the mud.

"We'll share, hey," he asked, "you promise?"

"Of course."

"Well, then, old man, have patience!"

A great moment! And one after another my matches went out, while the indefatigable beggar carefully explored the pavement. Soon, other individuals as blue with cold as he was, and intrigued by our conduct, had joined us. They came out from under the shrubs which are at the foot of Charlemagne's statue and, hearing what was the matter, began looking also. Some women came as well and also searched in the rain. I was tired and unhappy at the site of all those miserable people who, for five francs, silently prayed luck to be good to them and were watching each other covertly. Suddenly I could not stand it anymore. I gave up the search and went home very sadly.

"How pitiful!" I thought.

As I was undressing, the small gold coin, which had providentially fallen into a fold of my old trousers, rolled out of its hiding place to the floor.

I kept for a long time a painful recollection of those ten francs which I used instead of dividing them. I am still ashamed when I think about it. I asked for the beggar the next day of the passersby, at the same time, at the same place, but nobody was able to give me any information. Necessity kept me from insisting anymore. Days and years have passed and if now I think of that night only rarely, it is still very difficult for me to cross the Petit Pont without feeling a tightness around my heart

...

Everywhere in that damp quarter the same impression follows me, for no matter where I go I see myself penniless and tormented by a smell of warm chestnuts which aggravated my hunger. In the rue de Buci, on the quai Saint-Michel at the corner of the square, in the rue Saint-André des Arts, the smell intoxicated me, and filled me with envy but, as I watched myself as soon as I could see the bag and pan of the vendor, no one would have noticed my craving. What did I have to complain about? I had left Montmartre to work and to lead quietly in a corner the kind of life I liked. All the worst for me, or all the better. I was free. I had only to persevere. I had to. Only I had not always the twelve sous which my friends paid for their meals at the Montagne[175] and I had often to go without eating.

After a three days' fast which I spent in bed, in the rue Visconti, under a gable in the garret where I had taken my abode, I remember going out, at night, not knowing where. The very bitter cold stung me and I trembled; I had a painful humming in my ears, and the people I met stopped and looked back at me. Through some dark streets, running into each other like a long passage, I went toward the Seine, follow the quays, and crossed the river. A vague impulse drew me toward Les Halles. It was not yet the time when the hungry go scavenging amongst the garbage, and the spectacle of the well-swept and clean pavements absolutely discouraged me. I leaned against a door – I could not wait any longer – I was done up, vanquished, lost. Such a night! Unsteady on my legs, wandering here and there, lightheaded, I soon landed on a bench in the boulevard

[175] Carco later identifies this establishment as the Bal Vachier, located on rue de la Montagne-Sainte-Geneviève. The Montagne Sainte-Geneviève is a hill in the fifth arrondissement, and the rue de la Montagne-Sainte-Geneviève runs from the hilltop, where the Panthéon is located, down toward Métro Maubert-Mutualité. In his reminiscence about meeting Katherine Mansfield, Carco writes: "We used to go out in the evening as friends, haunting the dance halls of the Montagne Sainte-Geneviève or the small *cafés-concert* of the Place d'Italie and returning sometimes at dawn, after long walks on Boulevard de la Chapelle, I had no idea that one day our friendship would become so close." (My translation.) The original reads: *"Nous avions beau sortir, le soir, en camarades, hanter les bals-musette de la Montagne Sainte-Geneviève ou les petits cafés-concert de la place d'Italie et rentrer quelquefois à l'aube, après de longues promenades boulevard de la Chapelle, je ne me doutais pas qu'un jour notre amitié se resserrerait si étroitement."* Carco, *Montmartre à vingt ans*, Paris: Albin-Michel, 1938, p. 183.

de Sébastopol. A raw north breeze which sent gusts of dust into the air was blowing and it froze my legs. I was looking without seeing, listening without hearing, to the trams and the heavy market trucks rumbling by, when an old woman who had been haunting the neighborhood for a while came and sat down beside me.

She was a sordid creature with an old boa around her neck, its feathers flying in the wind, a ridiculous hat, mittens and a canvas bag. What did she want? Either I could not understand the words she said or else she was crazy. I drew away slowly.

"Well, are you coming," she said, looking hard at me. "Well? Come along ..."

She scanned my face, shook her head and asked:

"[You look clean, though.][176] What is the matter? It does not please you? ..."

"No, no," I said ... "Go away!"

And as she was hesitating:

"Don't you see," I cried suddenly, "that I am hungry?"

"What?"

"Oh, leave me alone!"

The old woman came closer and then, convinced I did not lie, went away silently and came back two minutes later with a big hunk of warm and appetizing bread which she laid without a word upon the bench.

It is really true but, at that time, I was a perfect idiot and I believed in all good faith that because I wrote verses everything ought to be given to me.

"I thought the same," said a comrade to me one day. "If I had not succeeded, you know, what a great failure I would have been!"

His words are right. "If I had not succeeded!" And yet it is better to succeed, even if one regrets it later on. And yet! ... To

---

[176] The original reads "T'as un genre propre, pourtant," which Boyd renders as "And yet you look straight."

succeed! ... Did we think about it? Moréas'[177] example – he lived at the brasserie and Max Jacob called him *Matamoréas*[178] – did not incite anyone to follow it. We dreamed about fame and little did we care about succeeding because Forain's[179] question: "Yes, but in what way?" put everything in proper perspective for us.

In the cafés on the boulevard Saint-Michel, at the d'Harcourt, at the Source, at the Vachette,[180] which was soon replaced by a bank, at the Panthéon with Bernouard and two or three friends he employed at the printing works, pleasure came first – as well as in the rue Dupuytren, where the *Belle Edition* was proud of owning an unworkable handpress and where we earned our living, the composing stick in our hands and a smile upon our lips.

[177] Jean Moréas (1856 – 1910): Greek poet and essayist, who moved to Paris in 1875 and founded the Symbolist movement in poetry. "He lived at the brasserie": Moréas was a habitué of the Café Vachette. According to Seymour S. Weiner, he was one of the writers that Carco admired, but the Greek poet passed away in March 1910, just three months after Carco had arrived in Paris and before the two men had a chance to meet.

[178] "Matamoros" is a slang term in Spanish for someone who boasts excessively about their achievements or abilities, often in an aggressive or arrogant fashion. A braggart, show off, or big talker.

[179] Jean-Louis Forain (1852 – 1931): Impressionist painter and printmaker from Reims who was a protégé of Degas. Forain befriended many writers, including Huysmans, Verlaine, and Rimbaud, from whom he received a first edition of *A Season in Hell*: an honor bestowed upon only six other "known recipients."

[180] Located at 27, boulevard Saint-Michel, at the corner of rue des Écoles. Café Vachette was created in 1855 and hosted the likes of Joris-Karl Huysmans, Stéphane Mallarmé, Jean Moréas, and Paul Verlaine. La Source was located about a half a block south, at 35, boulevard Saint-Michel. Café d'Harcourt was at number 47, adjacent to place de la Sorbonne. The Harcourt was the favored café of university students until the Germans shuttered it in 1940, following a student demonstration. It was then converted into a Nazified bookshop, which attracted very few customers. (For more on this incident, see Frederic Spotts, *The Shameful Peace*, p. 68.

Jou,[181] the engraver who was to become very well known later, taught me, and, fine work for a poet, I set up letter by letter in my spare moments verses of *La Bohème et mon coeur* which was about to be published. Alas! The composition over, we had no paper and an unexpected order decided my fate. I had to break up the type I had assembled and my small book of verse did not appear.

"Come and have a glass," Bernouard said then, to soften the blow.

And showing a handful of gold louis[182] which he had got for the damned order, he added, joyfully:

"Well, anyhow, we have some dough!"

It was something.

And, indeed, what we would not have done to acquire the "dough" when we had none! We sold everything, even the clothes Poiret[183] gave Bernouard on the pretext that he could

---

[181] Louis Jou (né Luis Felipe-Vicente Jou i Senabre; 1881 – 1968): talented Catalan typographer, engraver, and painter, who specialized in the illustration of luxury edition books. After working as a sign painter while a teenager, Jou expatriated to Paris in 1906. In 1908 he met the publisher François Bernouard, and together they founded La Belle Édition. Jou soon became acquainted with Apollinaire, Derain, Picasso, Van Dongen, Raoul Dufy, Cocteau, and many other bohemian figures that are chronicled in Carco's memoirs. After illustrating Anatole France's *Les Opinions de Jérôme Coignardto* (1914), he began to design original typefaces. In 1925 he created a workshop at 13, rue du Vieux-Colombier, where he continued to work until 1939, when he moved to Les Baux. Jou remained there for the rest of his life. See also Francis Carco and Jean Cassou, *Notre Ami Louis Jou*, Paris: M. P. Trémois, 1929. This limited edition contains numerous woodcuts by Jou, including a colored frontispiece.

[182] The "louis d'or": a twenty-franc gold piece issued after the Revolution. From King *Louis* XIII + *d'or* ("of gold").

[183] Known as *Le Magnifique* and "King of Fashion" who, in his own words, "dressed an epoch," Paul Poiret (1879 – 1944) was a celebrated French fashion designer and founder of the highly successful Maison Paul Poiret. In 1911 he rented part of his property at 109, rue du Faubourg Saint Honoré to his friend Henri Barbazanges, who opened the Galerie Barbazanges, a venue

wear them. I sang in backyards. Jou went around to the booksellers to collect big bills and Clarnet, a Romanian, tried nobly to get his relatives interested in our futile efforts. Nothing happened. I got English or Italian pennies for my songs. Jou came back empty-handed from his rounds, Clarnet led a joyous life and Bernouard tore his hair.

His fair hair, very long and brushed back, gave him an inspired air and assured his success with the ladies of the d'Harcourt – success not as a publisher, but as an artist – which entitled him to a lot of drinks. How did he get on? That was a mystery, but no one thought about it, because he was a real Parisian and had early been taught "music" as he said. The attractive young man knew and knew also how to prove it. Although he was older than we were, he looked without doubt the youngest of us and, at times, maybe the most romantic. A real personality: looking like a boy, very pale, very much awake, with blue eyes, sensitive, quarrelsome, funny, always master of himself and full of insolence. The only person who

for contemporary art. As part of the deal, Poiret was allowed to use the gallery for two shows per year. André Salmon was placed in charge of Poiret's *L'Art Moderne en France* in July 1916, which featured the first public exhibition of Picasso's *Les Demoiselles d'Avignon*, as well as works by Modigliani and Moïse Kisling; poetry readings by Max Jacob and Apollinaire; and musical performances by Erik Satie, Igor Stravinsky, and Georges Auric. Poiret is remembered for "freeing women from their corsets" and is regarded as fashion's "first great modernist," but after WWI his designs fell out of favor. He was soon reduced to abject poverty and attempted to support himself as a street painter or by selling his drawings in Parisian cafés. See Harold Koda and Andrew Bolton, *Poiret*, New York: The Metropolitan Museum of Art, 2007, pp. 13-14. Fernande Olivier devotes a chapter to him in her memoir, which includes a description of Poiret's visit to the Bateau-Lavoir, calling him "friendly" and "cheerful," and adding: "he deserved fame for his audacity, his generosity and his genuine feeling for art. He saw things on a large, a grand scale. His extravagant tastes were part of this." Olivier, *Picasso and His Friends*, pp. 115-116.

could intimidate him was the sheriff when certain bills falling due required his presence. I would then wrap "the boss" in a big roll of Arches paper, and he was present at the discussion unseen. In the end he would burst out, laughing uproariously. How many times have we laughed instead of being disheartened! How many times have we coolly let things take care of themselves! That was the most sensible thing to do. By a kind of miracle, just when we were the most in need of it, some author who could pay to have his work published would come and pay something in advance, or else a friend passing through Paris or a creditor moved by our distress, or a lady friend from the Quarter would take us to a restaurant. Nothing ever happened to us except providentially and such happenings, far from astonishing us, strengthened our hope that sooner or later everything in life is settled when it is least expected.

Our feasts were not very costly. A small bar in the rue Monsieur le Prince was sufficient. We feasted on cafés-crème and on buns, and then on fanciful drinks. That street, which Barrès[184] made celebrated at the time of the brasseries, was not very prepossessing. Some *bistrots*, some dark little shops, some hotels and third-rate houses of prostitution succeeded each other from left to right and its damp pavements, its panes thick with dirt, its untidy and unclean shop windows gave it all together a very unpleasant appearance.

It was in that street we met at night as friends of the girls and of the harpies who exploited them. We were very poor clients but we were welcome, they offered us drink and *mère* Charles, sitting in front of a brasero, told us her life. In exchange for

[184] Auguste-Maurice Barrès (1862 – 1923): French novelist whose nonrealist writing style was an early influence on Carco. As a politician, Barrès became increasingly right-wing during the Dreyfus affair (1894 – 1906). An anti-Dreyfusard, he authored anti-Semitic pamphlets that feature diatribes such as: "That Dreyfus is guilty, I deduce not from the facts themselves, but from his race." Tristan Tzara and the Surrealists held a mock trial of Barrès in May 1921.

stories and songs the white wine was poured ad libitum and we shared it with the taxi drivers in those desolate places. Then the ladies, who knew that we were poets, asked us to write acrostics for them and sometimes long letters to very respectable gentlemen.

"My darling," we would dictate, emptying bottles, for which none of us, for a very good reason, ever thought of paying, "I do nothing except think about you. Since you made me yours …"

"Ladies!" *mère* Charles would call.

Outside it was pouring rain. The wind blew and we felt tired and sleepy, sitting near those women who spoke incessantly about the Mondays at Convert, where they danced. A thick air filled the room, between its plastered walls, under the gas jets on the ceiling which lighted the room crudely. But what did it matter! We were under cover. We listened to the rain falling and to the verses of François Villon:

Vente, gresle, gelle, j'ay mon pain cuit[185]

They filled us with a greater and more delightful languor.

Must I be frank? No other place pleased us as much. It was a synchronization, in its ordinary setting of fans, divans, mirrors covered with writing, garlands, photos, of a very equivocal world, and it helped us to know that sort of world well and even then, whatever one might think, to describe it as it really was. Where could we have gone? There was not much choice

---

[185] "Wind, hail, frost, I have my bread baked." By quoting Villon — the homeless, exiled wanderer who finds a "home" only in taverns and brothels — Carco is establishing a context for his own "feeling at home" in the bordello. "The tavern and the brothel draw unto themselves all the homeless, the outsiders. This is where the peasant and the poor man and the criminal belong …" See Evelyn Birge Vitz, "Symbolic 'Contamination' in the Testament of François Villon," *MLN* vol. 86, no. 4 (1971), pp. 481-483, jstor.org/stable/2907647.

for us. Here or there, I mean, in the brasseries or in the strange shops of the Quarter, we would have found very much the same people. Shall we be blamed on that account? I don't care. My life is settled and I have neither the time nor the effort to waste on regrets.

And anyway even if *mère* Charles were obliging, perhaps we were freed from the obligations of the expense she incurred for us, for about New Year's we would pay our debt to her very handsomely. At New Year's I used to send my card and wishes to celebrated writers, and the cards which they did not fail to send me in acknowledgment "with their sincere thanks" I gave to *mère* Charles. She was more than delighted. She put all those valuable visiting cards around the mirrors in the place, and when clients asked her questions she pretended, for example, to know the Messieurs de Goncourt quite well, since they sent her cards.

In the rue de l'Echaudé-Saint-Germain, which we also frequented and where we took Mario Meunier,[186] who confessed and consoled the girls, love of literature made us call a certain house the Mercure de France and the proprietress Rachilde. At ours we were at home.[187] The good woman even

---

[186] Mario Meunier (1880 – 1960): French Hellenist and translator of antique Greek and Latin classics. Meunier was one of the founders of the literary magazine *Le Feu* and worked as the secretary of Isadora Duncan from 1910 to 1913. He was associated with esoteric spiritual groups, hence Carco's ironic depiction of him eliciting "confessions" from prostitutes. The Meunier text mentioned in the following passage, *Pour s'asseoir au Foyer de la Maison des Dieux* ("To sit at the Hearth of the House of the Gods "), was published in Paris by Albin Michel, in 1921.

[187] *Mercure de France*: A literary magazine established in the seventeenth century (originally called the *Mercure galant*), which was later reincarnated as a review (1890) and as a Left Bank publishing house associated with the Symbolist movement (1894). In 1995 it was absorbed into Éditions Gallimard.

Rachilde (née Marguerite Vallette-Eymery): French novelist and playwright associated with the Symbolist and Decadent Movement who

kept a room for me where I could write "my poems" and sometimes a young person under transparent veils would bring me a glass of champagne to help the Muse. Why did I not make better use of the calm quietness of such hospitality! Why was I not able to convince Rachilde that the work of a poet is not counted by the lines and that sleeping is often better than forced work! She did not believe me and from the poet I was in her eyes, I became a bad boy, I ceased to interest her and lost all my prestige.

Luckily Mario Meunier, with his long hair, his cane with its lapis lazuli knob, his episcopal hands and the big amethyst ring he wore on his finger, kept up the love for artists in the house. He was writing then a noble book of a very high philosophic import: *Pour s'asseoir au Foyer de la Maison des Dieux*, and, full of his subject, he would exchange ennobling thoughts with the proprietress. Soon one spoke only of God at the Mercure, and a certain customer who hid his real calling very badly under ordinary clothes, thought when he heard the conversation that he had been found out and called no more.

"What does it matter?" Rachilde said, "one lost, ten found."

wrote erotic novels. Although her work has been largely (and justifiably) forgotten, the publication of *Monsieur Vénus* (1884) caused such a scandal that she was tried for pornography in a court in Belgium, where the book was first published. Convicted in absentia, she was thereafter forced to remain in France to avoid imprisonment.

Here Carco is transposing the notion of a publishing *house* (*maison*) with a *house* of ill repute, the bordello, and concluding that he feels most *at home* in the latter establishment. "*Chez Rachilde*," writes Carco, "*nous étions chez nous*": "At Rachilde's, we were at home." (Boyd translates this as: "At ours we were at home.") Louis-Ferdinand Céline, another Montmartre author (and xenophobic fiend) from the same time and milieu would later write that publishers are pimps who force their authors to play the role of prostitutes, doling out a few measly francs while the pimp-publishers keep the lion's share of profit.

And indeed, enough people came without the poor uneasy man of whom the women had been afraid. Merchants, students, Arabs, bourgeois, workmen and a sacristan! The latter used to amuse us enormously every time he came. He waited till all "the ladies" gathered around him, then looked at them one after another and asked:

"How much?"

"Well, five francs."

"Ah!" He would sigh deeply, "five francs, it is expensive, I haven't got them ..."

"Go on ..."

"No, no," he would assert and, looking at the nudities which excited him, he would mutter: "What beautiful girls! Oh! ... what beautiful girls. You are magnificent, you know ..."

"All right, make up your mind."

"Make me a price," the sacristan would ask in a low voice. "What about two francs?"

"No. Five."

"Three. Look, I'll go to three franks ... Will you take them?"

By that time Rachilde was annoyed:

"Go to the devil! You won't get one of my women for less than five, miser, go, go away, get out!"

And the man, who had been waiting for this, went down the stairs four steps at a time, carrying away with him and treasuring the exciting vision.

Picasso, *Portrait of Max Jacob*, 1907, gouache on paper, 62 x 47.5 cm.

XI

These people were certainly a welcome change from Montmartre, where our young friends were models and mannequins, rather than humble girls without mind or imagination; they were less annoying, less tyrannical and scarcely stayed a fortnight in the same places, and they did not try to impose themselves upon us. Seeing them regularly making room for newcomers, we never had time to know them too well. They kept all their mystery; and the life they led away from the place where we met them was so difficult to define that, in spite of our blasé air, we felt a singular and hungry curiosity.

How, indeed, were we to get to know about the lives of these false creatures? They would wait till it was two in the morning, yawning and listening for the arrival of the taxi which was to call for them; then, in a thrice they would disappear till the next day. Some of them who lived in the hotels of the Quarter joined the knights of the sweater and cap at a café of rather doubtful reputation in the rue Mazarine, and when they saw us, they pretended not to recognize us. The gentlemen would stare hard without, however, trying to quarrel with us; they would drink and discuss their next "business." [188] Between them and us there were their women. They knew it and were not surprised on that account, but they opposed an unbending disdain to the tokens of sympathy we could offer them, never giving themselves away. And yet, in the café-bar of the Ancienne-Comédie, in the morning at the time of the aperitif, we met and sometimes,

[188] In the original text Carco uses the term "le coup," which Boyd translates as "business." He later employs the phrase *arrangeaient leurs 'combines'* ("arranged their 'schemes'"), which Boyd again renders as "to settle and plan their next 'business.'"

along with *mère* Charles, we clinked glasses with them. These gentlemen were together without their women, and although very little inclined to welcome us, they agreed to play the next round at *zanzi*.[189]

What a café that was! One could rub elbows there with all the bad boys at the rue de Buci, *patrons* in slippers carrying their net bags for marketing, sellers of rings and mirrors, thieves, fences and commissionaires. A peaceful and picturesque crowd of clients invaded it in the early morning. How many stories I heard, sorted details of human life. It has furnished me with the rarest material in the world for my need. Whatever the time, poets, bandits, police spies, and actors drank their *momimette*[190] and isolated themselves at different tables to settle and plan their next "business."

At the tobacco store, at the Café Mauguin, at the bar on the corner of the rue de Seine, the choice was less varied. Here, students and old painters; further away, smaller fry, elsewhere, ridiculous drunks, harpies, beggars talking or quarreling. With what could we compare this? There was in all those places a sickening dampness. The dirty walls, the greasy counter, the slippery floor, covered with cigarette butts, were far from attracting us, whilst at the café-bar of the Ancienne-Comédie, where these gentlemen began their day at twelve and tolerated our presence around the tables they had reserved for themselves, everything shone in the most beautiful way.

The case of the rue de Buci should be remembered, not so much because of its deplorable frequentations, but on account of its exceptional atmosphere and its setting, where André Salmon's heroes were still present and lived in the light of day.

---

[189] In the opening scene of Carco's novel, *Jésus-la-Caille*, a group of musicians gamble for drinks, shooting dice in a game called "Zanzibar." Thus, *faire un zanzi* = to play a game of Zanzibar.
[190] *Mominette*: slang expression for absinthe. From *môme*: slang for a kid or young girl.

We admired André Salmon; he was celebrated. Poet, writer, arts critic, his gifts awed us. As for his clothes, cut out of material with large checks, and his small hat perched on the top of his head, no one could wear them as he did. They were part of his aesthetic baggage, his program, his own idea, and beside Paul Fort,[191] dressed all in black, they opposed the theory of free verse, and other uncommon rhythms. That was obvious. Salmon paraded his colorful poem around the Quarter carrying it on his thin body, and all that he wanted to be talked about, advertised by his extraordinary attire, was reported at once.

We recited by heart the verses of the *Calumet*, on the very spot of the Pont-Neuf where the author had composed them:

> *Nous rentrions très tard, mêlant*
> *Des vers purs à des chants obscènes*
> *Et l'on s'asseyait sur un banc*
> *Pour regarder la Seine …*[192]

We evoked the spirit of Moréas, who used to take his favorite disciples to Les Halles. Salmon had written in dedicating his *Féeries* to him:

> *Plus tard, je connaitrai le sort des vieux poètes*
> *Que l'espoir de la palme, hélas I ne soutient plus.*
> *Je serai las, brisé, doigts gourds, bouche muette*

---

[191] Jules-Jean-Paul Fort (1872 – 1960): French Symbolist poet who edited literary journals with Alfred Jarry and Apollinaire. In 1912 he was bestowed with the honorific title, "Prince of poets." As noted by Ernest Hemingway in *A Moveable Feast*, Fort and his colleagues patronized La Closerie des Lilas, located at 171, boulevard du Montparnasse. The Cubists often attended Fort's soirees at this famous brasserie, which still exists.

[192] The opening lines of Salmon's poem "Fraternité": "We would return very late, / Blending pure verse with obscene song, / And we'd sit on a bench / To look at the Seine." From the collection *Le Calumet* ("The Pipe"), Paris: H. Falque, 1910.

Et pourtant glorieux de vous avoir connu,[193]

and we loved him all the more.

But indeed, in spite of appearances, we were devoted to poetry and we put it before everything else, having nothing else to keep our spirits up and therefore praising it loudly. What mattered our poverty? It only deepened the feeling which made us turn instinctively to Moréas and Paul Fort, who filled us with admiration. I do not want to anticipate. I shall return to the Prince of Poets and his Tuesday evenings at the Closerie des Lilas. Let us remain in the rue de Buci, with its strange aspect where, sometimes, inebriates asked us to witness how unhappy they were and dice players wanted to teach us their tricks. One evening, in a bar, a Negress before whom we were speaking about the Théâtre du Vieux-Colombier, came up to us and said:

"Don't go there. It is a theater run by Protestants who have the blues."

Who was that Negress? She drank with another young person in a red jersey who was called Pépé-la-Panthère and who lived by frequenting dancing halls. We met her at Bouscatel's[194], at

[193] "Later, I will know the fate of old poets / Whose hope for the laurel wreath, alas, no longer sustains them. / I will be tired, broken, fingers numb, mouth mute / And yet proud to have known you."

[194] Antoine ("Bousca") Bouscatel (1867 – 1945): French cabrette bagpipe player, who was first employed as a boilermaker and coppersmith. He later assumed ownership of the bistro Au Chalet, located on rue de Lappe, which he renamed Chez Bouscatel and transformed into a grand dance hall. André Warnod chronicles another one of his establishments: "All that's left for us to see is the Bal Bouscatel, at 11, rue de la Huchette; it's quite important, but it lacks both charm and color. Rue de la Huchette, however, is quite curious, and all around, the labyrinth of old streets has a lot of character; but the Bal Bouscatel is very peaceful, very tame. It must also be said that it is located right in front of a police station. So be careful when you hear someone bragging about committing incredible exploits in an 'Apache ball.'" André Warnod, *Les bals de Paris*, Paris: G. Crès, 1922, pp. 131-132. Carco

the old *père* Lunette's,[195] rue des Carmes, where she had certainly been mixed up with all the ups and downs of modern painting, and she sang, sitting in front of a salad bowl full of hot wine, these verses written by Salmon:

> *Quand elle est rev'nue aux Beaux-Arts*
> *Fatiguée de fair' le lézard*
> *Prendre des leçons d'aquarelle,*
> *Comme ell' voulait peindre des fleurs*
> *Et qu'il lui fallait des couleurs,*
> *J'ai vendu mes tableaux pour elle !*[196]

portrays the Bal Bouscatel in a passage that follows below, echoing Warnod's description of its regrettably "tame" atmosphere.

[195] "At the old *père* Lunette's": located at 4 rue des Anglais. The dangerous and disreputable nature of this cabaret has a long history. On 18 March 1888 the *New York Times* ran a story headlined: "Père Lunette: One of the Dens of Criminals," calling it "one of the worst dens of Paris." It was shuttered in 1908, after which it morphed into a restaurant called Au Caveau des Anglais, but the highly destructive flood of late January 1910, which almost breached the embankment of the Seine, led to its closing. Since Carco first arrived in Paris in January 1910, he would have known of the original *père* Lunette's only through secondhand accounts. As Nicholas Hewitt points out in his book on Montmartre, Carco was not adverse to this sort of literary artifice, and he frequently borrowed from the verbal chronicles of his contemporaries, weaving them into his own quasi-fictionalized memoirs. See Hewitt, *Montmartre*, p. 178. For more on the Paris flood, see "Remembering the Deluge: An Interview with Jeffrey Jackson, Author of *Paris Under Water* and *Making Jazz French*," featured in my *More Collected Couteau*, New York: Dominantstar, 2016, pp. 112-152.

[196] "When she returned to the Beaux-Arts / Tired of lounging around like a lizard / Taking watercolor lessons, / As she wanted to paint flowers / And needed colors, / I sold my paintings for her!" These and the following verses are from Salmon's poem, "Beaux-Arts."

The fantastic creature! Pépé-la-Panthère would laugh at the men, assert that she was free, and knowing also the song, would take up the second verse:

> *Elle était si gentille à voir*
> *Quand ell' peignait les arbr's en noir*
> *Que je l'appelais Raphael … le …*
> *Elle m'a tant vanté Corot*
> *Que je suis degouté d' Picasso*
> *J'ai changé ma manièr' pour elle !*[197]

"Bravo! Pépé!"
  The Negress went on:

> *Mais les copains de l'atelier*
> *Lui ont fait bien vite oublier*
> *La fidélité conjugale.*
> *C'est un massier de chez Cormon*
> *Qui l'a emm' née a Barbizon*
> *Après une vadrouille aux Halles.*[198]

And at last, Pépé and the Negress, joining their voices, would sing the end of this crazy song:

> *Et me voici triste, indigent,*
> *Sans tableau, sans femm', sans argent,*
> *Plongé dans la débine extrême.*
> *Pourtant il me reste à manger*
> *Une ou deux couleurs sans danger,*

---

[197] "She was so cute to see / When she painted black the trees / That I called her Raphael … le … / She praised, so much, Corot / That I'm disgusted with Picasso / For her, I changed my style!"

[198] "But her friends from the atelier / Made her quickly forget / Marital fidelity. / It was the treasurer from Cormon's studio / Who took her to Barbizon / After a stroll in Les Halles."

Oubliées par celle que j'aime ![199]

Thundering applause burst out. The two women bowed, drank their hot wine, and saying "thou" [*vous*] to the gentlemen of the caps, threw themselves in their arms and danced the Java.

We never heard the name of the Negress. As for Pépé, she was murdered on the boulevard Beaumarchais before the war, maybe by one of her dancing partners who, wanting to bring her back to the ordinary ways of life, had lost his time, his hopes and his most cherished illusions trying to convince her.

Poor Pépé! I see her still with her short skirts, her red sweater, her patent leather boots, her fair hair and her pretty face. It was a bad thing for her to be dependent on one of the gentlemen. She was setting a bad example. She was too inclined to laughter, to amuse herself, too easy, too different from the others; and I shall long remember the kind of satisfaction that some women in houses felt who declared, when, in a bar, they heard of her death through the papers:

"One less!"

Pépé dead, her absence left no emptiness at the rue de Buci, nor in the dancing halls, and no one except us missed her. We had had a very sincere feeling of comradeship for her. She was different from the professional girls of the rue Monsieur-le-Prince, having manners which those creatures lacked. Then we heard that, affiliated with a gang of counterfeiters of the Luxembourg, the unlucky Pépé had talked more than she ought to about her friends and that was the only reason which could explain her death.

At that time the famous gang was under lock and key, but occasionally we would still be accosted at night in certain bars

---

[199] "And here I am sad, destitute, / Without a painting, without a woman, in dire straits, Immersed in the extreme depths. / Yet I still have something to eat / And one or two harmless colors, / Forgotten by the one I love!"

by mysterious individuals who proposed to exchange five louis for eighty francs.

"Seventy," they would say to tempt us. "Don't you want to do it?"

"What do you think?"

They had in their pockets matchboxes which would hold five louis and as soon as one of us made the gesture of lighting his pipe, the boxes of matches would all come out and would be held out to us.

A prince I won't name – he is dead and died bravely during the war – was bothered daily by their offers. Wherever he went his dark complexion and his fuzzy hair attracted counterfeiters. They asked for him at his hotel, they pursued him, and finally, for a small sum, they would end by doing some business. And the prince threw the dangerous money away in the toilets and no one could say anything about it, when one night a beggar accosted him.

"No," answered the prince, who was drunk, "go away."

"Please, give me ten cents! ... moaned the beggar.

"No."

"Because," said the prince, "I am absolutely broke ... Look ..."

He turned out his pockets, some bread and some tobacco crumbs fell, his handkerchief, a bunch of keys and unluckily one of the damned matchboxes, which opened in falling, and the gold coins rolled on the pavement.

"Oh!" exclaimed the beggar.

The prince threw himself on the box, but the beggar had had time to pick it up and ran away as fast as he could.

"Give it back," shouted the prince. "Stop ... Stop ..."

He started running after the man when some policemen attracted by the noise joined in the chase. They seized the delinquents, took them to the police station where, on brutally searching the thief, a louis fell to the ground and broke. The false louis was made of glass. And the prince was jailed.

Is it for that reason that, with each gold coin that they received, the proprietors in the rue de Buci would take out of their drawers a gigantic hammer? No doubt. With such clients one has to be ready for anything. Poets were included in this category, because we were accustomed at that time to stand near the door on tiptoes, waiting for the propitious moment when we could make a getaway without paying.

The strangest person in that strange street was assuredly our friend Claudien, of whom I have already spoken. He lived in the Hôtel Jeanne d'Arc. Claudien, either through decency or laziness, hated our wild flights for a glass of three sous. He had the bills put down to him; then, always Olympian, he would tramp the streets looking for adventure. A great friend of the Negro prince that he had saved from the police, he would often be seen walking around till daylight in his noble company. However, Claudien spent his nights more often with Mario Meunier and myself. His monocle always created a sensation among the clients of the small bars. His conversation intrigued them greatly and even Mario was not far from taking him for Satan himself when he had been drinking too much. Why not? His nom de plume Claudien was very equivocal. Claudien what? Which? Mario would remain open-mouthed and ask with anguish whether he were dreaming, and suddenly, hanging on my arm, he would confide to me:

"Yes, he is the devil ... He is the devil!"

Mario was not wrong. The calmness and indolence of Claudien, an undefinable atmosphere of the supernatural, his yellow and shining eyes, gave him a very uncanny appearance. His body was very straight, but he walked bent on one side, swaying lightly as he walked; his beard as well as his eyes shown with a phosphorescent light very upsetting to look at ... Claudien gave way sometimes to sudden outbursts of rage for which he tried in vain to find a reason. If he were not the devil, he must have, at least, been one of his intimates after midnight, because at that time rare and astonishing things happened to him. He was a connoisseur of women and the ones he saw, when they were with him, felt inexpressible terrors. All of them, the lowest as well as the most innocent. However, it was to his room that the women went in the mornings; they climbed his stairs, pushed the door open and, without saying a word they would get in the bed or on the floor and all together they would go to sleep.

He who has not seen Claudien, naked in his "tub," surrounded by these creatures, some of them coming out of prison and pursued by the police, has seen nothing. He never pitied them. On the contrary. One would have sworn that he enjoyed their troubles coldly and that he took a cruel pleasure in tormenting them with his questions. His attractiveness was as strong as another force within him, more obscure, which repulsed and frightened them. Sometimes one, sometimes the other, predominated. These two conflicting aspects of him were never manifested together. In the daytime he frightened friends of his that were weak, and at night he inspired in them a nameless feeling. I am not inventing all this. With all that he was very detached, but the author of *Les Labyrinthes* showed himself the straightest and most faithful of men to all of his men friends. But where did he get his piercing voice, his shouts and his well-balanced enthusiasms? More than all else one spectacle was haunting him: boulevard de la Chapelle, behind the gratings of the dark hall and the tracks of Gare du Nord, where the thick smoke of the trains, their signals, blue, white, green or red, tragically complimented each other. The sonorous metal arch of the metro obliging him to raise his voice, Claudien would shout out loudly, before this active and desolate scene, the bitter taste which inspired him. We felt ourselves drawn towards that abyss with the shiny rails, with the innumerable lights until, little by little, vertigo would take hold of us.

Claudien had certainly written the most acute pages that exist about that setting. There is hidden in it a secret fire, without ardor or anger, as monotonous as hell and drier to the heart than one can imagine. [Have you read in *Labyrinthes*, this other poem which begins with these words:

> In this small room warmed with dry heat by a coal grate, almost all day long he darkly dreams of torture. Alone, he sinks into his reverie, brooding over his desires, akin, he would believe, to the blackish flame and the horrible smell of burning coal ...

and contains this desperate confession:

> An imaginary and ill-defined world is thus forming around him, a world of which he is the center and whose root is this evil instinct that he carries in his soul, silently approved by the dark and fetid fire, his only companion.][200]

---

[200] This entire passage in brackets is omitted from the Boyd translation. The original French text reads:

> Avez-vous lu dans Labyrinthes, cet autre poème qui débute par ces mots :

> > Dans cette petite chambre que chauffe d'une ardeur sèche une grille de houille, presque tout le jour il rêve obscurément de supplices. Seul, il s'enfonce dans sa rêverie, remâche ses désirs, parents, croirait-il, de la flamme noirâtre et de l'horrible odeur du charbon qui brûle ...

> et contient cet aveu désespéré :

He was always haunted by fire! It must have tortured him in secret, in that low-ceilinged room where I can still see him, lying upon my divan. It was my own room, rue Visconti; I had left it to him after the idea of committing suicide in it had got hold of me to such a point that I had to leave it.

Situated between two floors – on the right, in the commons of an ancient damp house with flagstones polished and worn by time, a narrow passage led to that room. Opposite, two policemen whose patrol duties followed each other were my neighbors, and on the left a very old servant was busy dying. There was always a policeman snoring beside me and that old woman, the rollers of whose armchair morning and evening kept scratching along the floor. No noise came from the street, tight between its gray houses, one of which had been Racine's and the other the well-known printing works of Balzac.

The carriages came slowly and very seldom, and at night the lamplighter was the only one who, with the very joyous Baron Maxzen, gave any signs of life.

But the baron frequently made so much noise that he disturbed the whole street.

Un monde imaginaire et mal défini se constitue
ainsi autour de lui, monde dont il est le centre et
dont la racine est cet instinct mauvais qu'il porte en
son âme, approuvé en silence par le feu obscur et
fétide, son seul compagnon.

XII

Will anyone understand that, thanks to the environment and the sticky dampness, anonymous sister of poverty, we lived extraordinary days on this side of the water? More than in Montmartre, the illusion of a maritime town, with its low pubs, its buildings at the corners with high prows, its poor population, its fog, its houses of prostitution, pursued us at each step. The sharp groaning of the ships' whistles that the wind sometimes brought and the soft breeze full of a sickening smell coming from the Seine made the illusion very real. At Montmartre, the howling of the trains, of both the Est and the Nord stations, aroused I don't know what presentiment and prevented us from heartily amusing ourselves.

"A great many travelers who stopped at the Lapin Agile, which was at that time, for all of us, a first-class waiting room," has written Mac Orlan, "had done their military service in Nancy. Montmartre and Nancy each held an end of the telephone wires, which explains why so few of us were surprised when they met at Domgermain, near Toul, in August 1914."[201]

Rue de l'Hirondelle, at Hubert's, la Bolée[202] – the Lapin Agile's competitor – offered a hitherto unexplored territory. The clients were anarchists, ex-jailbirds, students, songsters, thieves, milliners' apprentices and miserable women who feasted cheaply, not as in a first-class waiting room, but as in a third,

[201] Fort Domgermain is situated 400 meters above sea level on the banks of the Moselle, making it an ideal lookout post to monitor railways entering Paris and Verdun. During WWI it served as an army depot for delivering supplies to troops.

[202] As noted earlier, this was the Caveau de la Bolée, located at 25, rue l'Hirondelle, chez Hubert, whom Carco nicknamed "Hubert the Magnanimous."

amongst greasy papers, on sausages and tankers of cider. Between enormous whitewashed walls, barrels, broken down benches running along the walls, a few seats, unsteady tables, were all the furnishings. Two steps away from the Seine, which could be reached through the narrow and stinking passage of the rue Gît-le-Coeur, Hubert's porch opened like a night shelter where the low strata of humanity ate and drank. Inside there were always pale individuals, streetwalkers, poets and a doubtful old man whom a woman of easy virtue had horribly mutilated to punish him where he had sinned. A lamb which ate the cigarette butts covering the floor, as well as the sawdust, and which was rather fond of light wine, was attached to the establishment, as well as several thin and melancholy hunting dogs. Whom did one not meet at Hubert's! He had engraved on a stone upon the wall the list of the habitués, and the Americans who often came with a guide to visit his place could read beneath the inscription:

"Here have sat,"

names which added to the glory of the establishment and its proprietor. Among them, in company with the Tharaud brothers[203] and Jacques Dyssord,[204] mine came between François

[203] Jérôme Tharaud (1874 – 1953) and Jean Tharaud (1877 – 1952): French brothers remembered for their prolific coauthorship of novels, essays, and travelogues, whose writing often appeared in the journal, *Cahiers de la Quinzaine*, edited by Charles Péguy. By the 1920s their work on Jewish life became increasingly anti-Semitic, in parallel with the xenophobia of the broader society. See Virginia M. Crawford, "Jerome and Jean Tharaud," *Studies: An Irish Quarterly Review*, vol. 15, no. 58, 1926, pp. 204–216. Reprinted in *JSTOR*, www.jstor.org/stable/30093265. Commenting on the Tharauds' *Quand Israel est Roi*, Crawford writes: "The book is in effect an anti-revolutionary and anti-Semitic pamphlet – hence in part its wide popularity …"

[204] Jacques Dyssord (né: Édouard Jacques Moreau de Bellaing; 1880 – 1952): French poet, novelist, playwright, critic, and journalist, who associated with

Villon's and Jean Lorrain's.[205] Was that not in Hubert's favor? He loved poets, made room for them at his board, prepared everything for them, and lent them money surreptitiously. Tall, strong, sympathetic, still young, always there, the man whom we called Hubert the Magnanimous, has deserved well of contemporary French letters. He was proud of it and he always hid the small slate, upon which he wrote our accounts with chalk, when a client he did not know was near.

"How can I tell?" he used to say, "he might be a critic and an allusion in the papers might be enough to destroy your reputation ..."

Then, very rightly disgusted with critics, he would rub out the accounts on the slate and nothing more would be said about them.

Jacques Dyssord, who had brought me to this astonishing barkeeper who always wore an immense cap and a smock like a market gardener, knew well the kind of man he was. So he dedicated a piece of verse to him[:]

Pour célébrer l'honnête cabaret de la Bolée, sis rue de l'Hirondelle, jouxte la rue Gît-le-Cœur et dire le los de son bon maître[:][206]

> [*Vous tous qu'oncques ne vit la marâtre Sorbonne*
> *A la tête pelée et au téton désert,*
> *Qui, rêvant de Thaïs, couchez avec sa bonne,*
> *Escholiers du courant d'air;*

Apollinaire and André Salmon. During WWII Dyssord contributed to the collaborationist press.

[205] Jean Lorrain (né Paul Duval; 1855 – 1906): French Symbolist poet, novelist, and denizen of Montmartre nightlife. Nicknamed "the Ambassador from Sodom," Lorrain was unabashedly gay and a follower of dandyism. After contracting tuberculosis, he began to use morphine and ether.

[206] "To celebrate the honest cabaret of La Bolée, located on rue de l'Hirondelle, next to rue Gît-le-Coeur, and to praise its good master."

Maîtres en l'art subtil mais combien illusoire,
De maquiller la brème et de piper les dés,
Prodigues inventeurs, encor qu'après Gringoire,
Du breveté Système D.

Le grand cœur de Villon et celui de Verlaine
Gisent en cet endroit, jouxte où gisait le coeur.
Venez-y donc, vêtus de soie ou de futaine
Laissés pour compte des tailleurs.

Et venez-y aussi costumés de drap Joffre,
O poilus de tout poil sauf du poil à la main
Car c'est votre tournée et c'est Hubert qui l'offre.
Vous l'offrirez demain ...

Sur les tonneaux épars, lampez d'amples rasades
D'un cidre que, païen, il n'a point baptisé
Durant qu'un calvados qu'il estime moins fade,
Humecte son gosier blasé.

La ribaude aux seins durs et aux fesses grenues
N'y rencontre jamais cette « femme aux bijoux »
Dont le refrain prétend « qu'elle nous rendra fous
Avec des mines ingénues.

Mimi Pinson y vient, la dernière Mimi
Que guette Millandy au coin d'une romance,
Elle y chante parfois des airs très vieille France
Au vieux Pépère son ami.

Pépère est le patron de ce lieu débonnaire.
Il se couche fort tard mais il se lève tôt.
Philosophe toujours, joyeux drille naguère,

Il met parfois la poule au pot.

Que Dieu l'ait en sa digne et sa benoîte garde
Ainsi que notre Sainte Dame de Montretout
Et qu'entre la salière et le pot à moutarde,
Il prospère longtemps pour nous !

You all whom the stepmother Sorbonne never saw
With a bald head and a barren nipple,
Who, dreaming of Thaïs,[207] sleep with her maid,
Students of the drafty corridor;

Masters in the subtle but how illusory art,
Of disguising the bream and loading the dice,
Prodigal inventors, even after Gringoire,
Of the patented System Finagle.[208]

The great heart of Villon and that of Verlaine
Lie in this place, beside the rue Gît-le-Coeur.
Come then, dressed in silk or in coarse cloth,
Left behind by the tailors.

And come also dressed in Joffre's[209] cloth,

[207] Thaïs: a Greek *hetaira* and courtesan of Alexander the Great.
[208] "Prodigal inventors, even after Gringoire, / Of the patented System Finagle": Pierre Gringore (né Gringon): Fifteenth-century playwright whose mystery play about Louis IX, *Vie Monseigneur Sainct Loys par personnaiges* (1514), is considered his greatest work. The crafty character "Gringoire," a major figure in Hugo's *The Hunchback of Notre-Dame*, was inspired by Pierre Gringore. "System Finagle": the original line in French reads "Système D." The slang term *système d* or *débrouillard* refers to achieving something by devious, crooked, or crafty means, especially in the sense of "tricking" or "getting around the system." Hence, "finagle" is probably the English term that comes closest to its meaning.
[209] Joseph Joffre (1852 – 1931): French general and Commander-in-Chief on the Western Front from the inception of WWI until 1916.

O *poilus,* soldiers from far and wide except for the
lazy ones,
Although it's your turn to buy the next round,
In your honor Hubert is treating today;
You'll take care of it tomorrow ...

On the scattered barrels, gulp ample draughts
Of a cider that, pagan, he hasn't baptized
While a Calvados, which he considers less bland,
Moistens his jaded throat.

The strumpet with firm breasts and ample
buttocks
Never encounters there that "bejeweled woman"
Whose refrain claims that "she will drive us mad
With her innocent looks."

Mimi Pinson[210] comes, the last Mimi
Whom Millandy[211] spies upon when he's not
entangled in romance,
She sometimes sings passé, outdated French tunes
To old Pépère her friend.

Pépère is the owner of this debonair place.

[210] The protagonist of Alfred de Musset's 1845 novelette, *Mademoiselle Mimi Pinson: Profil de grisette.* A *grisette* refers to a young working-class coquette (in Mimi's case, a seamstress) who wears dresses made from inexpensive grey (*gris*) fabric. The sexually liberated, emotionally independent *grisette* was a well-known bohemian personage in the subculture of the Latin Quarter. Various other "Mimi" *grisettes* will make their subsequent appearance in the literary and popular forms of the day.

[211] Georges Millandy (1870 – 1964): Famous French singer, poet, and composer. His song, "Le Coeur de Ninon," was featured in Jean Renoir's *La Bête humaine* (1938). Millandy also authored an autobiography, *Lorsque tout est Fini. Souvenirs d'un chansonnier du Quartier Latin,* Paris: Albert Messein, 1933.

He goes to bed very late but he rises early.
Always philosophical, once a cheerful fellow,
He sometimes cooks *la poule au pot*.

May God keep him in his worthy and blessed care
As well as our Holy Lady of Montretout
And may he prosper long for us
Between the salt shaker and the mustard pot!][212]

These lines, dated September 1915, which touched Hubert to such an extent that he pinned to them on a wooden panel and hung them well in sight of everybody, were a witness to our friendship for that very good man. But, alas, he was not becoming rich in a trade where he was paid with rhymes. So, for a while, rather than close his doors or not give credit to the artists who needed it, Hubert, after midnight, left his house and went to the markets to work as a porter. He earned his living and ours, saying nothing about it, and we would find him afterwards, a glass in his hand, offering a round.

Some have not been fair to Hubert; he has been considered a joker much too often when he was above all a perfect philanthropist and a bon vivant. He incurred debts for us, shared his soup with poor people, treated them like princes, and then, astonished at their obstinacy, he would give them two francs to go and enjoy themselves across the way.

There, in an atmosphere of low prostitution, under a ceiling with water leaking through, was a kind of common room of which the heavy door was always left ajar. A baroque lantern of beaten iron giving forth a pink light was above it. And women who coughed and held their dressing gowns tight around them on account of the cold awaited mariners, sewer cleaners and petty officials who treated them to white wine. How careful one

[212] The entire passage set within brackets is absent from the Boyd translation.

had to be in leaving la Bolée not to enter that awful house! On the threshold a dreadful matron would call us, pull us by the sleeve and, once inside, we were stunned by what we saw, such lamentable sights that they seemed like hallucinations. Near the counter, an esthete with glasses, blue with the cold, pale, as thin as a skeleton, was howling:

> *J'écoute au lupanar la mazurka fervente*
> *S'éplorer tendrement sur les civilisés*
> *Que le rythme et le rêve ont dévirilisés*
> *Et qui, devant la mort, pâlissent d'épouvante.*[213]

There was also in that cursed place a Newfoundland dog that was offered drinks by eccentric gentlemen. The dog drank, and the impression stamped on us by those motionless painted women, that dog, the walls oozing a sticky dampness and the leprous lusterless mirrors, froze us to the marrow of our bones.

If there are in the world, in ports, places accustomed to human degradation which go beyond those that are near the Seine and spread around the rue Mazarine, where are they? I would like to know them in order to compare them with the rue de l'Hirondelle, because I do not think I exaggerate if I say that nowhere else can worse ones be found. In the winter evenings especially, when the wind blows, bringing in the rainy air mixed with snow, and the sharp whistles of tugs, there was no need to meet sailors on the loose to find adventure. It was there, all preened up, in the shops waiting for you. Near the police station of the rue de la Huchette, where in a narrow opening masts and smoke rise and hover above the water, several of those places are always discreetly ajar. He who has seen them keeps all his life an atrocious picture. Here, in the false luxury of

---

[213] "I listen in the brothel to the fervent mazurka / Tenderly crying over the civilized ones / Emasculated by the rhythm and the dream / And who, facing death, grow pale with terror."

garlands, dolls, gas, behind high frosted windows, women dressed in kimonos, their hair pulled away from their foreheads in the Chinese manner, were busy around the customers. In other places were solid servant girls or a pathetic creature sitting in her small compartment, her body wrapped in a woolen shawl. Further away were some half-colored women, some young girls from Belleville or Vaugirard, old women making signs, some of them behind windows with colored curtains, some in small shops made into bars. Their "Pssst!" sounded in the empty streets as the call in one's dreams of an impossible love.

Before the war one could count about twenty of those vile places, in addition to the hotels and the rooms where the women from behind the windowpanes spied the passerby. In the center, near the police station with the flag washed colorless by the rain, was a so-called family dancing hall where we went to dance. With Claudien and Mario Meunier, M. Bouscatel,[214] the owner of the place, received us with great ceremony and to charm us still more he would take out his flute, which he played magnificently. At the plaintive sounds of the instrument the couples would pair off and dance. We followed them with our eyes, carried away by the nasal sounds of the Java and, little by little, intoxicated with a very peculiar kind of drunkenness, we would leave with a thousand polite phrases. M. Bouscatel's was a very peaceful dancing place, much too peaceful for us. It opened straight off the street and its customers were for the most part humble working girls, small employees, soldiers and shop assistants. What a change it was, with its peacefulness, from the neighboring places where well-assorted couples seized each other savagely like animals and stared at us contemptuously as we passed. At M. Bouscatel's the girls let

---

[214] Based on the description that follows, this must be the Bal Bouscatel, located at 11, rue de la Huchette.

themselves go with lowered eyes. They were well-mannered and not once did we see anyone fighting over them.

And it is precisely on account of that quiet atmosphere that the dancing place did not attract us much. We preferred the smoky back room of a bistro in the rue des Carmes, where, on the slightest pretext, stupid rivalries and quarrels would arise. The red wine spilt on the tables, the meager and insufficient lighting gave that dive an intense character and when, with its resounding voice, the melodeon would start the first measures of a waltz, we felt carried away by it.

However, the best known of these dancing places was in the rue de la Montagne-Sainte-Geneviève opposite a creamery where I used to take all my meals. It was called Bal Vachier. One first entered a room, where the proprietor, enthroned behind a counter, watched the gentlemen and ladies and allowed them in or not as he liked. One had to be well-dressed to be permitted to enter. A notice, hung at the entrance of the very narrow passage which led to the dancing, asserted that fact. In big letters carefully written by an expert, one could read: *La tenue est de rigueur,*[215] and I must say that M. Vachier senior

---

[215] "Formal attire is required." In a previous memoir Carco notes that his use of the phrase "Le bal de 'la Montagne'" is an abbreviation for a dance hall on the rue de la Montagne Sainte-Geneviève: "It's the Vachier ball where you can still read this announcement on the walls: 'Formal attire required!' What attire! Opposite this ball, where the owner's son, Mr. Mimile, is the most renowned accordion player, you will find the small creamery where we used to have meals with Bernouard and various friends, for nine sous." We can assume this was the infamous Bal de la Montagne located at 46, rue de la Montagne-Sainte-Geneviève. A British guide book to Paris from 1903 breathlessly intones a dire warning about this venue, then known as Le Bal d'Octobre: "This is established in the back part of a wine shop, giving no indication on the outside of what goes on within. The place is frequented by the lowest class, so it is specially necessary for visitors and strangers to be on their guard. It has been stated that in certain parts of Paris there are refreshment bars and cafés where customers are served, and waited upon, by women only. There are many such, and this is one. A description of Le

knew how to command respect. His son, Milo, played at that time in the small balcony allotted to the musicians. He was an ace at it. He drew such music from his melodeon that the women went into ecstasies, ready to die. The tables were nailed to the ground, benches surrounded the shining floor and between two iron pillars, at the end of a string, another notice was posted with all the rules of the place. There were nights in that autocratically governed dive when everything was perfect. Then there were nights when guns would be shot off and the men and women would be forced to scramble to safety under the tables. Who had fired the shots? That was the secret of that dancing hall. Everything was meticulously and carefully arranged and suddenly battles would take place that would end in blood.

*

Why can't I as I write these lines prevent myself from thinking of my friend Jean Pellerin? He never frequented those dancing halls. He hated them. But, in spite of myself, in the rue de la Montagne-Sainte-Geneviève, I thought I was in Grenoble, where I loved the brasseries of the rue Saint-Jacques. Jean Pellerin lived in that street above one of them, the "Criterion." A somber passage led to a badly lighted stairway, one went up

Bal d'Octobre will serve for all, and is here given for the benefit of the English visitor, and should act as a warning not to go there." See George Day, *Pleasure guide to Paris for bachelors*, London: Nilsson and Co., 1903. For Carco's original text, see *Francis Carco Raconté par Lui-Même*, Paris: Éditions Sansot, 1921, p. 10, n. 1: "Le bal de 'la Montagne,' abréviation de la rue de la Montagne Ste-Geneviève. C'est le bal Vachier où l'on peut lire encore sur les murs cette annonce : La tenue est de rigueur! Quelle tenue! En face de ce bal, dont le fils du tenancier, M. Mimile, est le plus réputé joueur d'accordéon, se trouve toujours la petite crèmerie où nous prenions, avec Bernouard et différents amis, des repas à neuf sous."

in the dark, and then a door in the floor opened, everything would be lighted up and Jean Pellerin, holding a lamp very high, would joyously welcome me.

At that time, in the uniform of a secretary of staff, Jean Pellerin looked very tall, very thin, and he never sat down without folding one of his thin legs under the other as if he were ashamed of being so long. And he would look one straight in the face, smile, light a cigarette and seem to have no other affectation except the use of his hands which, very delicate and well cared for even amid the military routine, showed a care for elegance, neatness and natural grace. As soon as one knew the man, one recognized him in his writing. It was astonishing, it emphasized the resemblance, and when I read today the *Bouquet Inutile* published after his death, I found his tall, flowered and easy writing in the following verses:

Le premier frisson du matin.
Une cloche qui tinte.
Le songe est mort. Le feu s'éteint.
La lampe s'est éteinte.[216]

Alas, those young hands – which were writing not only, even in 1909, military orders – have stopped writing, line by line, those clear sentences and those verses which their author tried to fill with a rhythm which he executed to perfection. Even in very short poems which he carefully copied in a thin copybook, he had shown a great love and a great knowledge of his art. We exchanged our first writings with each other. We had great ambitions for the future and one for the present was to have new verses every day to show each other, a book which the

[216] "The first shiver of the morning. / A bell ringing. / The dream is dead. The fire is dying. / The lamp has gone out." Excerpt from the poem "Le premier frisson du matin," *Le Bouquet inutile*, Paris: Éditions De La Nouvelle Revue Française, 1923.

other had not read, or an anecdote which the other did not know. Charming times they were, in spite of my military service spent in barracks where I played at being a soldier, and the difficulties we encountered when we tried to get our writings published. We decided to begin a review. It came out. I remember that Jean Pellerin gave me the proofs in the jail of the Second Regiment of the Artillery where I was confined for some minor offense and where I was not so badly off.

"I went to see him," the mysterious Eve Arrighi said in the *Divan* – Jean knew her well – "and I went every day as long as he was in jail.[217] He had plenty of visitors and if the prisoner's parlor of the Second Artillery was not a very comfortable drawing room there were lots of friends and geniality to compensate. There one met, bringing books and cigarettes, the poet Maurice Morel, the beautiful Madame Paule L., Jean Pellerin, a lady well provided with charms called Lily and many others absolutely devoted to him. The young man looked well in his prison uniform. He was gay, he recited verses. I never found him discouraged, not once did he regret his escapades or complain. They were pleasant talks but, alas, cut short by the authorities. Carco was sent to Briançon in disgrace when he got out of prison."

To come back to our review, *Les Petites Feuilles*, it had one number only and it is very rare today.

Later on, when Jean Pellerin came to live in Paris, he stayed first in the rue Réaumur before he lived in an apartment near Montmartre. It was furnished at first only with a bed, a table, three chairs, a rocking chair and innumerable cases of books. In Paris, he remained the same Jean Pellerin, he wrote light verses in which he showed himself as he was, not seeking vain

---

[217] In 1908 Pellerin published his poem *"Octobre"* in *Les Petites Feuilles*, under the pseudonym "Eve Arrighi." Several other articles appeared under "Eve's" byline, including the one quoted here, from *Le Divan*. Carco continues the hoax by dryly remarking: "Jean knew her well."

successes, but ready to mock at himself and dance graciously for his own pleasure to the tune of a melodious fantasy.

Je ne me suis pas fait la tête de Musset,

he used to declare.

Je tartine des vers, je prépare un essai,
J'ai le quart d'un roman, à sécher, dans l'armoire ...
Mais que sont vos baisers, ô filles de Mémoire !
Vous entendre dicter des mots après des mots !
Triste jeu ...[218]

His irony was soon to take a less joyous tone. Out in the world he faced the necessity of earning his daily bread like the others. The poet learned quickly that to write beautiful verses is not enough. Jean Pellerin knew how to adapt himself to circumstances. Then his pen did not find in the inkwell the impertinent rhymes which it generally found there, but endless words and words which always finished by being the lines of a newspaper paragraph or an article, and were paid for. Till the war he signed in several papers, "Parisian evenings," tales, notes, interviews. It took all of his time but I knew that after midnight, the brilliant chronicler gave up his newspaper work to deliver himself to his temptation.

What better thing could he have done? Jean Pellerin was above all a poet and lived for poetry alone. How many times have I seen him reading Baudelaire, Verlaine, Mallarmé,

[218] The opening verse of Pellerin's poem, "La Nuit d'Avril," from *Le Bouquet inutile*: "I didn't make fun of Musset, / I'm churning out verses, / I'm preparing an essay, / I have a quarter of a novel, drying in the closet ... But what are your kisses, oh daughters of memory! / To hear you dictate word after word, / Sad game!" Seymour S. Weiner further elucidates the sense here when he remarks "Pellerin refused to make a display of himself like Musset and even mocked the poet." Weiner, *Francis Carco*, p. 72.

Rimbaud, Lautréamont, Guérin,[219] Apollinaire, Jean-Marc Bernard, Toulet, Allard, Tristan Derème![220] He sent his verses to small reviews, never talked about them and secretly nursed the idea of gathering in a volume those exquisite and sad stanzas of which I was not the only admirer.

Alas! Jean Pellerin never saw the book he had thought so much about. *La Romance du Retour* contains only one poem, beautiful and stirring. The others, after appearing in modest publications, had to be collected. After his death it was necessary in order to fulfill at last Jean Pellerin's ambition that I should offer to the public the work he had left us. May it keep for a long time its varied colors, its aroma, and its proud and sensitive form. It is not a festive bouquet, gathered in some middle-class garden, but one of those which comrades buy at the gates of the graveyard to lay upon the tomb beside which they uncover themselves. Humble flowers, although brilliant and carefully chosen, Jean Pellerin's verses are not the sort one forgets after reading them. They have the tone of youth, of his youth wounded by many losses, of his youth still alive, even though it weeps as it counts what is left of love and betrayal, after many years.

It was not I who wrote this:

> *Aujourd'hui je reviens et tel*
> *Qu'hier. La cloche sonne.*
> *La même cloche au même hôtel.*

---

[219] Georges-Maurice de Guérin (1810 – 1839): French nature poet whose works were imbued with pagan imagery and who died at the age of twenty-eight; author of *La Bacchante* and *Le Centaure*.

[220] Tristan Derème (né Philippe Huc; 1889 – 1941): French poet and politician who, along with Carco and Robert de la Vaissière, founded *l'École Fantaisiste*. Derème was the author of *Patachou, Petit Garçon*, a collection of poetry and prose said to have inspired Saint-Exupéry's *Le Petit Prince*.

Je ne revois personne.[221]

But if he could come back, how touched he would be to find that so many admirers know his name.

Picasso. *Apollinaire blessé*, 1916, graphite
pencil and conté crayon on paper, 31.3 x 23.1 cm.

[221] "Today I come back and, like yesterday, the bell rings. / The same bell at the same hotel. / And again, I don't see anyone."

XIII

If Montmartre and the Quarter had each their own cafés, the literary ones were more numerous on the boulevard Saint-Michel than on the boulevard Clichy. They have remained celebrated because, in place of a Bruant[222] who is still, when all is said and done, a real personality, Verlaine and his genius, Rimbaud, Moréas, Paul Fort, Apollinaire have left there enduring memories.[223] The Quarter only needs painters comparable with Lautrec, Degas, Picasso and Utrillo to equal Montmartre, but Matisse still lives on the quai Saint-Michel, Dunoyer de Segonzac and Derain in the same house in the rue Bonaparte and Marquet[224] as well, who noted upon his canvases the leadlike water and the sky of a small dead backwater of the Seine, the smoke and the tugs, is an artist of some quality. Shall we try to compare them? It is not necessary. However, if Montmartre excels on account of its picturesqueness, the

[222] Louis Armand Aristide Bruant (1851 – 1925): French singer, comedian, and cabaret proprietor. Bruant is perhaps best remembered for being the subject of Toulouse Lautrec's *Aristide Bruant in his Cabaret* (and of other poster art portraits), in which the celebrated *chansonnier* is depicted wearing his emblematic wide-brimmed hat, brilliant red scarf, dark corduroy suit, and trousers tucked into his boots. In 1903 Bruant purchased Le Lapin Agile from Adèle and Jules Jouy, placing Frédéric Gérard in charge of management. In an act of memorable generosity, Bruant bequeathed the cabaret to Frédé after his death.

[223] This passage could be literally translated as "Verlaine and his genius, Rimbaud, Moréas, Paul Fort, Apollinaire left memories on the Left Bank that will not perish."

[224] Albert Marquet (1875 – 1947): French Fauvist, whose style shifted back to a naturalistic mode (a volte-face similar to Derain's, although Marquet's later work explores landscape). Marquet studied under the symbolist painter Gustave Moreau at the École des Beaux-Arts, where he met Matisse. The two artists painted together, were roommates for a time, and developed a close lifelong friendship.

Quarter can claim a much more distinct character, although it does not appear on the surface.

I began frequenting the Vachette just in time to know Moréas and to hear him whistle without answering when some stupid person would talk to him about the Academy. In spite of his dyed mustache he looked wonderful and his speech, however insolent, was full of exceedingly good sense. To the young men who were around him, in the packed room of the Vachette, he would declare:

"Rely on principles."

Then, stroking his mustache and fixing his monocle solidly in his eye, he would add:

"They'll end by giving way!"

We feared him like the plague on account of his conversation, for at certain times he would pour out in no uncertain terms his hatreds and disappointments.

Whatever time it was, Jean Moréas always carried himself exceedingly well, though sometimes drunk, and was followed by the young men of the Quarter. He loved youth and women, and addressed charming compliments to them in verses which he improvised, like those he wrote for Marie Laurencin:

> *Qu'elle rie,*
> *Et, Marie*
> *Laurencin,*
> *L'or enceint*
> *Dans ses belles*
> *Prunelles.*[225]

Great Moréas! After him we deserted the Vachette which became a bank where much later I cashed my first check,[226] and

---

[225] "Laurencin" is phonetically similar to "*l'or enceint*," combining "the gold" (*l'or*) and "cradled" (*enceint*). Hence: "Let her laugh, and, Marie Laurencin, the gold is cradled in the apple of her eye."

went up the famous Boul'Mich', to the Closerie des Lilas where we assembled beside Paul Fort on Tuesdays,[227] in an indescribable uproar mixed with the shouts of the poets. It was a magnificent period. We drank. There were arguments. One added one's saucers to one's neighbors without any shame whatsoever and jumped at once into the discussion, taking sides …

Paul Fort's long hair, his sombrero, his black tie, his small coat buttoned right to the top, his simplicity, stood in contrast to the ornaments which women of all races, Swedes, Russians, Spaniards flaunted here and there under our eyes. Escorted by the giant Diriks[228] and the poet Napoléon Roinard,[229] Paul Fort would tell stories. He laughed, he sang, he emptied his glass and, as spontaneously as a child, kissed all his friends in turn. It was a pleasure to find him always in a good humor, welcoming everybody with open arms and making them feel happy. Time after time, bucolic, idyllic, familiar, Gallic, inventive, spirited and imaginative, Paul Fort enchanted us with his small tremulous voice. His eyes, which pierced one's soul and

[226] Under the headline "FAMOUS CAFE DOOMED; Vachette's, Resort of Poets and Painters, to be Torn Down," the 15 June 1913 edition of the *New York Times* reports: "PARIS, June 14. – All those who have passed any part of their lives cultivating literature or the arts in Paris will be sorry to hear that one of the chief landmarks of bohemian life in the Latin Quarter, the Cafe Vachette, in the Boulevard Saint Michel, is to be demolished in a few days' time, to make room for a bank." (See special section, p. 2.)

[227] "On Tuesdays the Picasso gang went to the Closerie des Lilas for the poetry and prose evenings which had been started and were run by Paul Fort, with André Salmon as the secretary." Olivier, *Picasso and His Friends*, p. 44.

[228] Karl Edvard Diriks (1855 – 1930): Norwegian naturalist painter who lived in France between 1899 and 1921. In 1920 Diriks was awarded the French Legion of Honour.

[229] Paul-Napoléon Roinard (1856 – 1930): French anarchist poet and author of *La Légende rouge* (1921).

inflamed one with the fire which lived in them, invested all his words with a charming enchantment.

One must have heard the Prince of Poets improvising about midnight, in his kingdom in the Closerie des Lilas, ballads which he did not write down, unlike most poetasters who are afraid of losing anything, to know what riches he possessed and distributed without counting. He was not only a man and a "very extraordinary one," he was inspired and gave ample opportunity for even the meanest heart to marvel at. In the street, under a gas lamp or the moon:

Comme un œuf dansant sur un jet d'eau,[230]

he never stopped pouring out his songs, and then he would push us suddenly into dark small cafés which he brightened by his presence.

The collaborators in the review *Vers et Prose* which he directed gave him his cues. Salmon with his angular profile, Guillaume Apollinaire, Guy-Charles Cros, Louis Mandin, Alexandre Mercereau, Fuss-Amoré, who was amused at everything, his friend Tancrède de Visan, Bersaucourt, Max Jacob, Gazanion and painters, boxers, critics and beggars who, like the wild animals in the legend, followed Orpheus and drank with him.

I remember that at the birth of his third child, the poet and essayist Tancrède de Visan[231] came to tell me the happy news and we drank for two days till Tuesday, when delirious, we met Paul Fort on the boulevard Montparnasse. Visan wanted to go home, but he was imprudent enough to show the few louis he still had in his pocket and Paul Fort seized them.

---

[230] "Like an egg dancing on a jet of water."
[231] Tancrède de Visan (né Vincent Biétrix; 1878 – 1945): French journalist and director of the magazine *Notre carnet*, who associated with the Cubists at the Closerie des Lilas.

"We are going to drink them," said the prince joyfully ... "all of them ... all ..."

It was late. A bistro – there are always some open even at the most unusual hours – welcomed us and the festivities continued. This bistro, a long passage filled with mirrors, benches and marble tables, which was called, I think, A la Villa de Dreux, was hardly big enough for us three, we were so overwrought. It did not matter! The libations went on and a terrible tumult of very eloquent voices rose, while to add to the noise, the drunkest in our crowd were breaking glasses and standing on chairs.

What happened then? I do not know, but I must have been amongst the noisy drunks, because I seem to remember, when my drunkenness had passed all limits, creating a scandal because someone had spoken ill of Rimbaud. I would allow no one to say anything against that poet. Also there was a splendid fight, at the end of which a boxer belonging to the prince's following literally stunned me and threw me out.

What an adventure! Lying on the pavement with blackened eyes, my right ankle dislocated, I came back slowly to my senses to shout again:

"Long live Rimbaud!" and to see Paul Fort, with his hands laid in a brotherly fashion upon my forehead, laughing and lamenting:

"Rimbaud?"

"Yes, long live Rimbaud!"

Hereupon a policeman, not understanding my enthusiasm, asked me to have the kindness to move on.

"Move on and be quick about it."

And as I was not obeying his orders quickly enough, he called another policeman and they dragged me, howling, to the police station. From the station, still howling, they took me to a hospital where an intern had to look after me, and the next day I found myself, my shoes in my hand, in a cab.

And every thirty yards I'd shout to the driver:

"Stop! Is there not a bar around that way?"

The man jumped out of his seat, got two Pernods, which we drank at the window peacefully, till the next bar. One can guess in what state we soon were for the coachman took Rimbaud's part since he was having free drinks and I was delighted to have convinced him without having my other leg broken. This man was surely well-born. Stopping his horse at my door, he refused to accept anything for the drive and hoisting me on his shoulders he carried me up to my room, to the amusement of the onlookers.

At that time, nine out of ten of our literary feasts ended that way. We were thus expressing our admiration for the poets who in their time had done far better; the next day it brought us to the attention of everybody in the Quarter and it increased our prestige enormously. But on that occasion it took me a month to recover and to put my foot to the ground.

I see myself again in a taxi with Rachilde, the one who had given me up as a poet, very much upset about my state. She paid the chauffeur to take me home.

As soon as she had left, I said to the man: "Take me to the Pascal." But there my manners must have been wanting in dignity, since, very disgusted, the boss put me to sleep in a small room and sent two bellboys to accompany me home in the morning. I slept two days and two nights like a brute and waking at last my ear was so sore that I felt it at once and I found inside a small piece of paper folded in four, buried deep in the drum. On it was written:

"Francis, you were dead to the world, so I took the money you had, fourteen francs in all. You can come and get it at the d'Harcourt." It was signed Gisèle and there was a P.S.

"I took that money because the other women would have kept it for themselves."

*

You will excuse me if I do not dwell longer on such scenes. Extravagances of that kind were not in very good taste, but what am I to do? I told the last episode to show the motherly solicitude of the young ladies of the Left Bank for poets, even when they were dead drunk. With them we were safe. They had founded a league for the defense of French comrades against the foreigners and helped us in crises. Indeed, having found a job as secretary, a rather well-paid job with Louis Vauxcelles,[232] I was so proud that one evening when drunk I stupidly started a fight with a very robust gentleman who got the better of me. All the ladies came to my rescue and helped me to avenge my honor. We all went to the police station and the next day Vauxcelles was very astonished by my appearance, and asked me how many days a week I could be serious.

"Every second day," I replied.

"All right," he said. "One day's feasting and one day's work!"

And as he was the kindest man in the world, he paid me a month in advance and said:

"I'll see you the day after tomorrow."

Who has pretended that God's goodness stops at literature? He is certainly not a poet and he lies.

An American reporter recently asked me: "What is the thing that has astonished you most?"

"I don't know."

"But yet ..."

The man embarrassed me. He watched me and waited, his notebook in his hand.

---

[232] Louis Vauxcelles (né Louis Meyer; 1870 – 1943): French art critic who coined the (pejorative) term Fauvism (in 1905, he called the painters aligned with Matisse *les fauves* or "wild beasts"). In 1908 he accused Braque of "reducing everything ... to cubes." The following year he referred to Braque's work as *"bizarreries cubiques"* (cubic oddities).

"Please," he said, "think ..."

"The thing which has astonished me most? Well," I said, "I think my being able to earn my living by telling stories which my parents would not have tolerated at table."

What other answer could I have given him? At twenty, one is convinced that a novel must be concerned with exceptional facts, and that is why we all have in our desks very ridiculous works that remain unpublished. Poor young men! We did not know much about life and we did not dare lay claim to it, while life is the only thing a writer has any claim to. Otherwise what reason would he have for writing? Young men can believe me. If they spend their youth learning from teachers, instead of learning by committing a thousand follies, they will grow old too quickly and they will not have later to brighten their old age any of the experiences one does not find in books. One must live first of all, even if one has to leave behind, as Dorgelès confessed in the *Boutique de Socrate*, "spoiled days, sterile efforts, missed loves, no other family than dishonest café keepers, no other roof than a damp house," because, he added, "when we smile today, it is about our troubles of yesterday."

Guillaume Apollinaire knew this, when at the marriage of his friend Salmon he got up and read:

> *Nous nous sommes rencontrés dans un caveau maudit*
> *Au temps de notre jeunesse*
> *Fumant tous deux et mal vêtus attendant l'aube*
> *Epris, épris des mêmes paroles dont il faudra changer le*
>   *sens*
> *Trompés, trompés, pauvres petits et ne sachant pas*
>   *encore rire.*[233]

---

[233] "We met in a cursed vault / In the days of our youth / Both smoking and poorly dressed, waiting for dawn / In love, in love with the same words whose meaning will have to be changed / Deceived, deceived, poor little

And indeed, one learns to laugh only by being alive and struggling, at the price of the hardest privations, perhaps in poverty and abandonment. Do you remember the hero of the road to Mandalay who sang while in irons, and so many others, including François Villon! That unfortunate one laughed, "weeping," and he did not hide the fact. Can we despise experience? It is thanks to what he had gone through that we went cheerfully through the narrow streets of the Quarter. All the time, even in that *"caveau maudit"* ["cursed vault"], which was to be the one where Guillaume met Salmon, we never despaired about anything.

That dive, in the rue Grégoire de Tours, was not wanting in picturesqueness. Its centered in a kind of bar where girls answering to the names of Yolande, Isabeau, Guillemette, Denise were waiting for patrons in a whitewashed, heavily rounded vault. The floor of beaten earth, coffers, heavy rings sealed in the stone walls and big hearts pierced with arrows, gave a very suitable appearance to that hell. We drank goblets of wine, smoked rank tobacco, and gentlemen hiding behind the pillars were dressed as authentic *Compagnons de la Coquille* with dirty and tattered raiment and leather coats.[234]

I have often recited in their company the verses of the poor *escholier*[235] Villon and thought I could see him, standing amongst the tables, ragged, his clothes stained with earth, like a

ones and not yet knowing how to laugh." From "Poème lu au mariage d'André Salmon," included in the collection *Alcools*.

[234] *Compagnons de la Coquille* or "Companions of the Shell": a term referring to the homeless and destitute who roamed the streets in ragged, tattered raiment and soiled leather coats. The phrase derives from the expression *mendier en coquille*: "to beg in a shell," referring to the act of begging while curled in a fetal position on the ground, thus resembling the shape of a shell.

[235] An archaic French term for a student.

dead man who has come out of a tomb, with black hands and sunken eyes.

> *Car ou soies porteur de bulles,*
> *Pipeur ou hasardeur de dez*
> *Tailleur de faulx coings, tu te brusles,*
> *Comme ceulx qui sont eschaudéz,*
> *Traistres parjurs, de foy vuydez;*
> *Soies larron, ravis ou pilles :*
> *Où en va l'acquest, que cuidez ?*
> *Tout aux tavernes et aux filles.*[236]

He was with us, singing his "Ballade de bonne doctrine à ceux de mauvaise vie" and those who did not see him still heard his voice resounding deeply in their sleeping conscious minds. We loved you so much, François Villon! We felt you so near to us, at the same table, your elbow against ours, or outside in the streets walking beside us till the moment when the day paled; straying dogs stopped and sniffed at us fearfully, silently, and then, frightened, ran away. Yes, it was you ... and you disappeared always without saying goodbye, so that a sudden strange feeling would make us count ourselves and look back saying:

"Well! ... Where on earth is he?"

---

[236] "Whether you are a false preacher, / Cheater or dice gambler, / Maker of counterfeit coins, you burn yourself, / Like those who make the same mistake twice, / Perverted traitors, devoid of faith; / Be you thief, plunderer, or pillager: / Where does the gain go, do you think? / All to taverns and to girls." The first of four stanzas from the poem "Ballade de bonne doctrine à ceux de mauvaise vie" ("Ballade of Good Doctrine to Those of Bad Life"), each of which ends with the refrain: "All to taverns and to girls."

XIV

The bad days were over. Thanks to Jean de Pierrefeu[237] and to Maxence Legrand,[238] my godfathers at Baptiste's, I was given credit at the pension Laveur[239] and I ate twice a day. What a pension that was! In spite of the smell of cats on the stairs and the simplicity Baptiste did things well. His regular patrons, who at once made a little elbow room for me, became my friends.

[237] Jean de Pierrefeu (né Pierre-Édouard Maurin; 1881 – 1940): a "Pied-Noir" French journalist who penned a positive review of Carco's novel, *L'Homme traqué* in the 7 July 1922 issue of *Journal des Debats*: "A sort of Russian adaptation of a picturesque, incisive, and clear talent ... inspired by both Dostoevsky and Bergson." (Quoted in the original French by Seymour S. Weiner, *Francis Carco*, p. 227, n. 26: "Une sorte d'adaptation russe d'un talent pittoresque, incisif et clair ... à la fois inspiré de Dostoiewsky et de Bergson.") Pierrefeu also authored controversial books that were critical of the WWI French military leadership. An ardent nationalist, he was a stalwart supporter of Marshal Pétain; and, under the Nazi occupation, was director of the journal *Les Cahiers de la Jeune France*, an ideological mouthpiece of the Vichy regime.

[238] Maxence Legrand (pseudonym of Alexandre Warschawsky; 1882 – 1916): novelist and playwright from New Caledonia and the author of *La fille de Caïphe* ("The Daughter of Caiaphas"), Paris: E. Sansot, 1907, who also contributed to various magazines, such as the weekly *L'Opinion*. Legrand's name is inscribed on the Panthéon, included in a list of writers who died for France.

[239] The pension Laveur: originally located at 6, rue des Poitevins, a thirteenth-century street in the sixth arrondissement. Number 4, rue des Poitevins hosted the Hotel de Thou, where, in 1587, Jacques Auguste de Thou, president of the Parlement of Paris and an avid bibliophile, created one of the most renowned libraries of the Renaissance. The pension Laveur, which featured lodgings and a restaurant, was established in 1840 and was set in a wing of the Thou mansion. As Carco notes in this passage, artists and political figures such as Courbet and Gambetta lodged at the pension during their student days or as newly arrived immigrants to Paris. It later relocated to 20, rue Serpente, just around the block.

Giraudoux,[240] Clouard,[241] Le Cardonnel,[242] Tardieu,[243] Ramond,[244] Blanc ... I forget some of them ... They were all delighted with the house, very much at their ease and very comfortable. And under a sleepy appearance Baptiste hid great finesse. He not only offered food to his clients, but coffee, alcohol, cigars and choice wines. That was his pride! Renewing the traditions of the place where Gambetta, Vallés[245] and Courbet, to name only three, had found the table always laid, he laid ours and treated us well.

From there we went to the Cluny[246] where, from the most obscure corner in the café, M. Albalat[247] saw us arriving,

[240] Hippolyte Jean Giraudoux (1882 – 1944): novelist, diplomat, and prominent dramatist of the interwar period, born in Bellac, France. Adaptations of his plays by Christopher Fry ("Tiger at the Gates") and Maurice Valency ("The Madwoman of Chaillot") led to his international recognition.

[241] Henri Clouard (1889 – 1974): French literary critic and author of *Histoire de la Littérature Française*, Paris: Éditions Albin Michel, 1947.

[242] Georges Le Cardonnel (1872 – 1941): Literary and art critic for *Mercure de France* and *La Revue universelle*, born in Valence. Brother of the poet and Roman Catholic priest Louis Le Cardonnel (1862 – 1936).

[243] Charles Tardieu: French scholar and journalist who served as a captain during WWI and contributed to journals such publications as *La Revue de France* and *Le Figaro*. During the Nazi occupation the Germans appointed him director of the collaborationist newspaper, *L'Écho du Nord* (1942 – 1944). In 1944 Tardieu was condemned for treason and sentenced to life imprisonment with forced labor.

[244] Édouard Ramond: author of *Histoires de Filles et d'Affranchis* ("Stories of Girls and Freed Slaves"), Paris: Les Éditions De France, 1925, which features an Introduction by Carco.

[245] Jules Vallès (1832 – 1885): French novelist and political journalist associated with the revolutionary Paris Commune of 1871, who wrote about social injustice and the struggle of the working class. Most remembered for his autobiographical trilogy, *L'Enfant*, *Le Bachelier*, and *L'Insurgé*, a chronicle of his early life of poverty and political engagement.

[246] Café-Restaurant du Musée de Cluny, located at 20, boulevard Saint-Michel.

without any pleasure. We sat beside him, listened to him and studied him.

They talked only about literature at his table and I must confess that I did not understand a word they said[,] and André Billy[248] [and] René Gillouin[249] put me to shame, for they were

247 Antoine Albalat (1856 – 1935): French novelist and literary critic for the paper *Journal des débats*. Albalat published his theories on writing and literary style in didactic treatises such as *L'Art d'écrire enseigné en vingt leçons* ("The Art of Writing Taught in Twenty Lessons") and *Comment il ne faut pas écrire* ("How Not to Write").

248 André Billy (1882 – 1971): novelist, memoirist, and biographer, who published over 11,000 newspaper articles. He was also the literary critic for *L'OEuvre* and a friend of Apollinaire. After Apollinaire was unjustly arrested for the theft of the *Mona Lisa* and then released from prison, Billy came to his aid by offering him the associate editor position for his new review, *Soirées de Paris*.

249 René Gillouin (1881 – 1971): an anti-modern, antidemocratic French intellectual, literary critic, journalist, and extreme right-wing politician from the Drome region, whose father was a Protestant minister. A habitué of the Latin Quarter, he soon became acquainted with the writers of the Café Vachette, led by Jean Moréas, and of the Taverne du Panthéon, where he befriended Bernard Grasset, his future publisher. In 1931 Gillouin was elected as municipal counselor; and in June 1937 as vice-president of the Paris Municipal Council. During this period he was known for his xenophobic and nationalist rhetoric. In his role as municipal counselor, in 1938 he advocated the banning of Jean Cocteau's play, *Les Parents Terribles*, regarding it as "immoral, anti-family, and antisocial." He denounced the "émigré" artists of Paris, calling them "métèques" (a derogatory term for "foreigner") and claiming that because of their presence "hundreds of French artists of good breed ... will vegetate." During the Nazi occupation he advocated the National Revolution ideology of the Vichy regime, with Pétain's motto *Travail, Famille, Patrie* having replaced the *Liberté, Égalité, Fraternité* ideals of the Republic. In 1940 he moved to Vichy and became even more closely associated with Pétain, producing radio speeches and articles for the him while availing himself of two rooms on the Marshall's floor at the Hôtel du Parc. Gillouin called for the nation to "banish from within it, and strip of all leading influence, individuals and groups who, for reasons of race or convictions, could not or would not subscribe to the

very much in the know, being newspaper critics of literature. They tried their articles on us, while Jean Giraudoux talked pleasantly behind his glasses and René Dalize[250] and Jacques Dyssord who had had no sleep, yawned.

The last named was the enfant terrible of the group. He was overbearingly proud of his unmentionable acquaintances. He was ceaselessly praising the merits of his pal Hubert and a certain Betty to whose place he took me to drink with [in the company of] women.

Never has a man showed more naturalness and gaiety in leading a fast life than Dyssord.

He appeared to have been born to shock respectable people, [and] this verse by François Maynard, which he recited with enthusiasm

> *Entre au bordel en plein midi !*
> ["Enter the brothel at high noon!]

primacy of the French fatherland." Despite such anti-Semitic rhetoric, Gillouin was one of the few in Pétain's circle to protest the rounding up and deportation of the Jews, and he wrote several letters of protest to Pétain. He eventually fell out of favor with the Vichy regime, particularly after the rise of his adversary Pierre Laval. In 1943 Gillouin fled to Switzerland, where he remained until 1948. After his return to France, he continued to contribute to extreme right-wing periodicals.

[250] René Dalize (né René Dupuy des Islettes; 1879 – 1917): French writer and close friend of Apollinaire, whom he befriended while they were children at school. Apollinaire later dedicated *Calligrammes* to him. Dalize was the author of *Le Club des neurasthéniques* (1912), first serialized in *Paris-Midi* under the pseudonym "Franquevaux": a witty novel about a club of nine members who are devoted to neurasthenia as a way of life. Dalize's promising career was cut short when he lost his life at Chemin des Dames, fighting in WWI, to the great distress of Apollinaire, who died the following year, a victim of the flu epidemic.

he had made his own, [even if it meant letting me] recite to him these verses of the same poet, bitter and disillusioned:

> *L'excès de chagrin a vaincu*
> *Celui qui jamais n'a vécu*
> *Que parmi les filles de joie,*[251]

[because] he laughed and answered: ["I know.]"

Compared to him I was an amateur or, if you like, a second-rater, for the extraordinary acquaintances of my good friend Jacques were varied and numerous. In the gambling saloons of the Quarter Saint-Georges he taught me how to eat for nothing and, not at all ashamed, he put into my pocket sandwiches and hard-boiled eggs which he had stolen from the buffet. Why should we have restrained ourselves? Jacques was living of his own free will a picaresque novel and when I saw him dressed in a coat much too large, a green waistcoat and black trousers, he sighed and confided to me:

"You did not know me in my splendiferous days. It's a pity, old man ... I had a diamond as big as that" – he pointed to a

---

[251] François de Maynard (1582 – 1646). The first verse is from a four-line poem that reads: "Entré au bordel en plein midi ? / Meuble-toi d'une concubine, / Et cherche, avec un front hardi, / La verolle et la cristalline." ("Enter the brothel at high noon? / Furnish yourself with a concubine, / And seek, with bold brow, / The pox and the clap.") By changing the question mark into an exclamation, Dyssord appears to be answering Maynard in the affirmative. The second verse, from the same collection, may be translated as: "Excess of sorrow has overcome / One who has never lived / Except among *les filles de joie*" (i.e., prostitutes). The complete poem reads as follows: "A sad mood dominates me. Everything annoys me, everything displeases me, and the sun, beautiful as it is, seems to have a gloomy face. My fate is full of cruelty and passes for the strangest novelty that one can see: excess of sorrow has overcome one who has never lived except among *les filles de joie*." From the collection *Priapées de François de Maynard*, Paris: E. Sansot and Cie., Editeurs, 1909.

hardboiled egg – "shoes made to order, silk underwear and suits! Five suits! I swear ..."

"Well, and then?"

"Well, then ... I sold everything to live ... everything ... the diamond, the clothes." Then, seized with sadness, he muttered:

> *Cet hiver fut des plus froids.*
> *Nous n'aurons pas tiré les rois.*
> *– Qui serait roi, qui serait reine*
> *De ma peine ?*[252]

"It is better not to write it, no one would believe me."

Every evening, as Mac Orlan has told when speaking of his youth, the drama of the key was enacted by a hard-hearted proprietor and my friend Jacques the poet. "The key was hanging from a nail under a number, on a board ..." and, added Mac Orlan, "It was lucky for me as well as others that that board was not able to register human voices."

Yes, lucky, but after all, what does it matter! The next day Jacques had forgotten all about it and had gone back to his wicked life. He rested by teaching a very well brought up girl who waited for him at the Métro Saint-Germain. Jacques would walk with her arm in arm, would take her where well brought up girls are not usually taken and, vain of the progress of his pupil, admired himself in her and would tell me of her exploits.

"There is in your life of many artists, writers and ex-pimps converted to a regular life," Mac Orlan once also said, "a period

---

[252] The third stanza of "Aveu Dénué d'Artifice" ("Confession Stripped of Artifice"; 1914), by Jacques Dyssord: "This winter was very cold. / We won't have drawn the kings. / Who would be king, who would be queen / Of my pain?" The third line refers to the tradition of "drawing the king" ("Tirer les Rois") during the celebration of Epiphany or the Feast of the Three Kings. That is, a "king cake" ("galette des rois") is baked with a figurine or bean hidden inside. The one who finds the hidden treasure in their slice is declared the king or queen of the celebration.

which the most cynical of them consider with indulgence and the others with a bitterness that the smiles of fortune – when fortune deigns to smile – cannot dissipate."

Well, we all know it, and it is better so, since, brought up to lead that dissolute existence, we are able today to show it as its really was and be forgiven. What harm was there in it? We never thought of its wickedness. We were busy being alive, and in spite of the darkest circumstances we never gave way. Think of it! To live was not so easy then, when we wrote only verse. We had to use all means, whatever they were, and very often we had to be content with such ridiculous sums that when we had to pay for something we were not very proud of ourselves.

Je ne vaux pas plus qu'un autre,

sang Jacques Dyssord,

Et ce n'est pas beaucoup dire;
Mais le mieux ou bien le pire,
C'est cet air de bon apôtre.[253]

And Jacques Dyssord is the author of the *Dernier Chant de l'Intermezzo* and I would give many celebrated volumes in exchange for that one, for I am sure that many more famous works cannot equal it.

Another poet of whom they made a saint, and who was one in his way, because he was struggling against some strange streak in himself, and who has left the most beautiful and the most harrowing poem about the war – Jean-Marc Bernard,[254]

[253] "I'm not worth more than anyone else, / And that's not saying much; / But for better or for worse, / is this air of a good apostle." The first stanza of "Aveu Dénué d'Artifice."

[254] Jean-Marc Bernard (1881 – 1915): French poet, journalist, and co-founder of the review *Les Guêpes*. As previously noted, Bernard was a member of *Les poètes fantaisistes*.

frequented the peaceful café of Cluny about the same time. He did not sit at the critic's table, but outside at a small table around which Clouard, Eon,[255] Le Cardonnel, Marcel Drouet[256] gathered to welcome in Marc to Paris. Jean-Marc Bernard, Dauphinois, lived in Saint-Rambert-d'Albon. I had met him at Orange, in front of the Great Wall, and then I had gone, one day, to his secluded house in Saint Lambert's where he lived with his mother. A very sincere affection sprang up between us. Dear, unfortunate Jean-Marc! That day, which began in Saint-Rambert, ended in Valence, where the poet had a liaison with a curious creature. She was the owner of a café near the cavalry barracks, not unattractive, and as clever in dispensing her alcohol as her love. Jean-Marc introduced me. He wrote verses for her, which he dated from the Brasserie de la Cigale, where I see both of us, amongst outrageously made up creatures, drinking and talking.

J'aime tes tristes yeux ...

Jean-Marc murmured and further, dedicating to Berthe this poem in which he reveals himself, he moaned:

Tais-toi ! Pourquoi mentir encore ?
Je ne demande rien : je vois.
Sous la honte qui me dévore,

---

[255] Lucienne Gaulard-Éon (née Lucienne Gaulard Conquet; 1885 – 1962): French poet and author of *Une Pierre au Temple* ("A Stone at the Temple"), Paris: A. Lemerre, 1914.

[256] Marcel Drouet (1888 – 1915): French poet and author of *L'Ombre qui tourne, poèmes* ("The Turning Shadow"), Paris: Dorbon aîné, 1912. Drouet was killed during military combat on the Eastern Front, in Consenvoye in Woëvre.

Je cache mon front dans mes doigts.[257]

In Paris, seeking a refuge from that awful liaison unworthy of an artist such as he, he tried to make up with another woman who would not change her life for him. Then Jean-Marc went from one café to another, from Les Halles to the Quarter, and full of bitter disappointment, spent his nights reciting versus without paying attention to anyone. The high boots he wore gave him the air of a gentleman farmer: his frank way of speaking, his enthusiasms, his feverish eyes, sometimes got him into trouble, but Jean-Marc would not avoid it and, shivering in the early morning which found us outdoors, he would sigh:

Que l'aube est froide après une nuit d'insomnie ![258]

Tristan Derème, whom Claudien and I had left to finish his studies at the lycée in Agen, and Jean-Marc as well sent me from the provinces poems they had just written and they were, in the poisoned atmosphere of the literary powwows of the time, like a breath of comforting fresh air. I was not mistaken. Those poems of Jean-Marc and Tristan Derème are today on every lip and I had then the merit – if it is one – of being the first to recognize them and to make them known in my group.

I am proud of it and rightly so, as I am proud of having foreseen about 1913 that Pierre Benoît would be the novelist he has become. Who could have foreseen it, at that time, when Pierre was a facetious civil servant in the Ministry of Beaux-Arts? Charles Perrot[259] had brought us together – and

[257] "I love your sad eyes ... / Shut up! Why lie again? / I don't ask anything: I see. / Under the shame that devours me, / I hide my forehead in my fingers."

[258] "How cold is the dawn after a sleepless night!"

[259] Charles Perrot (1887 – 1914): French poet and author of *La Plainte intérieure* ("The Inner Complaint"), Paris: Bernard Grasset, 1909. Perrot died on 13 October 1914 while serving on the Western Front at Arras.

Derennes,[260] who played interminable poker games with Pierre in a dusty brasserie in the rue Médicis. Near a goldfish bowl under the sleepy eyes of the Madame, *threes of a kind, full houses, flushes* were everything. Derennes was losing, Pierre winning and afterwards, the astonishing young man would see us home and recite from memory a whole act of *Polyeucte* or, without forgetting one stanza, the whole of the *Légende des siècles*.[261]

He was sending perfect parodies ... in verse to newspapers, unsigned, and also editing the *Grande Anthologie* in which everyone got their deserts and he had the time of his life playing with difficulties. *Le Double Bouquet* which he edited for a hard-to-please, mean and cosmopolitan owner, enabled us to get some money, thanks to him. But that money was soon spent in the shadow of the goldfish of the brasserie and we had often to wait several months before getting any more.

Pierre Benoît was then as he is today, bounding about, always in a good humor. He did not like the grave M. Souday[262] very much, whose name he would write in the following manner for his own amusement.

[260] Charles Derennes (1882 – 1930): French poet, novelist, and journalist, who also wrote in Occitan (a Romance language, spoken in southern France and parts of Italy and Spain).

[261] *Polyeucte* is a five-act drama by Pierre Corneille. Hugo's *La Légende des siècles* ("The Legend of the Ages") is a poetry collection composed between 1855 and 1876.

[262] Paul Souday (1869 – 1929): French essayist and biographer, who joined the newspaper *Le Temps* in 1892 and was in charge of literary criticism from 1912 to 1929. Initially antipathetic to the work of Marcel Proust, Souady underwent an extreme volte-face and became one of his earliest supporters, authoring a Proust biography in 1927. He also published critical studies and biographies of André Gide, Paul Valéry, and Théophile Gautier. When the French poet and novelist René Maran became the first Black writer to win the Prix Goncourt in 1921 (for *Batouala*), Souday remained vehemently opposed to the award because he was convinced that a Black man was incapable of being a genius.

DAY

———

PAUL

– Paul *sous* Day – even then wanting to mystify him.[263]

He was very fond of a certain kind of bitters, which Derennes also loved, and he held forth at the refreshment room of the Gare d'Orsay where we all met. Those Milon bitters had their story. They were used as stakes for our bets and Derennes was seized with such a passion for them, that he discovered ways to keep on drinking them, even though the aperitif hour was long over everywhere in Paris.

With a metro ticket, we would go to the nearest station and, each on a platform, we would wait for a train. The first one whose train came in had won, and at once we went back to the quai d'Orsay to drink, the winner free of charge, a general round of those bitters which made us sick, till the next day at least.

The only one who was very dignified all through the proceedings was Pierre Benoît. He was never drunk. However, after the fifth or sixth goblet of the bitter mixture, he would suddenly talk so loudly that our neighbors would have vertigo. He was always on time at his office, which he reached through narrow passages crammed with archives and fallen plaster. He made me think – as Colette so well described him – of an amiable and cunning rat, who, knowing better than anyone the corners and recesses of the ministry, would tread lightly, bobbing up and disappearing. To catch him they would have needed a whole pack of ushers ... and more! The ushers helped him to escape every time, and then ashamed of their clumsiness would reply when reproached: "What can we do with M. Benoît? We believe he is in one place and he is already in another."

[263] Paul Souday = Paul *sous* Day = "Paul under Day."

And the other was the *Buvette*[264] of the Chamber where as secretary to several deputies, Pierre was telling stories; it was also the warm and perfumed boudoir of Maurice Rostand, the brasserie of the rue de Médicis, the refreshment room of Gare d'Orsay or, how am I to know? the apartment occupied at the Hotel Brighton, by the owner of the *Double Bouquet* when he was in Paris.

He would appear everywhere he was least expected, amuse the audience with his prompt repartees and then quickly disappear. None of his intimates could have said how he spent his time outside the café and the ministry, or with whom he associated. He paid mysterious visits to Suarès,[265] whom he admired, to Barrès,[266] to some pretty women, and never calculating the part he brought to a friendship, lost whole days meeting people who pleased him. Whatever one may say, it was not the need of intrigue that decided his tastes. In spite of sacrificing part of his time to it and in spite of his love for practical jokes, it was only necessary to quote to Pierre a verse of Baudelaire or Racine to make him, neglecting at once the greatest enterprises, go on with the quotation and recite by heart the *Fleurs du Mal* or any tragedy one wished.

His remarkable memory never failed him. He exercised it constantly and then would go back to his [schemes][267] and complete them with the greatest care.

[264] A small bar or refreshment stand where drinks and snacks are served.
[265] Joseph Suarès (1868 – 1948): French art critic, essayist, and poet associated with the Symbolist movement. A friend of Pablo Picasso and André Gide.
[266] Maurice Barrès (1862 – 1923): French novelist, journalist, and deputy in the French National Assembly, known for his anti-Semitic and nationalist rhetoric. He was also a member of the French Academy.
[267'] Boyd translates "retournant à ses combinaisons" as "go back to his combinations." Although *combinaisons* can be translated as "combinations" in certain contexts, here it refers more to plans, schemes, or strategies rather than a literal combination of elements.

He very quickly found out that one of his good friends who liked to drink immoderately had left Paris during the war without giving any forwarding address. With the help of directories and the *Bottin*[268] Pierre got busy. He wrote to his friend's old address and told him to go and see a certain Mr. X., Chairman of the Anti-alcoholic League of a town which he named, adding that with a certain amount of tact, he would get some Pernod out of him as the man was very fond of it. Absinthe was absolutely forbidden. It still is. The friend believed Pierre. He went to the chairman of the Anti-alcoholic League and after bewildering him for a long time with his incoherent talk was shamefully sent away, because, at last, unable to endure it any longer, he had familiarly struck the man on the paunch, and said convincingly:

"Come on, don't be nasty now ... Hand over the green poison ... I swear I won't tell anyone about it."

Anything was good enough to amuse Pierre. He had just written *Koenigsmark*,[269] and, very much embarrassed, wondered where he could market it. With it under his arm, he tried several times to approach our elders who, repulsed by his handwriting, took good care not to read a line of that mass of paper, till the day when discouraged he handed me his manuscript. I remember it well, it was in the rue de Buci, at Boileau's, at the Trois Portes where Dumur[270] lunched with us. I spent the night making out Pierre's hieroglyphics, but the next day my opinion was formed and Dumur, to whom I gave *Koenigsmark*, published it in the *Mercure de France*. We had won the first

[268] The *Bottin Mondain*: a social register that listed the contact information of le Tout-Paris and of French high society, including aristocrats, artists, and politicians, and of other prominent, elite figures of.

[269] *De Koenigsmark à Montsalvat* (Paris: Émile-Paul Frères, 1918; translated as *The Secret Spring*, 1920): Benoît's first novel, awarded the Grand Prize of the Académie française.

[270] Louis Dumur (1860 – 1933): Swiss novelist, poet, playwright, and editor in chief of the *Mercure de France*.

hand. Pierre, thanks to his talent, did the rest, and my pleasure as well as that of his readers was perfect.

*

How little is necessary in life to decide a man's fate! I had discovered that with my first book, *Jésus-la-Caille*, and I still see myself mounting the stairs of the *Mercure de France* when a colleague who shall remain unnamed stopped me and asked:

"Are you going to see Valette?"

"Yes," I corrected him, "Monsieur Valette."

"Why? For a book?"

"I am going to submit this one to him," I said shyly.

"Well," said the other, "he won't read it. My dear friend, I just left my third upon his table. Give up all hope! ..."

A few days later, Paul Fort was marrying his daughter to the painter Severini,[271] there were great rejoicings at the Café Voltaire and I was invited. When Paul Fort is the organizer of festivities they at once assume immense proportions. And, indeed, when I arrived, the Prince of Poets was standing upon the piano and singing. The guests were drinking and congratulating each other and Marinetti whose magnificent white automobile showed off beautifully on the gray pavement of the place de l'Odéon was abandoning himself to futuristic joys.[272] He was breaking the china. It was splendid. Everybody

---

[271] Gino Severini (1883 – 1966): Italian painter and prominent figure in the Futurist movement. Severini expatriated to Montmartre in 1906, where he befriended Modigliani and became closely associated with other avant-garde artists and writers. In 1946 he published his autobiography, *The Life of a Painter*. Café Voltaire was located at 1, place de l'Odéon.

[272] Filippo Marinetti (1876 – 1944): Italian poet, founder of Futurism, and author of the first Futurist Manifesto (1909). With the Futurist's emphasis on dynamism and speed, it's amusing to recall Fernande Olivier's anecdote about spending an evening at Marinetti's hotel room, where he spoke to Picasso and Apollinaire nonstop for ten hours. During WWII Marinetti

was shouting himself hoarse celebrating this charming union. Parisian grace and the ultramodern Italian art! Then Paul Fort rapped for silence and asked me to "sing" a song. I agreed willingly. Apollinaire was watching me with his small eyes. I sang. It was a street song I had learned in the popular dance halls and it pleased them to such an extent that I had to come out with all my repertoire, to the great joy of a lady whom I did not know and who asked me my name.

It was Rachilde, wife of M. Valette, editor of the *Mercure de France*.

"Well, the boss knows my name."

"What, the boss?"

"He'll explain," I went on, flattered by Rachilde's insistence. "I took a novel to him ..."

"No, really?"

"Yes!"

"You bandit," Apollinaire said to me, when he saw me risking my chances thus. "Now you are in for it. You also, my little brother, will soon be one of the clan. That was a well-played hand."

"What do you mean?"

"I mean that Rachilde will keep after Valette till she gets your manuscript ... And she'll read it without waiting long, be sure of that. You can't have a better ally in the place than Rachilde ... wait ... and you'll see ..."

Guillaume Apollinaire had prophesized correctly. *Jésus-la-Caille* pleased the author of *Monsieur Vénus*, she made the *Mercure* take it and it was published within three months.

attempted to convince the Fascists to make Futurism the official state art. When it was criticized for being "foreign" and "radical," he declared that Futurism was purely "Italian" and that there were "no Jews" or foreign influences in the movement.

That is the way things came to pass. Without Rachilde, to whom I owe everything and who has not ceased to wish me well, I might still be playing one of "the young literati" in brasseries where fame is as bitter as gall or the dregs of an empty glass of beer.

> *La gloire éclôt, jaunit, se fripe*
> *Et se fane de l'aube au soir,*
> *Et j'aime mieux fumer ma pipe*
> *Que renifler son encensoir ...*[273]

Derème wrote to me from his province ... I understood what he meant and knew he was right. As a real romantic poet, because the school of that name deserves it, I would rather have my pipe, my quiet life and especially my friends than the vain noise of celebrity.

My friends never changed: La Vaissière, Tristan Derème, Jean Pellerin, Édouard Gazanion, Mac Orlan, Dorgelès, Mario Meunier, Pierre Benoît. I saw them often. I went to Montmartre to see some of them. I stayed in the Quarter to see the others and nothing in the world would have tempted me, except the prospect of seeing them. Getting up late and not daring, sometimes, to worry Baptiste, who had regular hours, I used to go to a bistro in the rue des Saint-Pères where I knew I would find Apollinaire still sitting at table and waiting for me. What a man he was! He would welcome me joyously, order soup and, although he was at the coffee stage, begin all over again to keep me company, and then go back to his pigeonhole.

His extreme stoutness, though it made him puff at the slightest effort, gave him an air of great authority. A gourmand in the best sense of the world, enormous, appetizing to look at,

---

[273] "The blooming glory yellows and withers / And wilts from dawn to dusk, / And I'd rather smoke my pipe / Than sniff its censer." Tristan Derème, *Le Poëme de la Pipe et de l'Escargot*, Paris: Émile-Paul Frères, 1920, p. 9.

he broke between his teeth the bones served to him, sucked them, covered himself with grease and, then, telling some story about a painter, made his chair groan under his weight without worrying about his fate. What did he have to fear? He looked like some big laughing god, so steady upon his base that, even if the chair broke, he had his big hassock to soften the shock. The more he ate, the gayer he became, with a physical gaiety which shown all over him. It was devastating. It had no limit and no setback. The most astonishing thing was that although heavy with meats, bread, wine and soup and the rest, which he had eaten twice over, Apollinaire was still able to work until evening in his apartment on the boulevard Saint-Germain, where his secretaries were waiting for him.

Under his roof, in a big room encumbered with books, small statues, cubistic paintings and Negro art, these gentlemen were ready, waiting for orders. Guillaume loved to be a tyrannical buffoon. He came in, looking very severe, took off his collar and his coat, then, filling a very light earthenware pipe, sat down. Then he began what he called the "poisonous work," because he did for several publishers very odd work and the best that could be said of it was that it was composed of clippings stuck on banking slips or pieces of paper, scribbled on by him or by others and painfully assembled. As the different chapters of the book began to fatten many covers, Guillaume became himself again. He would burst out sometimes into a heavy satisfied laugh and continue his work with scissors.

His laugh was his strength, his wealth, his fecund and powerful means of expression. No one who has not heard it, its thunderous quality, can have a real idea of Guillaume Apollinaire's work. It is the foundation stone for a building made up of rare materials, fables, gossip, new and sublime ideas, poetry, ordinary sayings, the whole worked into a mortar which only that marvelous man knew how to prepare, sweating over it for long hours.

He inspired real veneration and he deserved it, because of the original turn of his imagination.

Louis de Gonzague Frick[274] knows this. At that time, with a top hat, a monocle in his eye, and new gloves, the admiration – I mean the cult – he had for Apollinaire made him go every morning to see him. Gonzague Frick rang. Guillaume opened the door and saw his assiduous admirer, who bowed and asked:

"Monsieur Apollinaire?"

"That's I," the poet would answer.

Louis de Gonzague Frick then presented an apple to Guillaume, which he would hold out as the purest of symbols. Guillaume would take the apple and crunch it with pleasure.

Only to the author of *Alcools* could such an adventure happen, because, whatever has been said about him – even though he was a man and a very fat one at that, his appearance also indicated that he was one of those genii of the old German ballads, who, seeking a body to lodge in, had found his suitable ... Wasn't it like him to amuse himself by terrifying his first collaborator by making him copy whole pages of the dictionary which he then read with delight. He loved the comical and all kinds of jokes and at times he carried them very far. One whole winter he wrote to a woman dealer in odds and ends in the rue du Vieux-Colombier whose sly humor showed itself in the poems she put up outside her shop. Guillaume would read one of these poems, go back home, write an answer, post it and eagerly wait for the sequel. We went together in the evenings to see the new efforts of the woman and Guillaume, convulsed with laughter, would recite loudly the extraordinary verses.

[274] Louis de Gonzague Frick (1883 – 1958): French poet, literary critic, founder of several journals, and a close friend of Apollinaire, whom he first met at the Collège Saint-Charles in Monaco (Apollinaire dedicated the poem *Lul de Faltenin* to him). Frick appears in Jean Vigo's film, *Zéro de conduite* (1933), playing a prefect, and in Pierre Chenal's *L'Affaire Lafarge* (1938), in the role of a clerk. He's also portrayed in a painting by Marie Laurencin.

Voyez ce bon gros militaire
Glorieux de sa fourragère ![275]

the lady had written one day. Guillaume read the piece till the end – it was far from being complimentary – bowed and took me at once to a café.

"What a —" he said.

And I believe he was really annoyed.

That is all for the poet. The art critic was another matter because the profit one gets from the society of painters is more valuable than the criticism one makes.[276] Picasso had taught Guillaume that and had convinced him. "It is the time for masters," wrote the author of *Calligrammes* in his *Méditations Esthétiques*, and, further along in the same work, he added: "One can paint with what one wants, pipes, stamps, postcards, playing cards, candelabras, pieces of oilcloth, collars, painted papers or newspapers." We must not offend anyone. But since it was a question of painting, why did Guillaume neglect color on principle?

"The day the Cubists use color," he confided seriously to me, "they will be done for!"

One can see the paradox. Guillaume cultivated it carefully. He loved it. He owed to it his successes as a critic, when on the terrace of the charming Café de Flore, the painters sat around him and tried to make use of his teaching.

Guillaume also used to say:

"It is by the quantity of work furnished by an artist that one measures the value of a work of art."

[275] "Look at this big, hefty soldier, / glorious in his braided decorations!"

[276] "It is no coincidence that the main critic to pay significant attention to non-French artists before the First World War was himself a foreigner: Apollinaire.... He was the most active and important supporter and defender of modern art both before and even during the First World War." Kenneth Wayne, *Modigliani and the Artists of Montparnasse*, p. 26.

And he wrote on paper the most contradictory theories without worrying about the results.

These beautiful discourses, mixed with laughter, bear their fruit today, but Guillaume is not here anymore, alas, to help maintain through his life and his imagination the scaffolding of humor and truth which he worked up while serenely smoking his pipe. Salmon, who is very clever, took care not to add to his account such a heavy and badly balanced inheritance. He "passed his hand" and perhaps is quite amused to see Jean Cocteau making use of the legacy.

How good it is to live and to wonder at "the way of the world" and to see that, at bottom, the stupidity of certain sets is enough to amuse them. Without Jean Cocteau, who would have believed that Cubism would delight the snobs! He "got them," however, and that poet, born of Rostand with the *Prince Frivole* passes today as the couturier of the arts, as a precursor, as a – I don't know what![277] As a perfumed rhetorician, as a man

[277] By associating Cocteau with the playwright Rostand, Carco is perhaps suggesting that Cocteau's personal and artistic style is influenced by the same sort of outdated theatricality that one finds in Rostand's dramas. *Prince Frivole* refers to the title of Cocteau's second book, *Le Prince frivole* ("The Frivolous Prince"; 1910), a verse anthology. Carco was by no means the only one to critique Cocteau for being flighty, frivolous, and vain. André Gide once remarked "He is incapable of seriousness," while Picasso often regarded him as a buffoonish court jester ("Cocteau was born with a crease in his trousers"). Carco's characterization of Cocteau strongly contrasts with the more profound image he conjures of Apollinaire, whom he portrays as a serious, dedicated poet and critic worthy of respect. Carco will conclude the passage by lamenting Apollinaire's absence and suggesting that his lasting legacy is now being appropriated by others, notably Jean Cocteau. The latter is portrayed as a spurious inheritor, a "perfumed rhetorician," and a clever inventor of enigmas and rebuses, all of which implies a lack of substance and originality as compared to Apollinaire's more authentic vision. But one wonders if Carco may have been influenced in his views through his association with René Gillouin, who, as a right-wing politician, would later denounce Cocteau in the most vicious, vitriolic, and reactionary of terms. One also wonders what Carco would have thought if – while he

cleverer than most, the inventor of enigmas and rebuses, he is the beloved of all the old ladies and the very young men and his reputation – which is not negligible – rests in great part on the good jolly jokes of our dear Apollinaire, and for the rest, on Negro jazz and the mortuary setting of the fashionable *Boeuf sur le toit* and the still more fashionable Grand Ecart.[278]

was fleeing to Switzerland with his Jewish wife – he could have read Cocteau's diary at the time: "[Cocteau's] *Journal, 1942-1945* revealed to what an astonishing extent Cocteau went on living the same sort of life, professionally and socially, that he had had before the defeat. Out of the diary emerges a man totally self-absorbed, a solipsist who filtered everything through narrow personal interests. In the world of Jean Cocteau there was no war worth noticing, no Occupation, no cold, hunger or suffering, no disappearances or arrests, much less reprisal executions. The deportation of Jews in September 1942 was recorded in three pitiless words, *'Les juifs partent.'* ['The Jews are leaving.'] His record of the times gives the impression that the Germans he knew were visiting tourists rather than officers of the invading army of a cruel enemy. 'Long live the shameful peace!' he once said. And that, *grosso modo*, summed up his state of mind throughout the Occupation…. Cocteau's high opinion of Hitler is the biggest surprise to emerge from the diary. Yet perhaps it should not surprise, since both were men of the theatre." See Spotts, *The Shameful Peace*, p. 224.

[278] Le Boeuf sur le toit ("The Ox on the Roof"): a famous cabaret bar located at 28, rue Boissy d'Anglas, near the Eglise de la Madeleine. During its reign in the 1920s Le Boeuf would serve as the "cradle of modernism in French painting, film, and literature … The pianist Jean Wiener once recalled an evening at Le Boeuf in the early 20's: 'At one table were Andre Gide, Marc Allegret, and a woman. Alongside them, Diaghilev, Kochno, Picasso and Misa Sert. A bit farther on, Mistinguette, Volterra and Maurice Chevalier. Against the wall, Erik Satie and René Clair and his wife. Then I saw Picabia arguing with Paul Poiret and Tristan Tzara. Cocteau and Radiguet were saying hello at every table. Fernand Leger got up and asked me to play the 'St. Louis Blues' and, in passing, Moyses, the owner, told me that Artur Rubinstein would be in after his concert." See Frank J. Prial, "Heyday of Paris's Le Boeuf, Cradle of Modernism, Re-created at Gallery," *New York Times*, 15 July 1981, Section C, p. 17. The other legendary Jazz Age nightclub was Le Grand Ecart ("The Grand Split," also created by Louis Moyses), located at 7, rue Fromentin, near the boulevard Clichy. The moniker of this

That would have amused Guillaume a great deal and would not have troubled him much, he who carried upon his shoulders without weakening the sphere which bends Atlas and half smothers him. Maybe it is not the same sphere or this one is emptier and easier to manage, like those celluloid balls that children play with. Why not? Seeds in the inside make them sound like clown's bells and, according to the winds, they roll for the amusement of the onlookers, and the small athlete with his mad agility laughs under his faked burden, makes faces and trembles at the thought of being found out. Look at him. It is a miracle every time and when the sphere falls on the ground instead of saying, as did his good master Guillaume:

A la fin les mensonges ne me font plus peur,[279]

he stamps his feet, grows angry and pours out floods of tears, as empty as the ball he plays with.

I would rather have Apollinaire, his lies and his errors, than all the shameless mistakes with which his pupil, too clever for us, astonishes himself and which he expects will not grow old. Apollinaire, at least, was a real poet, a writer worthy of the name, and had moreover an inquiring and surprising mind. He lost himself in his love of art, and did not profit by it. I see him still at the end of the war, working hard at painful and mercenary jobs that barely fed him. Poor Guillaume Apollinaire! He remained on the breach, struggling till the last

trendy *boîte* is somewhat ironic; despite being "grand" it was also known as the smallest (and thus most exclusive) nightclub in Paris. As noted by Carco, "the still more fashionable Grand Ecart" catered to a chic and wealthy clientele.

[279] "In the end, lies no longer scare me." From the poem "Fiançailles" ("Engagement" or "Betrothal"), published in the review *Pan*, November-December 1908, p. 320-323, and later included in the collection *Alcools*.

moment, exhausting himself, tearing himself apart. Just like Moréas, who declared on his deathbed: "Classicists and romanticists, it is all a joke!" he has earned by his life, spent always in doing better and better, the right to be listened to and respected. If some have betrayed his memory and have methodically exploited him, thinking to belittle him, they are free to do so! Let them judge themselves! Apollinaire opened other vistas: a good many of us still know it, and that is why, far from going to seek what still remains alive of him in the bars beloved by Jean Cocteau, it is in Montparnasse that we shall find him.

*

Montparnasse owes its birth to Guillaume Apollinaire, who was the first to take us to Baty[280] and found himself joyfully welcomed everywhere. His presence in those places where the mixture of races brings an uneasy movement, created a sacred union of the arts, fixed it, crystallized it.[281] As soon as he spoke, Guillaume gave voice to the crowd of poets and painters who, as they listened to him, thought they were listening to themselves and bound their fate to his words. Before it could be noticed, as he sat beside his cousin Paul Fort, whose domain included the long Boul'Mich', Bullier,[282] the Luxembourg and

[280] Square Gaston Baty, a triangular-shaped "square" named after a Montparno theatre actor. A playground inside hosts a statue of the painter Chaim Soutine.

[281] Marcel Duchamp regarded Montparnasse as "the first truly international colony of artists we ever had." James Charters, *This Must Be the Place*, London: Herbert Joseph, 1934, p. 295.

[282] The Bal Bullier: a popular dance hall frequented by students, artists, and intellectuals, created by François Bullier in 1847, and located at 31, avenue de l'Observatoire, near the corner of boulevard Saint-Michel. "After the war I remember no more nights when howling students trooped from the Bullier to promenade *en monome* (Indian file, with a hand on each shoulder), the girls dropping their cloaks to dance nude on the tables of the Café d'Harcourt and the Café du Panthéon, amid laughter, bravos, witty sallies

the Closerie des Lilas, he traced the limits of his own which, from the Café des Deux-Magots where Jarry had once conferred upon him the order of the Gidouille,[283] spread through the rue de Rennes and the boulevard Raspail to the intersection of that boulevard with the boulevard Montparnasse. Had he not already sent his scouts towards Plaisance, where the custom officer Rousseau lived, and made the charming rue de la Gaîté his headquarters? Moréas recognized him, Moréas the sovereign of Les Halles and of the Vachette, who understood nothing else of this new spirit. But he had to admit it. Guillaume had a finger in everything. Painting and poetry decorated with two very noble jewels his cardboard crown and, as he drank mightily, very little was necessary to make his gang and the *"poisses"* [rowdies] all around shout at any time of the year: "The King drinks! The King drinks!" raising their glasses to join in a toast with him.

*

The Îles-Marquises was not an ordinary drinking place. It was close to the headquarters of the police inspector, where the poet Raynaud[284] looked after his colleagues and his usual "society," composed of painters, girls, models and pimps, was full of

flavored with *gauloiserie*, but without a rude or vulgar gesture." Charles Douglas, *Artist Quarter*, p. 137. Roger Shattuck sums up Le Bal Bullier as "a disreputable Latin Quarter dance hall for students and street-walkers." *The Banquet Years*, p. 26.

[283] Alfred Jarry (1873 – 1907): French symbolist writer, proto-Dada figure, and author of the play *Ubu Roi* (1896). The "Order of the Gidouille" was a fictitious award (with a nonsensical name) created by Jarry.

[284] Ernest Raynaud (1864 – 1936): Parisian police commissioner, leading poet of Jean Moréas' "Roman school," and a member of the extreme right-wing monarchist political party, *Action Française*.

respect at the sight of Guillaume and listened to him with open mouths.

It is because the dear fat man was never afraid of what he said and always celebrated the genius of the custom officer, that he astonished those gentlemen and ladies with his bright conversation. In the rue de la Gaîté a raffle of some of the works of the custom officer had not created a stir, it had even passed unheralded, until Guillaume, mounting his favorite hobbyhorse, appeared and changed everything.

During Apollinaire's time, the painting market was not what it has since become, but trading was already visible under the honeyed words, and the idiots were taken in by it. However there were still some people who were sincere. Guillaume did not lie. He was the first to suffer on account of his tastes and he was very much embarrassed when Dunoyer de Segonzac, for example, was sitting at his table and the aimless talk went on:

"Well!" said Dunoyer, who had been at the École des Beaux-Arts and who frequented Apollinaire's crowd, "I exchanged my one-eyed horse for a blind one."

He was not very much mistaken.

And indeed, I recall how little authority real artists like Dunoyer de Segonzac, Luc-Albert Moreau, Modigliani, had at the talks on Tuesdays at the Café de Flore. The two first mentioned have arrived since.[285] As for Modigliani he is dead and has reached since his death the first rank he should have occupied during his life.

[285] To "have arrived" = to have achieved success and acclaim.

XV

How painful it is for me to speak of the great poverty the unfortunate Modi had to struggle with till the end of his life. He lived first in Montmartre, then one saw him at the Rotonde,[286] drawing without ceasing in a notebook the pages of which he crushed and tore. A dealer had believed in him, had tried to impose him upon the public, had grown tired of him and finally had not renewed his contract. May God forgive him! Modi wandered in a hostile Paris, without money or hope, a red handkerchief around his neck in the winter instead of an overcoat, laughing at heaven and earth, like a cursed child. He struggled. He agreed to be imprisoned by another dealer who made a studio of his cellar, paid him some twenty francs every evening and quarreled with him very often. There seemed to be a curse on this very noble man. He was good looking, but alcohol and misfortune pulled him down; he was intelligent, but brutes managed him; proud and easygoing, he loved his art and served it passionately, but life humiliated him and in every

[286] The Café de la Rotonde opened in July 1911 at 103 (and then 105), Boulevard Montparnasse. During its heyday as a working class pub it was frequented by Picasso, Modigliani, Salmon, Apollinaire, Jacob, Derain, Vlaminck, Mac Orlan, Vaillant, Kisling, Ossip Zadkine, Charles Beadle, Beatrice Hastings, and many other avant-garde artists, writers, and denizens of the demimonde. La Rotonde is prominently featured in Charles Beadle's novel *Dark Refuge*, which contains one of the earliest fictionalized portraits of Modigliani, based on Beadle's frequent encounters with him. In *Artist Quarter* Beadle reports that "at the height of its fame" La Rotonde, with its "thoroughly cosmopolitan crowd," was nicknamed "the navel of the world." In her memoir Marevna reports: "One day Charlie Chaplin came in, wearing his bowler and swinging a black cape; the crowd surged toward him crying 'Charlot! 'Charlot!' and literally carried him upstairs to the restaurant. This was truly the apotheosis of the café. Lenin came in once, very quietly and without any ovations." Marevna, *Life with the Painters of La Ruche*, p. 35.

way, as if with a sadistic pleasure, made him pay for having the incredible audacity to pretend that he was born to a great destiny.

"You must feed the artists," he said, in the rue Campagne-Première to an Italian peasant woman[287] who kept a very humble restaurant where he went.

"And why should I feed them?"

"Because," Modigliani answered, "an artist can't earn his own living. He paints ... As for the rest? Pfft! ... How can you tell? Look."

And, doing an astonishing fresco on the wall, he would ask in a gale of laughter:

"You like that?... Really..."

"All right, sit down here and eat," the good woman would finally say.

The customers of the place, who were masons and day laborers with white smocks, would silently make room for the painter beside them on the benches and agree with him.

For several years, always hungry but always drinking, because people offer a drink much more easily than food,

---

[287] Rosalia Tobia (1860 – 1932): born in Picinisco, Italy, and remembered as the proprietor of a small bistro, Chez Rosalie, located at 3, rue Campagne-Première. The drawings Modigliani had given her in exchange for meals were carelessly stored in her basement and were later destroyed by rats. Rosalia arrived in Paris while employed as a maid for Princess Ruspoli. She also worked as a model for Odilon Redon, Bouguereau, and Whistler. Chez Rosalie was patronized mostly by bricklayers and other *ouvriers*, as well as by painters such as Modigliani (who occasionally slept there), Jules Pascin, Picasso, and Utrillo, and by the celebrated model, Kiki de Montparnasse. About four years after Rosalia's death Charles Beadle interviewed her son, Luigi Tobia, who was then living in Cagnes-sur-mer. (During this period Beadle was also living in the Côte d'Azur, teaching English in Grasse.) He reports: "Luigi also speaks of his mother not only throwing Modi's drawings into the cellar among the rats, but, in fits of rage during their frequent rows, actually burning them in the kitchen stove – even his sketch books." See *Artist Quarter*, p. 250.

Modigliani led the most foolish existence. Women, struck by his good looks, were dying for love of him, foreigners, humble girls, but Modi always left them before they could tie him down. His drunkenness broke everything as soon as he could feel the chain and then he would miserably go from one bar to another, where I met him, often, his pencil in his hand. He was a dark man who had kept, perhaps from his Italian origin, a very decided taste for endless discussions, politics, art and vermouth. His corduroy clothes, his wide-brimmed hat, his kerchief, his very quick repartee, almost lightning-like, and his laugh, which made him cough all the time, drew attention to him. But Modigliani did not care! He had no pride nor a trace of self-sufficiency and when, moved by his great poverty, we tried with misgivings to help him a little, he refused to take his poverty seriously.

An exhibition at Mademoiselle Weill's[288] to whom the painters, when they take her their pictures, sing to the same tune as *Mad' moisell' Rose*, this innocent verse:

Ah ! Mad' moisell' Weill-le,

[288] Berthe Weill (1865 – 1951): born into a poor Jewish family in Paris, Weill founded one of the most important art galleries in the early twentieth century. "In the first years of the century," writes Picasso scholar Michael C. FitzGerald, "only one gallery truly specialized in twentieth-century art – the Galerie Berthe Weill." FitzGerald, *Making Modernism*, Berkeley: University of California Press, 1996, p. 24. In 1900, after Picasso moved to Paris, Weill became his first dealer. In December 1901 she opened Galerie B. Weill (initially located at 25, rue Victor-Massé). The following year she arranged the first Parisian exhibit of works by Picasso and Matisse. Endowed with a prescient vision, Weill was an early supporter of the Fauves and Cubists, with a roster that included Suzanne Valadon, Utrillo, Vlaminck, Derain, Raoul Dufy, Diego Rivera, and, briefly, Modigliani (hosting his only one-man show, which was arranged at Zbo's request). As a result of the Occupation, she was forced to close her gallery in 1941. In 2022 the University of Chicago Press published *Pow! Right in the Eye! Thirty Years behind the Scenes of Modern French Painting*, a translation of Weill's autobiography.

J'ai un p'tit tableau, un p'tit tableau à vous offrir ...
C'est pas un' merveil-le
Mais payez-le nous et j'vous jur' qu'ça nous f'ra plaisir,
Mad'moisell' Weil ...[289]

An exhibition, I was saying, of Modi brought her her first success. But what an uproar in the street! The nudes of the painter could be seen from the outside and attracted the curious at once. Small errand boys, messenger boys, clerks, milliners' apprentices were jammed in front of the shop, literally crushing each other, and the police commissioner, astonished by the crowd, went also to the window and declared it was a scandal. It was an epic. By order of the police official, Mademoiselle Weill had to go to the police station, where she tried in vain to defend Modigliani. Nothing could be done about it. Traffic was suspended by the crowds and the admirable canvases had to be taken down from the walls,[290] and not one was sold, even at the lowest price.[291]

At that time through a sudden kindness of heaven, tired without doubt of worrying such a great artist, Modigliani discovered at the Dôme[292] a friend who shared his black and despondent poverty, ran around Paris and swore to make him

[289] "Ah! Mademoiselle Weill, / I have a little painting, a little painting to offer you ... / It's not a marvel / But pay us for it and I swear it will make us happy, / Mademoiselle Weill ..."
[290] When Weill asked the police commissioner, "Besides, what's wrong with those nudes, anyway?" his stuttering reply was a classic: "Those disgu– ... they ... they ... h-h-h-have *hairs!*" She concludes: "His shrieks of outraged prudishness clearly revealed a sick mind." See Berthe Weill, *Pow! Right in the Eye!*, William Rodarmor, trans., Chicago: The University of Chicago Press, 2022, p. 102-103.
[291'] Here Carco adds his own footnote: "One of them, a reclining nude, was sold for 22,000 francs in 1925 at the Salle Drouet." Roughly $1031.80 in 1925, the equivalent of $18,184.27 in 2024.
[292] The Café du Dôme and La Coupole were the other grand brasseries across the street from La Rotonde and Le Select.

celebrated. That friend never doubted Modigliani's genius for one second. To help him to live, he would have sold his clothes, his watch, his shoes, slept outdoors in the midst of winter and would have borrowed money from anybody at any rate. His name was Zborowski.[293] He was not yet a dealer, but a poet, and he lived in the rue Joseph-Bara in a tiny flat where Modigliani often slept and aroused the neighbors. What love Zborowski had for his painter! What a great and understanding admiration! He deprived himself of everything for him, of tobacco, food and coal. And little by little he was able to give Modigliani canvases, colors, a humble studio and a few hundred francs a month which at least enabled him to eat, even if poorly.

When one went to see Zborowski, he would run down to buy a candle and, setting it in the neck of a bottle, he would take you into a narrow room without furniture, bare, desolate, in a corner of which the painter's canvases were heaped. Lighted by the candle, Zborowski showed his treasures, stroking them passionately with his hands and devouring them with his eyes, then, fascinated, he would spit with disgust, talk agitatedly and curse the fate which crushed Modigliani. The more agitated he was the more naturally would the words come to his mouth to express his strange and splendid feeling before those nudes, those figures, those portraits painted without any care for schools, but in which the painter's pure and blinding art were manifested.

"Such poetry!" Zborowski would say ecstatically.

He would stop, walk around again and then suddenly:

[293] Léopold Zborowski (1889 – 1932): Polish poet, born into a Jewish family in Zaleszczyki, who endured great personal sacrifices to lend Modigliani support and become his art dealer, a profession in which he had no prior experience. He also represented Chaim Soutine, Utrillo, Marc Chagall, and Derain. After Modigliani's death, the value of his work skyrocketed and Zbo's collection reaped great profits, but as a result of the Great Depression he lost all his assets and died in poverty.

"Do you know," he'd say, "I took about fifteen canvases the other morning to a dealer, I wanted a little money – a very little, to give to Modigliani – and the dealer did not want to buy… He said to me: 'Take them away … I am not buying …' Why? I would have given him the fifteen canvases for nothing, if only he had shown some appreciation for the paintings. No … And they don't want them … How stupid they are … They are not yet accustomed … But you shall see … later … not even later – soon … they'll pay high prices for those canvases they don't want now … they'll all want Modigliani's … and meanwhile, he has no money, he is unhappy, he fills one with pity."

"Well," I said to him, "sell me that nude, will you?"

"You love it?"

"It is very beautiful."

Zborowski uttered a shout of joy and then bringing the candle nearer to the canvas:

"Look, how beautiful the painting is," he exclaimed, "and how … Watch! It is admirable … Yes, admirable, isn't it?"

I could see that.

"Yes, Zborowski, admirable. I agree with you. It is a masterpiece."

He turned toward me and, showing me the picture he had laid aside:

"To you," he decided, "I won't sell … I shall give it. Here … I give it to you … because you love it."

"And the money for Modigliani?"

"No … Take it, I am so pleased you love it … Forget the money question … Don't bother about that … Tomorrow a man is coming to buy some clothes … he'll give twenty francs. That will be enough …"

And he came with me to my house, carrying that magnificent picture and refusing even at the last minute to accept a very small sum which, not being rich, I tried to force upon him.

It was my first picture, but the concierge who cleaned my room, in the quai aux Fleurs,[294] almost fell dead the next day when she discovered that nude above my bed.

*

Unhappy Modi! Almost five years were necessary before, one after the other, the finest [aficionados] and the most enlightened decided to have him in their collections. Meanwhile they would not listen to Zborowski, they laughed in his face, or else they did not receive him, offended that anyone should try to mock them in that way. Zborowski did not mind. He would leave the painting, come back, and talk and talk, until the day when, following my own taste, I wrote in a Swiss review called the *Éventail* an article which brought Zborowski two or three Swiss collectors who, thanks to the exchange, bought some nudes of Modigliani for almost nothing.[295]

The one I had in my room filled me with delight and yet not one of my friends admired it. They all called me mad, an idiot, an imbecile ... I let them joke as much as they liked and without asking their advice I began to save some notes from my slender

[294] Carco lived at 13, quai aux Fleurs, on Île de la Cité.

[295] Francis Carco, "Modigliani," *L'Éventail*, pp. 201-209. "Carco's was the only article devoted solely to Modigliani during his lifetime. Published in *L'Éventail* a year and a half after the exhibition took place, Carco's article is essentially a review of the ill-fated one-person exhibition and of Modigliani's art in general. Written before Modigliani's untimely death and, hence before a romantic myth developed around him, this article is one of the purest, most sensitive, and insightful pieces of writing ever penned about the artist and his work by someone close to him. Carco calls most art 'a meticulous copy' and writes that Modigliani has moved away from naturalism towards an art that is more poetic, graceful, and expressive. He gives special praise to Modigliani's drawings and his abilities as a draughtsman." Kenneth Wayne, *Modigliani and the Artists of Montparnasse*, p. 67.

resources for which Zborowski sold me other paintings by Modi and shouted it to the housetops.

What delight I felt in the mornings, in the quai aux Fleurs, when I woke, amongst those nudes with milky and orange flesh, under their blinking eyes and their magnificent forms! Two windows in a corner offered through their light the clean fresh landscape of the Seine. The shrill cries of tugs, the smoke, the panting of the motors upon the river surrounded me like a dream. In the summer, especially, when the open windows let a warm sun come in with the smell of the big trees, golden and rustling, from the point of the Île Saint-Louis, a light drunkenness would seize me. With half-closed eyes, I saw the blue sky, the mirroring waters which threw to the ceiling a thousand circles within circles and sometimes – the moving flight of pigeons – a warm and soft caress, folding and unfolding wings whose shadows hardly appeared. Everything was delightful to me. Everything kept me late in bed in a serene immobility when the beautiful burning day's youthfulness and my own faced each other and thought of nothing. What could I have wished more charming and more agreeable! I had these nudes in my home like a lover, they were women I loved and I felt alive beside them. And they were alive: their presence excited me, as the sun rising high in the sky filled my room with wonderful fire.

If I tasted the full measure of that happy tide, which is to real love what music is to poetry, I owe it to Modigliani; because at the same time, I imagined his dreadful life, his passion to paint, and I closed my eyes. He was standing there, looking at me and asking me as he did one winter's night, when half drunk:

"You? ... You love my painting ... Hey? And why? Do you understand it? ... You love it? ... As you love women? ... So! So! So! ... Yes ... That's it ..."

Every morning the same delight was waiting me, or else, when I had bought something new, I would wake ten times during the night to light my lamp and grow absorbed in the inexpressible contemplation. It was like an enchantment, but such a singular one, so subtle, so voluptuous that, in remembering it, I almost regret those days when I owned nothing and I was the richest man alive amongst my paintings and the scattered pages of my first novels.

Once upon a time Max Jacob lived in the house where chance had sent me two years before the war,[296] and the concierge remembered him very well. What an extraordinary woman that concierge was! She commented on everything and when frequently she would find me in bed in the great greatest disorder, she'd say to me:

[296] Max originally rented a room at 7, rue Ravignan but was evicted "for abuse of ether," since the flat was constantly filled with foul-smelling fumes. By January 1912 he was living at the Bateau Lavoir, right under Picasso's studio. That July he moved to Maurice Raynal's old *chambre* at 53, rue du Chevalier de la Barre. After an extended stay in Quimper, in January 1913 he returned to the Raynal room but then moved a few blocks away, to 49, rue Gabrielle, around the corner from his previous residence on rue Ravignan. He would remain there until he left Paris for good in 1921. (See Rosanna Warren, *Max Jacob*, pp. 167-190.) A *petite chambre* filled with bric-a-brac on the top floor of this rue Gabrielle building housed a retired legal clerk named Léon Angély (1848-1921): one the first Parisians to purchase work by Picasso. The two probably met during Picasso's first trip to Paris in 1900, when Isidro Nonell, an artist friend from Barcelona, shared his room in this same building with Picasso. A speculator of modest means, Angély also purchased Utrillos, Modiglianis, and other modern masters well before they had achieved recognition. Yet, he was almost completely blind. Legend has it that a young *gamine* named Joséphine accompanied "Père" Angély on visits to the artists' ateliers to serve as his "eyes." According to John Richardson, Picasso eulogized Angély and Joséphine in his "blind Minotaur" series (which portrays a young girl leading a blind Minotaur through a labyrinth), culminating in his most remarkable engraving: *La Minotauromachie* (1935). For more on this myopic visionary, see Rob Couteau, *A Blind Man Crazy for Color. A Tribute to Leon Angély: Illustrated by Picasso's Model and Muse, Sylvette David*.

"It is wrong, sir, to change all the time. Certainly ... and do you want to know what I think? The lady you had yesterday was much better than the one you had today."

"Please mind your own business."

"All right, sir ... And, as for those paintings, what an idea!"

"That's enough ..."

"No."

And the delightful creature would compare my Modigliani's to the landscapes the gentleman on the fourth floor had in his apartment ... landscapes where one could at least recognize something, while those horrible women ...

"Those beauties!" She would exclaim. "Ah! la! la! They look like ..."

"What?"

"Yes, sir!"

I had to get up and chase her away and she, very dignified, would open the door and call for help.

"Go to the devil!" I would shout, "and leave me alone!"

"All right, all right!

"You heard me?"

"And your mail, who will bring it up?"

"All right, bring up the mail," I answered, "but don't let me see you anymore. Put it under the door."

"Righto!" the old woman would answer.

So, punctually, when I was trying to work, Madame Delescalier[297] climbed my stairs softly, pushed a paper under my door as I had told her to do, and I picked up the paper and grew furious, for on it was written in big letters:

First mail: NOTHING!

Sometimes I would laugh at her, for my concierge's zeal for my welfare went so far that she would write on the pages of my manuscripts very motherly recommendations:

[297] A *jeu de mot*: "Madame de l'escalier" = "Madame of the staircase."

They would read: "Sir, take some orange flower tea as an infusion, very hot. Orange flower makes one sleep."

No one would believe it, but it is true, that woman, under the pretext of doing my room, would come in without warning and, seeing me at my desk, would mutter, as if seized with great admiration:

"What, you are working, let me look at you, sir, I won't disturb you ... Please let me ... It is so unusual ... "

And no matter how angry I grew, she did not leave the place. So, full of rage, I would dress and go out, while during my absence she would invite into my room the other tenants of the house and with them laugh to her heart's content about my "scandalous" pictures.

The stories she told about me defy the most inventive imagination. I was a monster, I did not pay her for her work and I made love to her. What else? She never stopped painting me in such a flattering and striking manner that my neighbors would always run away when they saw me on the landing. Not one would answer my greeting. I was pointed out, and if I came in at the break of day and in a good humor, Madame Delescalier announced my arrival by incredible yells and, to humiliate me, shut herself up in her narrow den, imitated the walk of a drunkard and shook her fist at me.

And yet she was a good woman and kindly as soon as she stopped being odious, because she took such good care of me that she would come up in the morning to tell me if it had been freezing:

"Put on your heavy overcoat, sir, it is terribly cold ... "

And if by any chance I were coughing, she went to the chemist and came back with a big bowl of tea, plasters, camphorated oil, aspirin tablets, potions and twenty drugs for which I had to pay afterwards.

XVI

There are thirteen letters in "quai aux Fleurs" and as I lived at number thirteen, Max Jacob told me it was lucky and that I ought to believe in it ... Yes, maybe, very lucky ... But I became superstitious very quickly. On the right, on the quai, Héloïse and Abélard's house not only sheltered a police station, but also Jean Dorsenne[298] the poet, and the engraver Louis Jou, who lived there, and I often waited to see Jou at his balcony before deciding what I was going to do with my day. If he did not show himself, I had to be content to look at four wild ducks which from the pale winter sky let themselves fall on the water like drops of ink ... or again, I would count the barges which were drawn in the wake of small, panting, squat tugs ... Four barges, four ducks and Louis Jou ... I could attempt anything ... If those were not forthcoming I would replace the ducks by the cops, or by the buttons missing on my clothes and I would go out happy.

Alas! How many avatars, how many polite refusals from editors, I had to endure in spite of all my calculations, and what stubbornness I needed to keep from getting tired of it. I never gave up. I went to the newspapers to offer them my tales for

[298] Jean Dorsenne (né Étienne Troufleau; 1892 – 1945): French poet, novelist, and journalist, born in Algeria, whose father was a literature professor. In 1922 Dorsenne and his wife, Micheline Picard, sailed from Rouen to Tahiti, remaining there until returning to Paris in 1926, where Dorsenne was employed by *L'Intransigeant* and *Le Figaro*. He published several novels influenced by his travels, such as *Mauruuru Tahiti, Un fils de cannibales, La Vie sentimentale de Paul Gauguin*, and *Les and Amants sans amours*. During the Nazi occupation Dorsenne refused to collaborate with Vichy-controlled newspapers and instead joined the Resistance. In 1942 he was arrested and imprisoned in Germany, then transferred to Sonneburg prison, in Poland. He eventually ended up in Buchenwald, where he died of pneumonia.

which, when they accepted them, they paid five francs. I wrote poems. I was happy to be alive. What a pleasure! In spite of being sent away from almost every place where I went to work, what did it matter? I accepted my fate and, far from being discouraged, I would gaily say to myself:

"Un jour viendra !"[299]

and dismissed my troubles.

If it had not been for the rent which, when due, generally found me high and dry and obliged me to borrow money from Hubert or from my acquaintances in the rue de Buci, it would have been too much luck. But what? The rent! I was accustomed to it and, moreover, the debts one contracted at Hubert's were paid for in songs. Why should I worry about them now? It would be rather late in the day. And in any case we were all in the same fix at the same time and never once did we blame Fate for not smiling at us, because we believed in her.

Do you remember, Mario, that night of Christmas Eve festivities when we stayed for three hours at the terrace of the Deux-Magots in front of a cold bock as cold as death, wet and shivering? It was raining. Such a beautiful night! And how it remains engraved in my memory. You slept at Rodin's house, at Meudon, as you were his secretary, amongst marbles which frightened you when you awoke in the night. Rodin had given you a holiday and all the money we had was a franc between us. Yes, in spite of that it was a beautiful night! So sad with the lanterns of the taxis and cabs, so bitter and so wet! A fresh smell impregnated it! The smell of the dripping horse chestnut trees and also the smell of victuals in pork-butchers' shops. We walked by without stopping, our hands in our pockets; we were young. We talked about our books, our friends, we recited poems to each other. And the wind heavy with water, the lights,

[299] "A day will come!" but more in the sense of "My day will come!"

the dark streets of the Quarter inspired us to such talk that, instead of feeling very poor, we felt the contrary, for eternal hope lived within us.

Remember ... but what is the use! We spent so many nights that way, that one more or less, what did it matter. It was life, as one of us said and he was quite right. With Claudien, who followed his demon, if we had to count the lost hours we would never stop. And yet I have forgotten none of our enthusiasms, our curiosities, the sincere friendship which bound us together and still does, our frankness, our generous flights. What did the rain, the north wind, the daily disappointments matter? They had no hold over us. They did not discourage us. Derain one evening confided to me:

"When things do not go well, I take my bike and I go away to Marseilles for a month, for a change of air."

"To Marseilles?"

"Or Cassis."

We did not go so far away, because we had no bikes and instead of having a change of air we were obliged to breathe always the same air in the rue de Buci and still managed to thrive on it.

It was at that time that a very extraordinary young man joined our group and I took to him at once on account of his mocking ways. He signed short articles in small reviews with the mysterious Christian name of Zavié, which the typesetters persisted in printing Zavie. As a joke, "Za la vie, Za la mort!" became the rally cry of our crowd. Bernouard had uttered it instinctively as a boy of the streets and that cry suited our new friend so well that he answered to it gracefully, but to revenge himself he called in a sinister tone "Francis Carcere Duro!"[300] and played tricks on me.

---

[300] The phrase "Carcere Duro" translates from Italian into English as "Hard Prison" or "Tough Prison."

That was his weakness; he played them on everybody and laughed afterwards only if they succeeded. The lock which fell on his forehead, his cold assurance, gave Emile Zavié a curious resemblance to Napoleon when he was young. He had the quick look, the reserve and the shyness of the young artillery lieutenant and when he let himself go, he would quickly regain his composure. What did one know about him? Nothing or almost nothing. He worked at Bernouard's in the afternoon, correcting proofs, spoke very little, left us about six o'clock, and was invisible till the next day, when he came back to the press and smoked cigars. If sometimes he wrote verses in secret, he never showed them to anyone. Verses? He pretended to be able only to dictate letters and to give a more correct turn to certain sentences submitted to his final judgment, or to answer, when Bernouard published a small book, *Les Regrets de Futile*:[301]

"Is silence not preferable?"

Bernouard annoyed him with his affected and untidy methods, bewildered him and I must say that the difference in the characters of those two astonishing gentlemen was so marked that it afforded us plenty of amusement.

So, proud of having learned by heart a quatrain about Bernouard, Zavié recited it:

> *Le soir où Bernouard, dédaigneux et futile,*
> *Dit à son secrétaire, effroyable nervi :*
> *"Soignez mon orthographe et corrigez mon style,"*
> *Fut le plus beau jour de Zavie.*[302]

---

[301] François Bernouard, *Les Regrets de Futile. Poèmes* ("Futile's Regret"), Paris: A la Belle Édition, 1912 (with a Preface by Marguerite de Charmoy).
[302] "The evening when Bernouard, disdainful and futile, / Said to his secretary, a dreadful henchman: / 'Take care of my spelling and correct my style,' / Was the best day of his life." In this last phrase we have a play on

The man in question asked coldly: "Is that yours? You know yourself perfectly."

"How is that?"

"Yes ... a *nervi* [henchman] ... a real one! ..."

And the resemblance to Napoleon disappeared instantaneously, because, unluckily, that day Emile Zavié wore a purple tie, a blue shirt, a beige waistcoat which proved that the boss was right.

But after all, a *nervi* – after Napoleon – was much more on my own level and it made me fonder of Zavié. He did not protest. I even thought that he was going to tell me an awful secret but he regained his self-possession and taking me off with him, demanded:

"You also prefer the *nervi* to Bonaparte?"

"Maybe!"

"Well, that's all right ... although Bonaparte ... Ah! Bonaparte! ... Napoleon!"

"Don't worry!"

"Yes, yes ... I must ..." he said.

"But why? On account of what?"

"On account of Stendhal," he answered, blushing with shame. "You know there is no other writer like him in the world. He is the greatest. He came from Grenoble like ... like your friend Pellerin ... and so, you see, to have dreamed only about that, to have loved only that, and then have that crackbrained Bernouard to allow himself ..."

He spoke and he gesticulated to such a degree, he who was generally so calm, so reserved, that I could not repress my laughter. Zavié looked at me, shook his head, and as I urged him to take things gaily:

words: "Sa vie" = "his life." Thus, *Fut le plus beau jour de <u>Zavie</u> = Fut le plus beau jour de <u>sa vie</u>*.

"Come and have a drink," he grumbled.

And he pulled me by the sleeve into a cheap restaurant as I was looking for a small café.

In that small restaurant it was almost totally dark. Wooden tables without tablecloths, shiny benches, a counter full of plates and half pitchers of light red wine, a pigeonhole for the napkins, filled up a big room which looked like the refectory of some seminary. There was sawdust on the floor. Upon the walls, the pale reflection of a gloomy day which filtered through the windows into the room and filled one with stupor and distrust.

"Monsieur Zavié," said a sleepy voice, "here already!"

"I have not come to eat, it is too early," answered my companion. "Light the gas, please, and give us some wine ..."

The gas was lit.

"It is amusing," I said to hide the painful impression which held me by the throat. "It is rather clean ... I did not know this place."

"I know it only too well," said Zavié bitterly.

He sighed and added: "I have been eating here for five years. One must have a good digestion."

"Of course!"

"Five years!"

He leaned towards me and continued, lowering his voice:

"I don't call it eating. I call it feeding oneself, and afterwards, I go regularly to the Havas Agency[303] to earn during the night enough to pay for my room, my laundry and my rations. Could you do it?"

"It is too depressing."

"And it is damp and above all it is sordid. The people who come here are almost all unemployed, poor derelicts who drink this sickening wine. To your health!"

[303] A French press agency founded in 1835, which instituted billboarding campaigns in 1923.

"Yes," I said, after having emptied my glass. "As a wine ..."

"The eats also," replied Zavié, looking at me sadly and proudly: "There you are, you see... in the morning, I write for myself; in the afternoon I scribble at Bernouard's and up till two or three in the morning I slave away at the agency ..."

"How do you manage it?"

"I have to do it."

I was thunderstruck and, suddenly understanding what price my friend had to pay daily for the right to live outside of realities, he appeared to me so different from all the others, that I did not dare laugh anymore and I only shook him sympathetically by the hand.

It was no laughing matter indeed! A sickening smell as of dirty military quarters prevented my mirth, and I told myself that Zavié was mistaken, that he was wrong not to risk everything rather than to live that mediocre existence which wore him out. At his age one plunges into the water, one does not think about a cutlet. Cutlets come of themselves or they do not come at all, that's the way it is, at least one's life does not depend on a cutlet, and the chances are great in any case. Why not take a chance on the cutlets? It is no use giving up before one has to.

"Do you really think so?" he snickered.

"I am sure of it."

"Yes, you are," said Zavié bitterly.

"Try first!"

"No."

"No? Listen," I went on, "I have cried with hunger like you and hunger does not frighten me. You see... one does not die of hunger."

"It may be!" he answered.

And beckoning to the [waiter], he paid for the half measure of wine; then, as it was time, or almost time, for him to sit down to his meal he ordered:

"One boiled beef, one cabbage, one coffee.

"Heavens! This discovery taught me to understand Emile Zavié perfectly. His attitudes, his airs, his romantic ways of avoiding all explanations, I understood them and his secret was not comforting or exciting. The more I preached to my friend, the more he evaded me, and when one evening, in the square Saint-Germain, he found one franc near a bench and put it in his pocket, the gesture he made revolted me:

"Twenty sous!" exclaimed a beggar woman who had seen Zavié pick up the small coin.

"Yes," said Zavié ... "Why? Is it so astonishing?"

"Sometimes I have the luck of finding two sous if I search well ..."

"That's not bad.

"I should say not!"

And as I was waiting to find in that strange young man an impulse I could approve, he took out the franc from his pocket, assured himself it was a good coin and, very sure of himself, said:

"It is always twenty sous I find; I would not take the trouble to bend down for less."

Then thinking I was not watching him, he threw the small coin on the ground at the feet of the poor woman and turned on his heels in a very Stendhalian way.

That's how we were. We imitated either Stendhal or Villon and would rather have killed ourselves than give up those affectations to which we adopted ourselves so easily. Whatever the hour of the night or the day, our affectations came first and I do not know that we should blush for it or if – regretting that time – we have not the right to a kind of legitimate pride in telling ourselves that those were the happy times and in laughing about them.

Why should we lie? Without that love, life would have offered us a long and sad series of difficulties of all kinds, privations, and discrepancies, and more than once courage would have failed us. Courage? The reason for our existing and with it the bitter conviction that the career of letters needs good brains far less than an ostrich stomach and a hard hide.

Frédé taught us that by writing upon the shutters of the Lapin this inscription full of good common sense:

"The first duty of a gallant man is to have a good stomach."

It is true that that was in Montmartre but we remembered the lesson and it was very useful to us later on in life.

If it had not been for that, when one evening Roland Dorgelès, knowing that I was without any resources in Paris, brought me to the *Homme Libre*, Clemenceau's paper,[304] and had me appointed its art critic, would I have accepted that work for fifty francs a month? The Tiger paid badly. Nevertheless, I was assured of at least fifty francs and I rejoiced. André Billy worked on the same paper. He probably was earning more than I was and behind his horn-rimmed spectacles he was already the man that nothing disturbs. His elegance floored me. His cold manner, his polite ways, his kindness, when he tried to dissimulate, and the walks we sometimes took, following the boulevards to the Left Bank, enlightened me about him. But how was I to exchange my nature for his! I could not do it. But wisely, gently, Billy warned me about life and taught me how to husband my resources and not waste my time and strength.

[304] Concerned that France was ill-prepared for war with Germany, in May 1913 Georges Clemenceau founded the *Homme Libre* in order advocate for rearmament and an increase in munitions production. Following government censorship and suppression of the paper in 1914, it reappeared under the title *L'Homme Enchaîné*. Known for his fierce rhetoric, Clemenceau was nicknamed the "Tiger." Besides serving two nonconsecutive terms as prime minister, he published a fictional story, "How I Became Presbyopic" (1894), which was illustrated by Toulouse-Lautrec.

What work we had on the *Homme Libre*! Jean Pellerin also worked there. He edited a literary letter, on the second page, near mine, in which he wrote about painters, and with the help of our friendship, those fifty francs a month Clemenceau paid us for a daily article appeared magnificent, because to earn them Jean Pellerin and I met once a day in the offices of the paper.

Dorgelès, Billy, Pellerin ... To the number of my friends I soon added Adrien Bertrand[305] who "did" the Chamber for the paper and, as an artist, wrote for himself poems which he published in obscure reviews with very few subscribers and no readers. Adrien Bertrand was somebody and the most loyal comrade I have ever met in that circle where, with the exception of Gombault,[306] secretary to the editors, no one could stand me.

[305] Adrien Bertrand (1888 – 1917): French novelist, poet, and short-story writer whose most surreal antiwar fiction was composed while he was bedridden in a military hospice, slowly dying from complications from his wounded lungs. Before the war, he worked as a journalist for papers such as *Paris-Midi* and *L'Homme Libre* and founded the literary journal *Les Chiméres*.

Despite his pacifist beliefs Bertrand joined the French cavalry in WWI and earned a reputation for heroism. Hit by shrapnel from a German shell in October 1914, he was told that his lungs were permanently damaged and that he would soon perish. He lingered on for the next three years while continuing to write. In 1916 he won the Prix Goncourt for *L'Appel du sol* ("The Call of the Soil"), an antiwar novel that ridicules a blind belief in patriotism. In the weeks before he died he completed *L'Orage sur le jardin de Candide* ("The Storm over Candide's Garden"), a collection of four stories that expands upon the same theme. The bulk of his writing was posthumously published.

[306] Georges Gombault (né Joseph Weiskopf; 1881 – 1971): Parisian journalist whose father immigrated to France from Bavaria; editor of publications such as *L'Aurore*, *L'Oeuvre*, and *La Lumière*. Gombault was also involved in the creation of Clemenceau's paper, *L'Homme Libre*. While he was a student at the Sorbonne, he supported Captain Dreyfus and was a founding member of the League of Human Rights (1898); he later served as vice president of the League, from 1946 to 1968. In June 1940, a few days after the French military defeat, Gombault traveled with his son to London. On 2 August *Le*

First of all, we were poets, we had recognized each other, and we accomplished the work that was imposed upon us without seeing in it anything more than drudgery, whilst the others, trained in journalism, thought more about its advantages and did not believe in pure literature.

I had then luckily published in the *Mercure*, *Jésus-le-Caille* and that led me, even in the eyes of the chief, to be considered less a reporter than a writer and still less an amateur. But my novel was not thought a very good one in the house and Adrien Bertrand, who had written an article about it, could not get it printed. He had to become angry and to assure the editor in chief that if the *Homme Libre* refused his copy he would leave the staff to assert his rights, and my reputation grew on account of that incident. Indeed, from column writer I became one of the copywriters. I was sent to the suburbs to describe in attractive terms crimes, accidents and suicides. I was sent to see the big pearl merchants who were in the limelight, politicians, concierges, burglars, to graveyards, what else? I interviewed strikers who would not say anything; generals who sent me about my business and when the anniversary of the theft of the *Joconde* made it a topic of the day, I interviewed Monsieur Bonnat himself, the director of the Louvre,[307] who would not let me open my mouth and relentlessly drove me away.

Matin newspaper published an anti-Semitic article about Jews who had left France earlier that year, and his name was included on a list of Jewish bankers, *fonctionnaires*, merchants, industrialists, and journalists. After the war, he was employed at *France-Soir* as a political commentator.

[307] In the original French version of his memoir, Carco never identified Bonnat as "the director of the Louvre." Instead he writes: "J'interviewais des grévistes qui ne voulaient rien dire, des généraux qui m'envoyaient faire f... et quand l'anniversaire du vol de la Joconde revint à l'actualité, chez M. Bonnat, en personne, qui ne me laissa pas placer un mot et me chassa honteusement" ("I was interviewing strikers who didn't want to say anything, generals who told me to fuck off, and when the anniversary of the

What a lovely profession journalism is! All my running about came to naught, my reporting had no life in it and "I got it" every time, because, instead of relating things to the readers as they wanted to hear them, I gave them my impressions, which were very interesting but which did not give them any tangible facts and were not what they wanted.

It happened one evening that, after a long campaign led by the president about flags at half-mast in Athens, I don't know what good Catholic admiral having ordered that they be lowered on Good Friday, it was discovered that the order authorizing that manifestation had appeared in the paper *La Croix*. What a windfall for the house! The boss was in the seventh heaven. Mandel, an elongated shadow of a squat Clemenceau, was rubbing his hands with glee and five or six ministers present backstage were getting ready to strike a big blow. The whole press, electrified by articles of extraordinary violence, [was] busy with the hare the boss had uncovered. It was talked about everywhere and I was probably the only one

theft of the *Mona Lisa* came back up in the news, at Mr. Bonnat's place, in person, who didn't let me get a word in and shamefully chased me away").

Earlier in the passage Carco says that he'd recently published the Mercure de France edition of *Jésus-la-Caille*, which was released in January 1914. The *Mona Lisa* was stolen from the Louvre on 21 August 1911, so we can assume that the upcoming "anniversary" of the theft occurred in August 1914. At that time Henri-Camille Marcel was the Louvre director, serving in the post from 1913 – 1919. The "Monsieur Bonnat" that Carco refers to was probably Léon Bonnat (1833 – 1922), a French academic painter who succeeded Paul Dubois as director of the École des Beaux-Arts in 1905. Although largely (and justifiably) forgotten, Bonnat was a popular painter at the time, and his naturalistic style drew support from Émile Zola and Théophile Gautier. Bonnat began his professorship at the École in 1882, and his students included Toulouse-Lautrec, Edvard Munch, Georges Braque, Thomas Eakins, Raoul Dufy, and John Singer Sargent. But there is no record of a "Bonnat" having ever held the post of Louvre director, and it remains uncertain why Boyd or her publisher altered the text in this way.

who, amid all that agitation, was serenely ignorant of what the thing was about.

"Carco," somebody shouted, "put on your hat and coat and hurry to the *Croix*."

"All right," I said ... "I am going ..."

"And bring back the number which had the order in it."

I looked at François-Albert, who was in charge of us all in spite of his sickly appearance and his boyish manners, and I asked very innocently:

"What order?"

I created a nice scandal. I was insulted and humiliated. A journalist who does not read the papers? That was a little bit too much.

"You'll have to read them," said François-Albert.

"Of course ... certainly.

"You'll have to begin with the *Homme Libre*. I suppose you never even peep at it?"

"Never."

"It does not interest you?"

"That is to say," I try to explain politely, "it does interest me ... yes ... but what would you have me do? To swallow the boss's sermon every morning is really too much for me. He is never pleased with anything. He grumbles all the time. In the morning, when I get up, I am generally in a very good humor, I don't want to spoil it with the boss's grumbling."

"Just as you like!" said Mandel in a honeyed voice as he came into the room unperceived by me. "You'll read Clemenceau, my friend ... otherwise ..."

What could I say? I was obliged to submit, but at the end of the week, disgusted with myself and the others, I went to François-Albert, who had asked me every evening what was in the boss's articles, and told him sadly:

"It is impossible ... I swear to you I did my best ... but to go on under those conditions, thank you ... I had rather throw the whole thing up."

And I left.

Of the two I was the free man as I discovered when the next day I saw from my window the Seine running between its quays, shaded by its trees, shining with a thousand silver spangles under a luminous sky. I was free, I was not tied down anymore! In the morning, I climbed the narrow stairs of my friend Daragnès, who was humbly engraving his woodcuts in front of the blue waters of the river while a file of boats went by one by one.

What a deliverance! Beautiful books, work accomplished with joy and calm, far from politics and stupid jobs ... I understood, I had found my way and Daragnès, who was preparing a series of drawings for *Jésus-la-Caille*, gave me copies of his first works. I have them still, they are rare. They are very rare, since the edition was not published and it is as a friend, not as a bibliophile, that I wish to say how much I owe to him who helped me to stabilize my life and I will always remember everything he has done for me with great affection.

XVII

And there I was! I had to live on "papers" about painters, on paragraphs and accounts of exhibitions that Vauxcelles accepted for *Gil Blas*. At the *Mercure*, Valette advanced me my first royalties. I was in heaven when July ended in stupor and consternation.

War, the awful war, was declared. Suddenly everything seemed to have been swept away, brushed away. At the *Gil Blas*, with Pellerin and André du Fresnois, a kind of exaltation took hold of us, threw us into the street like everybody else and made us join with ardor all the other young men who were going, without knowing it, singing, to their death. Women felt it already, everywhere around them. They were grave and on the boulevards formed immense processions, carrying banners and flags, following each other and shouting to the heavens. Preceding these parades, pastry-cook errand boys, boys on their bicycles, old gentlemen prey to a tragic delirium were dashing madly to and fro and the enormous human waves driven by their fate went forward, breaking against closed shops, cafés black with people, and roared at the top of their voices in a rhythmical three-beat measure:

"To Berlin! To Berlin!"

The day was coming to an end as those black gesticulating masses made up of salesman, employees, workmen, bourgeois, closely bound to each other by an inexpressible enthusiasm, passed under our eyes. In the gray light they raised a great cloud of dust and others appeared from everywhere and fell into step. "Jewish volunteers" one could read upon a huge wooden board amongst the banners of athletic societies. People saluted them as they passed.

"Long live the Jews!" shouted the onlookers, without any distinction of class or party.

Jean Pellerin and I looked at each other.

"Yes, long live the Jews!"

"And long live France!" shouted André du Fresnois, standing on a chair.

He had taken off his hat and almost deathly pale, so strong was his emotion, he followed with his nearsighted eyes, this parade of men of all ranks who, answering the general approval with a great clamor as they approached the place de l'Opera, started to sing with a thousand virile and hoarse voices:

La Victoire, en chantant, nous ouvre la barrière,
La Liberté gui-i-de nos pas.[308]

"Andre!" Jean called ...

Du Fresnois did not hear him. Still standing upon his chair, his whole being one with that mob, he, who ordinarily was so disdainful of crowds and who was ruled by the mind only, communed with the mob and consented to his own sacrifice. Then Jean Pellerin took hold of my arm, tightened his grip and pointed to our friend.

"Look at him," he said in a low tone ... "Look ... He won't come back!"

"Oh, yes, he will!"

"No, no," said Jean, whose presentiment filled him with great distress ...[309]

---

[308] From the first stanza of *Le Chant du départ*: "The victory song opens the gate for us; liberty guides our steps. And from the North to the South, the warlike trumpet has sounded the hour of combat. Tremble, enemies of France, kings drunk on blood and pride; the sovereign people advance: tyrants, descend to the coffin!"

[309] As mentioned in an earlier note, du Fresnois was killed on 25 August 1914, and his body was never recovered. Pellerin died from tuberculosis

And he climbed up beside André du Fresnois on the same seat, drew him towards him and for more than an hour held him in a brotherly embrace and du Fresnois may have understood for he stopped shouting.

Beside me, deaf to the applause, which came from the terrace of the Napolitain, like a continual fire of machine-guns, André du Fresnois's sweetheart was standing mute and motionless. Did she also have in that awful moment the presentment that André would soon be killed? I did not dare speak to her, but when my two comrades stepped down from their chair and approached us, my impression was confirmed and we went our ways.

I must not be accused of having written these lines after du Fresnois's disappearance. He was already no longer amongst us! The look I saw behind his misty glasses impressed me so that it still haunts me and recalls to me the time when I first felt it.

Night was coming. Through the avenue de l'Opera I went back to the Left Bank in a tumult still greater and more chaotic. The buses swayed heavily under their burden of people, the taxis were lined up as if they were frightened by the human avalanche, and from the tall lamps, the light, spluttering and crackling on incandescent carbons, illuminated a Paris which was upside down. Then, little by little, the streets became calmer. They were almost deserted when I arrived home, at nine o'clock, in the quai aux Fleurs, where I took from a drawer my draft papers, my military book and about twenty francs which, with the small change I had in my pocket, were all my riches at the time.

How awful it was to breathe the air of that hot summer night with the clear sky above. I was like the others, that is to say, I

contracted during the war. Thus, their embrace embodies an even more chilling, foreboding aspect.

had no control over my actions. I was prey to a kind of folly and pushed on heedlessly through the streets which again became animated and were filled with thick, black waves of sacred fury. At the Brasserie Cyrano in the place Blanche some friends were waiting for me.[310] We drank with the women, with their men, paying our turn after others, excited, throbbing. Those gentlemen were more serious than we were. They stared, their eyes blinked at the passersby and with hands in their pockets, they answered none of our questions. Afterwards we went down the rue Blanche and we saw, but too late to intervene, the quick attack made by three thieves on young men from whom they stole their money. Suspicious individuals surrounded us for a moment and then ran away. They went up to men and women at street corners, robbed them quickly, and, running away as fast as their legs could carry them, made another attempt a little farther away. In the place de la Trinité parades were formed. We accompanied them, between a double rank of onlookers who waved their hats and their handkerchiefs and escorted us shouting. Everywhere in the mob pockets were picked shamelessly, there were battles and slowly the enthusiasm diminished.

I remember very distinctly of what the howling crowd around me was composed. There were very young men, hatless women, salesmen, men with caps and corduroy trousers, mothers with their sons and a band of gangsters, happy to be able to shout at the top of their lungs. At times, when they were tired of singing the *Marseillaise* or the *Chant du Départ*,[311] undeveloped voices began another tune, and all, electrified,

---

[310] Located at 82, boulevard de Clichy, nestled a couple of doors away from the Moulin Rouge, at place Blanche. In the 1920s Café Cyrano became the unofficial headquarters of the Surrealists.

[311] "La Marseillaise," the national anthem of France, was written in 1792 during the French Revolution. "Chant du Départ," composed in 1794, also served as an anthem for the Revolution and as a rallying cry for liberty, equality, and fraternity.

howled it. Very often our advance would be retarded, we stamped our feet where we were. Songs that were in vogue rose from the streets ceaselessly in a fantastic heaving in which, holding each other feverishly by the arm, we walked and leaped and danced about.

On till midnight, drifting hither and thither along the boulevards to the Madeleine, the place de la Concorde, we never stopped until I broke away from the rank in which I was held prisoner and by way of the boulevard Saint-Germain reached the Quarter. But it was the same everywhere, the same crush. Students with velvet tam-o'-shanters bore at the head of the processions flags, lanterns, inscriptions, and mannequins with pointed helmets, and they shouted like madmen:

"To Berlin! To Berlin!"

An echo of a thousand voices answered them. One heard only that enormous, incessant shout, and in the bars as the steps of all these men resounded on the sonorous roadway and hammered at one's heart, women with fantastic headgear came to the windows and applauded vigorously. In front of the d'Harcourt, in front of the Brasserie du Panthéon and of the café opposite, the crowd completely jammed the boulevard. The flags that waved overhead stood still higher in the wide living folds, billowing with a hellish palpitation. They spread, sometimes when the light of the peaceful gas lamps came through a tree like a sieve, like an immense shroud and swayed mockingly. I think I see them still at the top of their poles unrolling their sinister and capricious caresses. They floated gracefully, twisted suddenly. Under their folds, moving like a scythe amongst the ripe corn, one would have said that already many young foreheads bent down brushed by an invisible hand.

But they soon stood up again, those smooth foreheads which death had marked before their time. They stood in front of him with a ferocious confidence that made me weak and hopeless. I saw flags no longer, but a horrible shroud with a long train red with blood. Why did not a voice come from that human flock to denounce the abominable and useless massacre which tomorrow was going to take place on the fields where the smell of earth and fruits is the only one permissible? One voice only would have been enough perhaps to change all that or, at least, to give to the immense gift of all those lives in their flower a more poignant and deeper significance ...

And there was no one, there was no one ... Only shouts, songs, more shouts, unheard clamorings ... Preceding me, a man about twenty-five, his shoes hanging by their laces around his neck, was dancing as if in a delirium. He stamped his feet, seized with a mad ardor, and the two women who held out their arms to him laughed as they led him away.

Following them I went through the crowd, keeping close, as if henceforth they would lead me through life and save me from my awful thoughts. That man was right. He was ready to live one more night, not in tears and despair but in the pleasures he would lose before he had had enough of them. Yes, he was right. And I went down, no longer wondering, the very narrow stairs of the Bar du Pantheon, entered, sat down and ordered a drink.

It was a strange setting. I did not recognize it at once, as the tables pushed back into corners left a much bigger space than usual for dancing. An orchestra played a tango and the men, pressing their partners to them in silent ecstasy, tried to dance it properly. They were all young and they all carried their knapsacks of brown leather, they looked without seeing, fixedly, in front of them, while I, caught by that enervating tune drawn out by the violins, was humming:

"C'est le dernier tango !"

There was a comical incident; a customer of the bar who was watching for her friend, cried out when she saw him coming:

"Ah, there he is, my Belgian boy!"

At that word the music stopped as if by enchantment and everybody shouted in unison:

"Long live Belgium! Bravo! Bravo!"

The Belgian's face was worth seeing. He appeared very much moved, bowed and thanked people. An old gentleman, very fat and very blond, offered champagne and the rejoicings went on.

But I went out of the bar and into the blue night. The heavy foliage of the trees of the boulevards and of the Jardin du Luxembourg spread over the crowd that sensuous and strong odor of humus and greenery which fills the hearts of the town dwellers with a heavy dissatisfaction. Higher than the tumult, one felt something pressing down upon us its inexpressible weight. Tragic night of a harrowing sweetness, it was no compensation for all the men and the women whom the war was cruelly pulling apart. As the night drew to an end, a strange feeling was taking hold of all those human beings. A stupor, vague at first, but little by little stronger than they, stunned them. The shouting stopped. The last groups broke away and while the market trucks went down the roadway toward Les Halles the dawn appeared and, without our noticing it, impregnated everything with the pale and surprising presence of day. Suddenly coming back to reality, counting the hours, the most courageous looked their fate face to face and I remembered that a month before an old woman who told fortunes by palmistry, on the terrace of the Closerie des Lilas, had stood, without saying anything, so frightened she was on discovering what she alone could see.

"Well, little mother? What is the matter?" but our questioning had been in vain.

The old woman, with her arms raised to heaven, had begun to weep.

What had she read in all those hands that announced death? What was the mysterious sign which she could not mistake? I would have liked to find that woman again to ask her ... no. In spite of myself, stupidly tightening my fists so that I would not be tempted to learn what no man perhaps must know, I put them in my pockets and went away quickly.

It was then that, thinking of my parents, who lived far from Paris, and who must have spent the night in getting my brother ready and in writing to me, an awful distress seized me. I was alone, terribly alone, in the streets, abandoned by everyone and struggling with fatigue. I felt absolutely done in. I had no more courage and when I went into a small café I saw myself in a mirror, as pale as death, with reddened eyes.

"Have some coffee, my boy, with a dash of rum to get rid of that. Will you?" said the beer seller to me.

"Yes, with some rum."

The place was full. Leaning against the counter, a man who had been drinking a small glass of *schnick* [Schnapps] kept drying his lips and, looking at him darkly and silently, a poor pale woman was waiting beside him. The man, whose hand trembled, went on ceaselessly drying his mouth and the woman not to rob him of his energy kept still. Suddenly he seized her in his arms, kissed her savagely, and she kissed him in return, folded him in her arms, till, disengaging himself, the man went to the door, opened it and disappeared.

"Oh, God!" moaned the poor woman.

Her neighbors went to her help, but she was huddled on the floor, dead, one more victim of the awful God who willed everything, exacted everything and remained indifferent.

Outside in the light, which was becoming brighter, military doctors, dressed in elegant uniforms, were walking down the boulevard; they were hurrying to the Gare de l'Est, on foot, because there were no taxis and no tramways. Almost children, all of them, or very young men, proud to show themselves in brown leggings, new caps, velvet collars, proud to go, on that golden morning, to the great war, a suitcase in their hands. What sadness we felt, all of us in that bar, in seeing them pass that way, near that woman lying dead on the floor, while a policeman came running up. How discouraging! And the paraders, who were going home in small groups of five or six, trailing their flags, dirtied by the filth of the streets, filed slowly by. They were drunk for the most part. They walked unsteadily and some of them, with their raucous voices and with the piteous stubbornness of drunken men, insisted upon shouting when they saw us looking at them:

"To Berlin ... ! Yes ... yes ... To Berlin! Yes, by Jove! To Berlin! To Berlin!"

*

All that day, I spent my time with my comrades, saying goodbye to them. One of them, the poet Édouard Gazanion, never left me. He bought me a flask and, filling it up with Pernod, lent me some money and prowled around with me till nighttime.

Paris seemed like a different city. One met an incredible number of men all of whom were going away, running towards the stations, and, although overburdened with parcels, still looking exalted. Hither and thither, horse patrols went around the streets. Companies, trucks full of arms, munitions, mounted batteries, squadrons, made way for themselves through the crowd, and the crowd applauded them. On the boulevard du Palais, a spy was arrested as I stood by to see an artillery regimen, which, with its interminable processions of Seventy-fives, the gunners seated on the gun carriages, crossed the water and disappeared. Horsemen whose mounts carried flowers in their harnesses showed grave faces. They did not answer the cries that rose as they passed. The wheels creaked. Cannons jumped in the ruts of the road like mysterious playthings, the number of which was astonishing ... And there were more ... and still more. These young men whose muskets reached the top of their caps above the coats rolled around their necks, pained me, as I followed them with my eyes, for the expression on their beardless faces was older than they, and hardened their features.

Alas! when night came the first news of the war added to the disorder. People fought over *La Patrie*,[312] the events commented upon, and the announcement in Paris of the pillage of German houses, excited the old men, who, speaking about their own time, saw this as a revenge – their revenge – and made long speeches. The thing that touched them least of all was the assassination of Jaurès. Jaurès?[313] It could not be helped ... They had no time to mourn at such a critical moment, but, haranguing an audience who listened to them without understanding them, those speechifiers said, in the sacred name of statistics, that three times a man's weight in bullets was necessary to kill a man.

"So," said an old beau, talking to a fat man, who standing in front of him, was willing to listen to him, "you, for example ... you will cost the Germans a ton of munitions, at least! ... They won't be able to economize where you are concerned!"

"Ah! yes ..."

And as the fat man thought about something else:

---

[312] *La Patrie* ("The Homeland"): A popular Parisian paper, known for its conservative, nationalist views and for attempting to shape public opinion during WWI.

[313] Jean Jaurès (1859 – 1914): socialist politician who advocated for social justice and the rights of workers and the disenfranchised. Jaurès attempted to promote internationalism and was opposed to militarism, the arms race, and imperialism. He was assassinated on 31 July 1914, shortly before the outbreak of the war, by a right-wing nationalist.

"Go on," said the old Beau Brummell.[314] "Have some spunk! Have some spunk! ... Dying is nothing when one knows what one is dying for ... nothing, my friend. Believe me, upon my word, because, if I were the age ..."

Those extraordinary individuals had crowds around them and, an unbelievable fact today, they went on talking ceaselessly and no one stopped them. In the cafés, in the buses, in the streets, near the stations, they excited people to go and be killed as if there were nothing unusual in it. Had they any idea of what a war can release in the way of horrors degradations when they spoke that way? They did not know. They believed, as everyone did, that this time the end would come quickly, since the Belgians and the English were with us against the "pointed helmets" and that, afterwards, Victory crowning our sacrifices, an era of peace and prosperity would be offered to the surviving ones. God forgive me, that era so long announced we have now, and even if it corresponded in all points to the picture painted by the zealous orators of the first days of the mobilization, no one would have wanted it, if they had known the price we have had to pay for it.

[314] A reference to George Bryan "Beau" Brummell (1778 – 1840), a celebrated dandy and friend of the Prince Regent and future King George IV. Brummell eventually fell out of favor and was forced to seek exile in France. During Britain's Regency era he was celebrated for his trend-setting, fashionable dress and piquant witticisms. When Brummell was snubbed by the Prince Regent at a private masquerade ball, he turned to Lord Alvanley and, referring to the masked Prince, asked: "Alvanley, who's your fat friend?" In the decades following his expatriation to France, numerous collections of Brummellian anecdotes and aphorisms appeared in print, many of them fictitious, including the series *Traité de la vie élégante* (1830), published by Honoré de Balzac.

Maurice Asselin, *Portrait de Jean Pellerin*, 1920, 41.3 x 32.8 cm.
(Musée de Grenoble – J. L. Lacroix.) Jean Pellerin was born on 24 April 1885
in Pontcharra, about twenty-five kilometers northeast of Grenoble. A
French poet and founder of the Fantaisiste school, he met Carco during his
military service in Grenoble. He died in Châtelard, near the French-Italian
border in the Alps, on 9 July 1921, from tuberculosis contracted during the
war. Carco assembled and edited a posthumous collection of Pellerin's
poetry, entitled *Le Bouquet inutile* ("The Useless Bouquet"; 1923).

XVIII

Indeed, after du Fresnois, after Marcel Drouet, Charles Perrot, Louis Pergaud,[315] Jean-Marc Bernard, on the eve of the armistice Guillaume Apollinaire succumbed and, later, Jean Pellerin, from the consequences of that horrible war from which my brother Charles, major of his year at the École Polytechnique also did not come back. When I think of it, and picture him again, the best of our family, that child whose remains I had to gather at Blercourt, near Verdun, his death is still vivid to me and tears me to pieces. The graves of the cemetery smelled like sinks. *Sidis*[316] had opened them, and were working hard with picks, like damned souls, to break the coffins that were floating in water. But the covers gave away, and in their muddy uniforms, our poor dead appeared in the warm day of the living. Spread under heavy regulation coats, they had to be taken piece by piece out of the holes, and their remains were laid down, while all swallowed their tears, in new coffins, on mattresses of sawdust on which the black water which dripped from the sheets ran anew. An abominable and yet a very noble and necessary ordeal. No one shrank from it. Those gray masses, petrified by the water in which they had lain so long, gave back to the bodies a semblance of human appearance, but in our

[315] Louis Pergaud (1882 – 1915): French poet and novelist, most remembered for *La Guerre des boutons* ("The War of the Buttons"; 1912), a novel later adapted for the cinema (*La guerre des gosses*; 1936) by director Jacques Daroy. Pergaud was killed by "friendly fire" in April 1915 while stationed behind enemy lines.

[316] The Sidi (aka Sheedi, Siddhi, or Habshi): an ethnic minority group in Pakistan and India, primarily descended from the Bantu peoples of the Zanj coast in Southeast Africa. The Battle of Blercourt lasted from 22 August to 11 September 1914. It was part of the larger Battle of the Frontiers, which marked the initial phase of World War I on the Western Front.

hands they were so heavy that our hearts failed us. To the end, nevertheless, each one bringing to the task a kind of mad exaltation, we went through the most painful formalities and I saw that the shell which had reached my brother had made only a very small hole, very neat, without breaking anything in his exposed cranium.

In spite of summer, of the tender light of day, everything around seemed imbued with a great sadness, from the woods crowning the heights, whence I knew that on the night of the twenty-first of June 1916, the one I was mourning had been sent to Blercourt, no noise came. One heard only the silence of those green hills, or that valley halfway up where the cemetery stands and which, peaceful and not deep, offered in every direction well-balanced perspectives. The poplars bordering the road, the low plain, soft, fresh as spring water, composed a happy landscape which, little by little, acted upon our tortured nerves and calmed them. And I thought of my brother Charles whose intelligence was the wonder of all his friends and professors at the École Polytechnique, and I said to myself that he was no more and that, great as his mind was, my twenty-two-year-old brother had been struck by God in the head.

Who would not have felt as I did, while, one after another, the heavy trucks, loaded with coffins, drove down amongst the bushes? They rolled on, leaving behind them a long ribbon of blue smoke which, as they went, disappeared, volatilized. Then the trucks themselves could not be seen any longer and the impression that life and death also will disappear was almost sweet to me, because, within myself, memories of which the witness was no longer there to stir the ashes, were also dissolved without any hope of renewal. Everything was escaping me, as if purposely to impress upon me the moving lesson which I had had and which, already, linking itself with other facts, was sinking further and further into my memory and pushing slowly towards that abyss which we all have in our subconsciousness.

*

Memories? Yes ... Nothing more. Gay or sad, as light as the smoke I had seen mixed with the atmosphere, from the height of the small Blercourt cemetery, they have no other power than to evoke for the friends of my youth years which never will be given back to us. May those friends understand me well and in far and distant time may they so confound themselves with the innocent portraits I have drawn here, that they add to the resemblance. As for those who have disappeared, lock, stock and barrel, it is between them and my conscience. I have tried to show them much as they were at the time when I knew them. Not all despised their contemporaries with the same great aloofness of the unlucky Léon Deubel who, before he committed suicide, wrote:

> *Et le poète qui s'éveille,*
> *Fiévreux d'entendre ses chansons*
> *Se prolonger par les buissons*
> *Sur le point d'orgue d'une abeille,*
>
> *Comme un héros de sa cité,*
> *Fait de la chose transitoire*
> *Une sonore éternité.*[317]

[317] "And the poet who awakens, / Feverish to hear his songs / Resound through the bushes / To the climactic melody of a buzzing bee, / Like a triumphant victor, / Makes of the transitory / A reverberant eternity." Léon Deubel (1879-1913), French poet from Belfort, endowed with precocious talent, who was traumatized by the sudden death of his mother when he was only six years old. Deubel was forever haunted by his only memory of her — viewing her corpse on her deathbed — and composed the following lines when he twenty-one years old: "Life echoes like a step / That has strayed from the road, / And the shadow shines like a vault / From which

Far from it! Neither Pellerin, nor Jean-Marc, nor Guillaume ... What did they care about the future? They were alive. They loved life. And Modigliani himself, who is certainly the one whose name had but to wait for death to reach

Aux époques lointaines,[318]

he thought of it only to laugh.

However, we were to lose him in his turn, in that winter of 1920, and he died in hospital saying: *"Cara Italia!"*[319] Although he was not French, his art had found with us its flowering, its grace, its rhythm, its clearness, its measure. The year before his

you will not escape." Deubel was also incapable of alleviating his embitterment over the banalities of life. Unable to adapt to the mundane obligations of quotidian existence – impoverished, starving, and lacking adequate external support – he burned all his manuscripts and threw himself into the Marne, committing suicide at the age of thirty-four. His corpse was retrieved by bargemen; in his pocket were six sous. One of his contemporaries, the poet and novelist Léon Bocquet, eulogized him thus: "He died for never having looked at life except with the hallucinated eyes of dreams ... He seemed like a sleepwalker among very practical and busy people ... He turned his back on life in order to be less distracted from his inner dream ... He immersed himself so deeply in the absolute that he ended up no longer discerning the necessities and contingencies of the earth, the world, or its laws ... And he believed he had fulfilled his day well as soon as he produced a beautiful verse." Deubel is often regarded as a *poète maudit*: a damned seer working in the cursed tradition of "misfits" such as Rimbaud and Baudelaire. A collection of his verse entitled *Regner: Poemes* was published in 1914, by Mercure de France.

[318] "In distant epochs." From Baudelaire's *Fleurs du mal*: "I give you these verses so that if my name / Happily arrives in distant epochs ..."

[319] "Beloved Italy!" For an in-depth exploration of the challenges caused by Modi's pulmonary tuberculosis, see Dr. Henri Colt, *Becoming Modigliani*. Colt uses a "medical through line" as the spine for this innovative biography.

death Zborowski had sent him to Nice for his health, and Nice is not a place for artists and still less for sick people and there, although Zborowski was paying, this incomparable painter worked. He lived, in the rue de France, in a hotel for prostitutes where these "ladies," knowing him to be tubercular and too poor to afford a model, posed in his room after their friends were gone. What an existence! Zborowski told me about it afterwards. One of those women who asked nothing from the painter for posing was caught once by the man who kept her and he asked for money. What could Modigliani do? He had only canvases that nobody wanted and it was the same with Zborowski. Sell them! To whom? Several well-known writers refused to give a sou. Others, better advised, bargained. For twenty francs they bought a picture or even two and told Zborowski, who begged them to help him save Modigliani:

"Well, it is only customary. A painter does not need to lead a wild life, if he is poor. Let him worry! Why does he not live in Paris?"

"But he is very ill," Zborowski would say to them. "He spits blood."

He was thrown out. He was sent to some [aficionados] of the town who are crueler there than any other place and they kicked Zborowski out without being moved in the least by his plea. He found the same welcome everywhere, cold and insolent. One could have sworn that till the end stupidity and vanity would go against the man who believed in his painter and that he would become disgusted. But Zborowski had seen much worse; when living with Soutine, in a studio in the Cité Falguière, Modigliani had had to sprinkle the floor with insecticide to escape from bedbugs, roaches and vermin which were plentiful in the studio, and Modigliani, who was to become the hero of the novel of Georges-Michelle, *Les*

Montparnos,[320] slept on the ground beside his comrade. They lived so for many long months, stoics, putting up with all their ills and drinking to forget them. Then Zborowski rented a garret in the rue Racine for him at the Hôtel des Etrangers and Modigliani arrived very early at his friend the poet's to paint; meanwhile his friend, to give him the indispensable necessities, ran about Paris from dawn till night and came back exhausted.

"Well, how goes it?" Modigliani would ask. "Did you sell anything?"

No, he had sold nothing, but to hide from the painter the hopeless result of his quest, he had borrowed forty sous in the Quarter and bought some bacon and red beans which he cooked and shared with Modi. All one winter they fed on red beans only, and the painter did not even have a canvas, so he painted figures on the wall, upon a door – they still exist – and, annoyed at not being able to do better, he sat in a corner of the room and waited for the poet's return.

In Nice he found no one worthy enough to be interested but he never stopped encouraging Modi, inspiring him and keeping him up to the mark every day, even if he had to get rid of everything he owned, his trunk, his old coat and his shirts. He went almost naked to Marseilles where he sold for five hundred francs fifteen canvasses which Modi had given him and sent him the whole of the money, keeping only the cost of the trip. He went back, he searched for a studio, and finally found in the rue de la Grande Chaumière one where the painter was able to settle afterwards. Zborowski needed a great deal of tenacity and faith to struggle and work as he did for Modigliani! Did the

[320] Michel Georges-Michel (1883 – 1985): Parisian painter, novelist, and translator who authored over one hundred publications. His novel about Modigliani and Jeanne Hébuterne, *Les Montparnos*, was published in 1924 by Arthème Fayard. The cover features a brightly colored gouache by Picasso of the *Three Musicians*. Georges-Michel served as an artistic advisor for Sergei Diaghilev's *Ballets Russes* (1913 – 1929) and organized Picasso's first exhibition in Rome, in 1917.

painter realize it? I don't know. As it is, in that studio which was not even furnished, the painter thought himself free from care for a while. Little by little his pictures were being sold. I have spoken of Swiss collectors; there were some in Paris but they did not pay big prices and Modigliani, who had had a baby girl by his mistress, struggled and starved as before. Whatever he did, however he tried to ward off his fate, the latter still had bitter days in store for him and ill-luck pursued him relentlessly.

It was then about November 1919, that, undermined by the illness which was to carry him away, Modigliani felt his strength leaving him. He worked only by an overwhelming effort and, as he drank more and more, the liquor helped to weaken his constitution and that effort broke him. Zborowski asked him more than twenty times to go and rest either in the South or in a sanatorium, where a doctor who was his friend would look after Modigliani for nothing. But he refused. He wanted only to walk about the streets and thus augment his weakness, which kept increasing daily. He coughed dreadfully and when people insisted that he should leave his studio:

"No ... No ..." he would reply, "leave me alone."

December arrived quickly. Modi, who did not know he was so ill, talked of packing his brushes and of going to Italy in the spring with his young sweetheart and their child.

"There," he would say, "I have my mother."

Against all advice, he worked in the studio without a fire, brought his pictures to Zborowski, asked him to sell them and then torn by a cough which racked him for hours at a time, ran away and avoided people. In January, Zborowski found him in bed, with a high fever. He shivered upon his uncomfortable divan and tossed about restlessly. He did not want to see a doctor, who, when called by Zborowski, came nevertheless and ordered him to be taken at once to a hospital.

"Italia! Cara, cara Italia!" the painter kept repeating as he was being taken away.

He fainted on the way. But in the rue Jacob, in one of the rooms of the Hôspital de la Charité, he regained consciousness and, his fever increasing, fought wildly and babbled verses all night in his delirium. The next night he was dead.

I put it to those who have known, loved and admired him, if, as soon as Modigliani was dead, we did not know at once that his reign was beginning. It does not require any explanation. In a moment the news was all over Paris. Kisling came to tell me. He told me how the painter's mistress, pregnant for the second time, with the courage of her despair, had thrown herself upon her lover's body, and had refused to be separated from him. She had to be taken away by force and returned to her parents in the rue Amyot. We begged them to take her back and to watch over her for several days for the gentle creature was so much in need of their care. Kisling was greatly upset. He asked me for my mite for the funeral, noted it down upon a sheet of paper where already a dozen names were inscribed and accompanied me to the hospital. Watched by his friends, Modigliani's corpse was covered with flowers and, under the flowers, a thick fair curl rested on the dead man's breast.

"It is hers," I was told, in an awed whisper. "His mistress, she cut a curl from her hair when they forced her to go."

From everywhere came comrades, dealers, humble people, owners of dives and models. They were all thunderstruck. With Modi, the last bohemian of his generation – which had not been coddled by life – bohemia in the best sense of the word was disappearing. We felt it. We were very sorrowful, and the next day, when, still bewildered by what had happened during the night, Zborowski and Kisling told us that Modigliani's mistress had thrown herself out of one of the windows of her parents' home and that the latter had refused to take in the corpse, an indescribable horror overcame us.[321]

Behind the hearse which, through a supreme irony, was covered with very expensive flowers and wreaths, an astonishing crowd followed. There were many painters, women, writers, the whole of Montmartre, the whole of Montparnasse, all united in a supreme homage to the memory of the departed friend who, during [his life of happenstance and disorder],[322] had been deprived of more things than anyone else. Anecdotes were told. People talked about the work he left behind and following the procession, I saw in the ranks the friends of the unlucky Modi. They had all succeeded since the old days. They had all grown older and fatter. Some of them were celebrated, others were going to be: Picasso, Salmon, Max Jacob, Blaise Cendrars ... All were there. They denied nothing in the past. On the contrary. With Modi they were burying their youth, and the policemen who, on the way, clicked heels and saluted, perhaps were the same who, so many times, had taken Modi to the police station and who now certainly had no idea that their salute appeared in our eyes a rather belated but public reparation.

It was Picasso, who, as always, drew from that spectacle the lesson it had for all of us, because, turning to me, and pointing first to the hearse where Modigliani rested under mountains of flowers, and then to the policemen at attention, he said softly:

"You see, he gets his revenge!"

---

[321] Amedeo Clemente Modigliani (12 July 1884 – 24 January 1920) was only thirty-five when he perished; Jeanne Hébuterne (6 April 1898 – 26 January 1920) was just a few months short of her twenty-second birthday.

[322] Boyd mistakenly translates "durant son existence de hasard et de désordre" as "during all his life of hazards and poverty."

Modigliani, *Le Pèlerin* ("The Pilgrim"), pencil on paper, 42.5 x 24.5 cm. The drawing is featured in a Sotheby's catalog for Sale 6019, held in New York on 17 May 1990. It quotes a passage from *Artist Quarter* in which the pseudonymous author says that Modi represented him with "the head of a hunting dog protruding between my thighs." The catalog adds: "There are three similar drawings of young pilgrims in private collections, but none include the dog." Modigliani biographer Pierre Sichel "ascribes much of the [*Artist Quarter*] biography ... to Charles Beadle ... He attributes the anecdote concerning *Le Pèlerin* to Beadle rather than Douglas." Sotheby's dates it 1916-1917, but Beadle was in New York by November 1916, so 1914-1916 is more likely, when his friend Beatrice Hastings was involved with Modigliani. In 1915 Beadle published his novel *A Passionate Pilgrimage*.

Locations of Various Meeting Places

Au Chalet: rue de Lappe (later known as Chez Bouscatel)

Au Clairon des Chasseurs à pied (aka Spielmann's): 3, place du Tertre, Montmartre

Auberge Bouscarat. See Hôtel-Restaurant Bouscarat

Auberge de la Marine. See Hôtel-Restaurant Bouscarat

Auberge de l'OEuf Dur et du Commerce: Saint-Cyr-sur-Morin

Au Caveau des Anglais. See Cabaret du Père Lunette

Aux Billards en Bois: at the corner of 2, rue des Saules, and 18, rue Saint Rustique

Bal Bouscatel: 11, rue de la Huchette

Bal Bullier: 31, avenue de l'Observatoire, near the corner of boulevard Saint-Michel

Bal Vachier (aka Bal de la Montagne): 46, rue de la Montagne-Sainte-Geneviève

Bateau-Lavoir: 13, rue Ravignan, at place Emile Goudeau

Brasserie Cyrano: 82, boulevard de Clichy, at place Blanche

Brasserie du Bon Bock: 2, rue Dancourt, at the foot of Sacré-Coeur

Cabaret du Père Lunette: 4, rue des Anglais

Café de Flore: 172, boulevard Saint-Germain

Café de la Rotonde: 103 and 105 boulevard du Montparnasse

Café de la Source: 35, boulevard Saint-Michel

Café d'Harcourt: 47, boulevard Saint-Michel, facing the Taverne du Pantheon

Café des Deux-Magots: 6, place Saint-Germain des Prés

Café du Dôme: 108, boulevard du Montparnasse

Café-Restaurant du Musée de Cluny: 20, boulevard Saint-Michel

Café Vachette: 27, boulevard Saint-Michel, at the corner of rue des Écoles

Casse-Croûte: 1, rue Paul Féval

Caveau de la Bolée: 25, rue l'Hirondelle (chez Hubert)

Chez Bouscatel: rue de Lappe (formerly Au Chalet)

Chez Manière: 65, rue Caulaincourt, on the northern incline of the Butte

Chez Père Azon: 12, rue de Ravignan

Chez Rosalie: 3, rue Campagne-Première

Chez Vernin: 8, rue Cavallotti

Closerie des Lilas: 171, boulevard du Montparnasse

Grand Café-Restaurant Voltaire: 1, place de l'Odéon

Grand Ecart: 7, rue Fromentin, near the boulevard Clichy

Hôtel du Tertre. See Hôtel-Restaurant Bouscarat

Hôtel-Restaurant Bouscarat: 2, place du Tertre, at the corner of rue du Mont-Cenis

L'Ami Emile: at the bottom of the rue Ravignan

La Belle Gabrielle: 12, rue Saint-Vincent, at the intersection of rue du Mont-Cenis

La Coupole: 102, boulevard du Montparnasse

Lapin Agile: 22, rue des Saules

Le Boeuf sur le toit: 28, rue Boissy d'Anglas, near Eglise de la Madeleine

Le Napolitain (aka Café Glacier Napolitain): 1, boulevard des Capucines

Maison Bouscarat. See Hôtel-Restaurant Bouscarat

Moulin de la Galette: 83, rue Lepic

Moulin Rouge: 82, boulevard de Clichy

Pension Laveur: 6, rue des Poitevins

Restaurant du Coucou: 7, place du Calvaire

Taverne du Panthéon: 63, boulevard Saint-Michel (and 26, rue Soufflot), facing the Café d'Harcourt

Vassilieff's canteen (aka la cantine de Montparnasse): 21, avenue du Maine

Auberge de l'OEuf Dur et du Commerce: Saint-Cyr-sur-Morin

On left: Au Clairon des Chasseurs à pied (aka Spielmann's): 3, place du Tertre, Montmartre

Aux Billards en Bois: at the corner of 2, rue des Saules, and 18, rue Saint Rustique. Bottom photo by Eugène Atget, 1 January 1922.

Bal Bullier: 31, avenue de l'Observatoire, near the corner of boulevard Saint-Michel

"In the rue de la Montagne-Sainte-Geneviève, where Bernouard and I were learning to set type and to print books …"

Carco refers to "Le bal de 'la Montagne,'" run by a Monsieur Vachier. The most infamous "Bal de la Montagne" was located at 46, rue de la Montagne-Sainte-Geneviève, pictured above. It is now the location of the Violon Dingue.

Photo of rue de la Montagne-Sainte-Geneviève by Eugène Atget, 1898.

Cabaret du Père Lunette: 4, rue des Anglais

Café de la Rotonde: 103 and 105 boulevard du Montparnasse

Café d'Harcourt: 47, boulevard Saint-Michel (facing the Taverne du Pantheon)

Café de la Source: 35, boulevard Saint-Michel

Café du Dôme: 108, boulevard du Montparnasse

Chez Rosalie. "Montparnasse was a special place for foreign artists in the first decades of the twentieth century. Hundreds of artists from dozens of countries lived there. They socialized and theorized at a handful of cafés and eateries: the Closerie des Lilas, the Café du Dôme, Café de la Rotonde, Chez Rosalie, and at Vassilieff's canteen. They lived in studios within a hundred yards of the Carrefour Vavin, and in the Cité Falguière or at La Ruche. They avoided the all-powerful École des Beaux-Arts in favor of the independent academies of Montparnasse that catered to foreigners [...] It was in this highly charged cosmopolitan atmosphere, with the broadest range of international and cultural stimuli, that Modigliani lived and where his art matured." Kenneth Wayne, *Modigliani and the Artists of Montparnasse*, New York: Harry N. Abrams, Inc., 2002, p. 29.

Grand Café-Restaurant Voltaire: 1, place de l'Odéon

CAVEAU DE LA BOLÉE

Caveau de la Bolée: 25, rue l'Hirondelle (chez Hubert)

Chez Manière: 65, rue Caulaincourt, on the northern incline of the Butte Montmartre

Dufayel Department Store: 26, rue de Clignancourt, which featured a 180-foot dome crowned with a searchlight and a theatre that seated 3,000

Hôtel-Restaurant Bouscarat: 2, place du Tertre, at the corner of rue du Mont-Cenis

Ground-floor restaurant at the Hôtel Bouscarat

Lapin Agile: 22, rue des Saules

Le Boeuf sur le toit: 28, rue Boissy d'Anglas, near Eglise de la Madeleine
(Top: the bar. Center: interior, 1922. Bottom: the restaurant.

Le Napolitain (aka Café Glacier Napolitain), 1, boulevard des Capucines

Moulin de la Galette: 83, rue Lepic

Restaurant du Coucou: 7, place du Calvaire

Another view of Restaurant du Coucou

Taverne du Panthéon: 63, boulevard Saint-Michel (and 26, rue Soufflot), facing the Café d'Harcourt

Francis Carco's Complexity:
An Afterword by Christopher Sawyer-Laucanno

When Rob Couteau asked me whether I would consider writing an Afterword to his new and revised edition of Francis Carco's *From Montmartre to the Latin Quarter*, I had to tell him that I had little familiarity with Carco's work. I had only read a handful of poems and forty years ago his 1925 noir novel *Perversité*. But then Rob sent me a PDF of his extensively annotated and scrupulously researched English-language edition, and I was hooked. Couteau, again, as he did with Charles Beadle, has made available for discerning readers another much-too-neglected book of great distinction.

Francis Carco is hardly a household name, even among the literati, but he should be. Carco, as Couteau admirably demonstrates in reissuing *From Montmartre to the Latin Quarter*, has written one of the great memoirs of poets and painters in Paris from before the Great War until the early 1920s.

Indeed, I was stunned by the tenderness and even humor Carco exhibits in recapturing the vicissitudes and triumphs of his friends from that period, including, among many others, Utrillo, Picasso, Jacob and Modigliani. I expected vividness but also, given what I knew about and had read before of Carco, a fair amount of raunchiness and even cruelty. Which is not to say that Carco sugarcoats the realities he describes. In fact, he unflinchingly depicts the poverty afflicting these formidable creators, and the squalor in which these artists were forced to reside. He does not dwell on these details, but rather on the kindnesses, the generosity and belief each of his friends exhibited in the face of very precarious circumstances. True empathy and acute sensitivity pervade the book. Aside from Robert Graves' *Good-bye to All That*, I can think of no other memoir that brought tears to my eyes. But Carco's description of the death of Modigliani had me weeping. And then, moments later, I was reveling in the last lines of the book, which focus on Modi's funeral procession:

> People talked about the work he left behind and following the procession, I saw in the ranks the friends of the unlucky Modi. They had all succeeded since the old days. They had all grown older and fatter. Some of them were celebrated, others were going to be: Picasso, Salmon, Max Jacob, Blaise Cendrars ... All were there. They denied nothing in the past. On the contrary. With Modi they were burying their youth, and the policemen who, on the way, clicked heels and saluted, perhaps were the same who, so many times, had taken Modi to the police station and who now certainly had no idea that their salute appeared in our eyes a rather belated but public reparation.
>
> It was Picasso, who, as always, drew from that spectacle the lesson it had for all of us, because, turning to me, and pointing first to the hearse where Modigliani rested under mountains of flowers, and then to the policemen at attention, he said softly:
> "You see, he gets his revenge!"

Let me explain why *From Montmartre to the Latin Quarter* surprised me so much. Carco's reputation is largely built on his sinister novels excavating, with intense realism, the Parisian underworld, or *milieu*, populated by pimps, queers, prostitutes, gangsters and thieves. In these works, two aspects of his writing stand out for me, make him different from most early noir writers: first, his ability to examine in detail the psychology of

The cover of Georges-Michel's novel about Modigliani and Jeanne Hébuterne, illustrated by a Picasso gouache: a rarely displayed variant of the *Three Musicians*.

his damaged characters, revealing their inner selves and their deep, often conflicting emotions; second, his use of *argot* which adds a vivid dimensionality to his descriptions and dialogue.

His early novel *Jésus la Caille* (1914), which I recently read, is an intense portrayal of a milieu that predates Genet by decades. This richly-layered novel features Jésus, a male sex worker, who is also enthralled with Fernande, a prostitute whose wretched life is ensnared between her sadistic pimp and a seriously troubled police informant. Violence is continually present, or just around the corner, so that the entire novel is infused with an air of constant malevolence and apprehension. Carco demonstrates an amazing ability to get inside the heads of each of his characters, and to his credit is never apologetic about who they are. They simply exist, just as the denizens of the impoverished streets and squalid bars Carco knew well, existed. He has no interest in assuaging any moral expectations on the part of his readers.

While seemingly detached from moral observation, one can't help but feel, as Couteau explains so well in his Introduction, that Carco also takes a certain delight in obsessively observing the misery of his characters. In *Perversité*, for instance, the sordid lives of his characters and perversity of plot are told with so much detail that it appears Carco relishes writing about the destruction of his creations. In *Perversité* Emile, a self-effacing office clerk, and Irma, his prostitute sister, with whom Emile is secretly in love, share a cramped apartment in a tenement house populated by prostitutes. Emile largely manages to ignore how his sister makes her living, until she takes up with Bébert, a violent pimp, who quickly uncovers Emile's timidity. Delighting at the discovery of Emile's weakness, Bébert proceeds to bully him (and Irma) relentlessly. Emile, in turn, takes up with Belle-Amour, an older prostitute neighbor, on which he reenacts the treatment Bébert has been inflicting on him and Irma. The ultimate tragedy of the novel is that Emile

Maurice Utrillo, *Place du Tertre*, 1911, oil on cardboard
mounted on cradled panel, 54.29 x 73.34 cm.

purchases a gun to kill Bébert but ends up killing his beloved Irma instead.

Carco writes so vividly and so unrelievedly about the abuse, that I found I had to stop reading from time to time to recover from the ardent misanthropy on display. Or to be blunt: I found myself squirming a lot.

In 1915 Carco had a brief affair with Katherine Mansfield, who wrote two stories about him. Her 1915 story "An Indiscreet Journey," based on an actual four-day visit Mansfield made to see Carco who was at the front during the war, does not probe deeply into "the little corporal" (Carco). Indeed, the focus is as much on the other soldiers in the café as it is on the relationship. But between 1915 and 1918, Mansfield decided to examine Carco's dark side which she reveals without reservation in her 1918 *conte à clef* "Je Ne Parle Pas Français."

Sadism, masochism, homosexuality, cuckoldry, prostitution, pimping: Carco's themes. But also, his actual obsessions as well, if we are reading Mansfield correctly. The narrator, Raoul Duquette, a Parisian writer and pimp based on Carco, recounts bits and pieces of his life while ostensibly telling a tale of Mouse (Mansfield) and Dick Harmon (John Middleton Murry, Mansfield's husband) within the context of carefully describing himself. Mansfield's brilliance is the way she reveals so much about each of her characters through their own words and actions. At the beginning of the story, in Paris, Duquette and Dick form a tight "friendship" based on their love of literature. When Dick announces he must return to England, Duquette is both furious and hurt. It's evident that his attraction to Dick is hardly brotherly. But then when Dick brings his lover Mouse back to Paris, Duquette's true character begins to emerge. His voyeur instinct comes full forward, as does his derisory view of those he watches. He compares himself to a customs officer who thrills at examining those inspected to force them to reveal what it is they have to declare. As the narrative progresses, the

Jules Pascin. *Pierre Mac Orlan*, 1924, oil on canvas, 92.1 x 73 cm.
Metropolitan Museum of Art.

contrast between the preying Duquette and his far more innocent victims, Dick and Mouse, becomes more evident, as does Duquette's delight in the destruction of their relationship. It is a story worthy of Carco; in "Je Ne Parle Pas Français," however, it is Carco who is mercilessly dissected.

That Carco was complex as a writer and human is indisputable. That he could write such a sensitive book as *From Montmartre to the Latin Quarter* as well as author his gruesome noir novels is decidedly contradictory. My sense is that the side of Carco who wrote poetry – lyrical, post symbolist, evocative of nature and weather – the *"poète de la pluie,"* as he was dubbed by his contemporaries, is the writer behind the memoir. His sensitive attention to detail in his poetry is mirrored in the *souvenirs* of his friends, their creations and their times; his tremendous love for art and artists, on display in his homages to Villon, Verlaine, and Rimbaud in his poetry, is what guides his empathetic observations in *From Montmartre to the Latin Quarter.*

Jean Rhys, an acute observer of human nature who translated *Perversité* into English, and who spent a fair amount of time in Carco's Paris, wrote from the point of view of an unnamed narrator in her 1927 story "The Blue Bird" this observation which seems to sum up a good deal of Carco's dual vision: "Montparnasse is full of tragedy – all sorts – blatant, hidden, silent, voluble, slow – even lucrative – A tragedy can be lucrative, I assure you. On any day of the week you may catch sight of the Sufferers, white-faced and tragic of eye – having a drink in the intervals of expressing themselves – pouring out their souls and exposing them hopefully for sale, that is to say."

In the end, we are glad for both Carcos. He was truly a literary giant. All praise to Rob Couteau for helping contemporary readers in English rediscover this important figure. Due to Couteau's copious and detailed and revelatory research, an entire panorama into the world of art in Paris – particularly that of Modigliani's circle – is opened to us. Replete with new and fascinating discoveries about both Carco and Modigliani, this edition immensely advances our knowledge of art and artists, collecting and trading during an important period in European art history. To his credit, Couteau even manages to identify for the first time what exactly were the Modigliani pieces in Carco's possession, and even the prices they fetched at auction. These are valuable details, the result of Couteau's willingness to keep digging into the archives, and then digging more. A rich portrait emerges that expands exponentially on Carco's already detailed memoir.

This is a gift for which I am admiring and grateful.

Christopher Sawyer-Lauçanno is the author of *The Continual Pilgrimage: American Writers in Paris, 1944-1960, E. E. Cummings,* and *An Invisible Spectator, A Biography of Paul Bowles.*

Modigliani. *Caryatid*, c. 1914, limestone, 92.1 cm. high; 41.6 x 42.9 cm. at base. Originally owned by Pierre and Dollie Chareau, from 1939 – 1951. Purchased by the Museum of Modern Art from Dollie Chareau through the Buchholz Gallery in 1951.

Francis Carco Bibliography

P: poetry. **N**: novel. **NL**: novella. **S**: tales and short stories. **P**: plays.
M: memoir. **B**: biography / fictionalized biography. **C**: critique. **E**: essay.
R: reportage.

Instincts. [P] Paris: Le Feu – Union Française d'Edition, 1911.

La Bohème et mon coeur. [P] Niort: [Imprimerie Clouzot], 1912.

Charles-Henry Hirsch. [C] Paris: E. Sansot & Cie, 1913.

Chansons aigres douces. [P] Marseille: Collections des Cinq, 1913.

Au Vent crispé du matin. [P] Marseille: Collections des Cinq, 1913.

Jésus-la-caille. [N] Paris: Éditions du Mercure de France, 1914.

Les Innocents. [N] Paris: La Renaissance du Livre, 1916.

Badigeon aviateur. [N] Paris: L'Edition, 1917.

Les Malheurs de Fernande. [N] Paris: L'Edition, 1918.

Les Mystères de la morgue ou Les Fiancés du IV arrondissement. [N] Paris: La Renaissance du Livre, 1918.

Scènes de la vie de Montmartre. [N] Paris: Éditions Arthème Fayard, 1919.

Bob et Bobette s'amusent. [N] Paris: Albin Michel, 1919.

La Poésie. [C] Paris: Edward Sansot, 1919.

L'Équipe. [N] Paris: Émile-Paul Frères, 1919.

Au coin des rues. [S] Geneva: L'Éventail-Kundig, 1919.

Petits airs. [P] Paris: Ronald Davies, 1920.

Maman Petitdoigt. Souvenirs d'enfance. [M] Paris: Ronald Davies, 1920.

M. De Vlaminck. [C] Paris: Éditions de la Nouvelle Revue Française, 1920.

Francis Carco raconté par lui meme. [M] Paris: R. Chiberre, 1921.

Maurice Utrillo. [C] Paris: Éditions de la Nouvelle Revue Française, 1921.

Les Humoristes. [C] Paris: Paul Ollendorff, 1921.

Mon homme, pièce en trois actes. [T] Paris: J. Ferenczi, 1921. (In collaboration with André Picard.)

L'Ami des filles. Paris: Ronald Davis, 1921.

Rien qu'une femme. [N] Paris: Éditions Arthème Fayard, 1921.

Promenades pittoresques à Montmartre. Paris: Edition Léo Delteil, 1922.

Les Chercheurs d'or. [T] Paris: Lecture pour tous. (In collaboration with Jacques Richepin.) 1922.

Panam. [P] Paris: Librairie Stock, chez Delamain, Boutelleau et Cie, 1922.

L'Homme traqué. [N] Paris: Albin Michel, 1922.

Verotchka l'érangère. [N] Paris: Albin Michel, 1923.

Le Gentleman. [T] Librairie du Théâtre français. (In collaboration with Alfred Savoir.)

Quatre poèmes. [P] Paris, Armand Huart. (In collaboration with Philippe Chabaneix.)

Maurice Asselin. [C] Paris: Éditions de la Nouvelle Revue Française, 1924.

Tableau de l'amour vénal. Éditions de la Nouvelle Revue Française, 1924.

Le Nu dans la peinture moderne. [C] Paris: Crès et Cie, 1924.

Avec les filles. [E] [Facsimile edition of the manuscript]. Paris: Edouard Champion, 1924.

Instincts, Promenade pittoresque à Montmartre, Panam. [P] Libr . Stock, 1924.

Visite à Saint Lazare. [R] Paris: Chez Madame Lesage, 1925.

Le Couteau. [NL] Paris: A l'Enseigne de la Porte Etroite, 1925.

Perversité. [N] Paris: J. Ferenczi et fils, 1925.

J'avais un secrétaire. [NL] Paris: À La Cité des Livres, 1925.

L'amour vénal. [E] Paris: [no stated publisher; later published by Le Diva in 1926; revised edition, Albin Michel, 1927], 1925.

Ces Messieurs-Dames. [C] Paris: R. Davis, 1926.

Le Roman de François Villon. [B] Paris: Plon-Nourrit, 1926.

De Montmartre au Quartier Latin. [M] Paris: Albin Michel, 1927.

Rue Pigalle. [N] Paris: Bernard Grasset, 1927.

Poemes retrouvés. [P] Paris: À la Cité des Livres, 1927. [Only 350 copies.]

Nuits de Paris. [R] Paris: Au Sans Pareille, 1927.

La Légende et la vie d'Utrillo. [B] Paris: Marcel Seheur, 1927.

Les Vrais de vrai. [NL] Paris: Au Sans Pareil, 1928.

Supplément aux dialogues des courtisanes de Lucien. [E] Paris: Éditions du Trianon, 1928.

Images cachées. [R] Paris: Éditions de la Roseraie, 1928.

Argot du milieu. [R] Paris: Albin Michel, 1928.

Complémentaires. [M] Paris: Emile Hazan et Cie, 1929.

Huit jours à Séville. Paris: Émile-Paul Frères, 1929.

Notre ami Louis Jou. [R] (In collaboration with Jean Cassou.) Paris: Éditions M. P. Trémois, 1929.

Printemps d'Espagne. [R] Paris: Albin Michel, 1929.

La Rue. [R] Paris: Albin Michel, 1930.

On ferme. [NL] [Privately printed.] Paris: Pour les Amis du Docteur Lucien Graux, 1931.

Les Enfants du malheur. [NL] Maastricht, A. A. M. Stols, 1930.

Prisons de femmes. [R] Paris: Les Éditions de France, 1931.

Gilberte. [NL] Paris: Émile-Paul Frères, 1931.

Le Destin du François Villon. [C] Paris: A La Cité des Livres, 1931.

Suite espagnole. [R] Paris: Les Éditions de la Belle Page, 1931.

Quelques-unes. Paris: Pro Amicis, 1931.

Traduit de l'argot. [R] Paris: Les Éditions de France, 1932.

La Belle Amour. [S] Paris: Les Éditions de France, 1932.

Paul Bourget. [C] Paris: Félix Alcan, 1932.

L'Ombre. [R] Paris: Albin Michel, 1933.

Pour faire suite à La Bohème et mon coeur. [P] Paris: Le Divan, 1933.

Palace Égypte. [R] Paris, Albin Michel, 1933.

Contes du Milieu. [S] Paris : Éditions de France, 1933.

La Lumière noire. [R] Paris: Albin Michel, 1934.

Mémoires d'une autre vie. [M] Paris: Albin Michel, 1934.

Amitié avec Toulet. [M] Paris : Le Divan, 1934.

Souvenirs sur Katherine Mansfield. [M] Paris: Le Divan, 1934.

Ténèbres. [R] Paris: Albin Michel, 1935.

Pages choisies. Paris: Albin Michel, 1935.

La Dernière Chance. [R] Paris: Albin Michel, 1935.

Brumes. [R] Paris: Albin Michel, 1935.

La Rose au balcon. [P] Paris: Philippe Chabaneix, 1936.

La Route du bagne. [R] Paris: Ferenczi, 1936.

Petite suite sentimentale. [P] Paris: Émile-Paul Frères, 1936.

Les Hommes en cage. [R] Paris: Albin Michel, 1936.

Le Bain. [R] Paris: Bonthoux, 1936.

Blumelein 35: Les Confidences du Lieutenant S. de Barrière. [R] Paris: Albin Michel, 1937.

A l'amitié. [P] Paris: Émile-Paul Frères, 1937.

L'Homme de minuit. [R] Paris: Albin Michel, 1938.

À voix basse. [M] Paris: Albin Michel, 1938

Montmartre à vingt ans. [M] Paris: Albin Michel, 1938.

Envoûtement de Paris. [E] Paris: Bernard Grasset, 1938.

Le Cinéma. [R] Bonthoux, 1938

Souvenirs de Montmartre et d'ailleurs. [M] Fayard, 1938.

Verlaine. [C] Paris: Éditions de la Nouvelle Revue de Critique, 1939.

Bohème d'artiste. [M] Paris: Albin Michel, 1940.

Heures d'Égypte. [R] Paris: Edouard Aubanel, 1940.

Nostalgie de Paris. [M] Geneva: Éditions du Milieu du Monde, 1941.

L'Ombre. [P] Villeneuve-lès-Avignon: Seghers, 1941.

Barraud. Un peintre chez lui. [C] Zürich: Éditions Galerie Beaux-Arts, 1943.

Surprenant procès d'un bourreau. Geneva: Éditions du Milieu du Monde, 1942.

L'Ami des peintres. Geneva: Éditions du Milieu du Monde, 1944.

La Danse des morts comme l'a décrite François Villon. Geneva: Éditions du Milieu du Monde, 1944.

Les Belles Manières. [R] Geneva: Éditions du Milieu du Monde, 1945.

Les Jours et les nuits. [P] Paris: Textes Prétextes, 1946. [Only 250 copies.]

Mortefontaine. [P] Paris: Émile-Paul Frères, 1946.

Dignimont. [C] Monte-Carlo: André Sauret, Éditions Du Livre, 1946.

Vertès. [C] Rosamond Frost, trans. New York: Athenaeum Publishing Co., 1946. [Deluxe edition, artwork of Vertès, with Carco's accompanying text.]

Ombres vivantes. [M] Paris: Éditions de la Galerie Charpentier, 1947.

Montmartre vécu par Utrillo. [E] Paris: Éditions Pétridès, 1947.

Poèmes en prose. [P] Paris: Points et Contrepoints, 1948.

Morsure. [R] Paris: Ferenczi, 1949.

Romance de Paris. [E] Paris: Société des Francs-Bibliophiles, 1949.

Francis Carco. Une étude par Philippe Chabaneix, inédits, oeuvres choisies, bibliographie, dessins, portraits, facsimilés, Paris: Éditions Pierre Seghers, Collection Poètes d'aujourd'hui 1949. (Assembled by Philippe Chabaneix.)

Rêverie dans Amsterdam. [E] Avignon: Pour F. M. et ses Amis, 1951.

Francis Carco vous parle. [M] Paris: Denoël, 1953.

La Belle Époque au temps de Bruant. [E] Paris: Gallimard, 1954.

Compagnons de la mauvaise chance. [R] Geneva: Éditions de Milieu du Monde, 1954.

Poésies complètes. [P] Paris: Gallimard, 1955.

Utrillo. [B] Paris : Bernard Grasset, 1956.

Rendez-vous avec moi-même. [M] Paris: Albin Michel, 1957.

Carco in English-language Translation:

The Noose of Sin. [*L'Homme traqué*.] [N] Emile Hope , trans., London: Jonathan Cape, 1923.

The Hounded Man. [*L'Homme traqué*.] [N] Alex Jorand, trans., New York: Thomas Selzer, 1924.

Perversity. [*Perversité*.] [N] Jean Rhys, trans. [although the translation was falsely attributed to Ford Madox Ford], Chicago: Pascal Covici, 1928.

Vertès. [C] Rosamond Frost, trans. New York: Athenaeum Publishing Co., 1946. [Deluxe edition, artwork of Vertès, with Carco's accompanying text.]

Only a Woman. [*Rien Q'une Femme*.] [N] Ralph Manheim, trans., New York: Berkley Publishing, 1953.

Rue Pigalle. [*Rue Pigalle,*] [N] Frances Frenaye, trans., New York: Avon Publications, 1954.

Depravity. [*Les Innocents*.] [N] Lowell Bair, trans., New York: Berkley Publishing, 1957.

Frenzy. [*Jésus-la-Caille*.] [N] Lowell Bair, trans., New York: Berkley Publishing, 1960.

Streetcorners: Prose Poems of the Demi-Monde. Gilbert Alter-Gilbert, trans., Copenhagen: Green Integer, 2004.

From Montmartre to the Latin Quarter. Edited with Annotations and an Introduction by Rob Couteau [*De Montmartre au Quartier Latin*] [M]. Afterword by Christopher Sawyer-Lauçanno. New York: Dominantstar, 2024.

INDEX OF PEOPLE AND PLACES

passion and his influence on the art world enhances a survey that should be required reading and acquisition for any serious art history student and the libraries catering to them ... Readers also receive revealing inspections of the process of interviewing artists and capturing their historical impact, adding to *A Blind Man Crazy for Color*'s importance as a survey that goes beyond a singular biography of an art enthusiast to delve into the world of artists, art appreciation, and muses ... Serious art libraries should consider this extraordinary recreation of artistic ambitions against all odds a mainstay that stands out in many different ways." – Diane Donovan, *Midwest Book Review*.

SELECTED POEMS

"There is a deep tenderness in these words, mingled with the sadness of age. If one goes back to the early poems addressed to Edda Maria Sangrígoli, one can find the tenderness there, too, as it is in his work as a case manager for the poor and homeless. There is much to admire in Couteau's oeuvre, but this tenderness stands out among so many things that make reading his work clearly an important experience."
– Ed Foster, founder of Talisman House Publishers, and editor
of *Talisman: A Journal of Contemporary Poetry and Poetics*.

"*Selected Poems* features 101 poems, 40 of which have been printed in numerous print and online journals since 1985. The rest are new to this collection and represent a satisfying blend of old and new works designed to appeal to newcomers and prior fans alike. Rob Couteau's works are diverse. They follow no set poetic structure, even defying some of them when the muse strikes and special needs indicate that the subject is more important than poetic form ... His inspections of artistic, literary, and social issues are astute and compelling. Don't anticipate set structures, uniform poetic approaches, or singular subjects. *Selected Poems* offers a freewheeling approach to poems and life alike and is a thought-provoking, evocative gathering of works recommended for literary readers not bound by convention or rules."
– Diane Donovan, *Midwest Book Review*.

MORE COLLECTED COUTEAU: ESSAYS AND INTERVIEWS, WITH AN INTRODUCTION BY JAMES DEMPSEY

"Couteau's essays are informal, fervent, and well-versed examinations of the work or author at hand. At their best, they include fascinating insights into the significance of a writer like Hubert Selby ... The interviews are uniformly strong and include conversations with Michael Korda on T. E. Lawrence, Justin Kaplan on Walt Whitman, and Robert Roper on Vladimir Nabokov. Not all of them focus on literature: author Jeffrey Jackson covers the 1910 flood of Paris and why it's relatively forgotten, and Robert De Sena, in one of the best interviews, discusses his life as a gang member turned community activist. Couteau's passion and wealth of knowledge are obvious throughout the book ... and should appeal to many readers."
– *Publishers Weekly Select*.

"The Renaissance Man is a multifaceted individual whose fingers are in just about every pie you could imagine, fostering a variety of abilities and mastering many quite well. His expertise is wide-ranging and there's seemingly no limit to his subject, as is demonstrated in *More Collected Couteau: Essays and Interviews*, which gathers Couteau's insights and encounters with a diverse range of individuals ...

The joy of reading Couteau's work lies as much in his penetrating, crystalline language as it does in the works or figures being examined, and so readers receive a wide-ranging treat that examines victims, vengeance, mortality, and immortality through an inspection process that educates even those unfamiliar with the subject: 'Selby once said: "There is no light in my stories, so the reader is forced to turn to his own inner light" to make it through this journey. I now realize this is only partially true. The great beacon in his demonic oeuvre is that of the artfully crafted line and the immense vision of wholeness and transcendence that lurks behind it. Selby's empathy is there, omnipresent, even while recording the darkest hues of black. The utmost depravity is portrayed with the noblest verse.'

After proving his prowess at the essay form, he turns to the heart of the collection: its interviews ... One of the pleasures in this collection is that readers needn't have prior familiarity with the writers' works. Couteau provides that familiarity by the structure of his interview questions, which probe the foundation beliefs of each figure … From the possibility that Nabokov suffered unconscious doubts about his own value that led him to insist that the world acknowledge him as a genius to the underlying patriotism of counterculture icons who were commonly seen as rebels ('Ginsberg continually affirmed that, essentially, Jack had always been a sort of patriotic American,' says Sawyer-Lauçanno. 'This had never not been part of who he was. It was patriotic to get into an automobile made in Detroit and drive across the country'), both essays and interviews are designed to make readers think about underlying psychology, social perceptions, and cultural change.

Readers seeking not just a literary presentation but a lively analysis of selected wordsmiths and their lives and influences must add *More Collected Couteau* to their reading lists. It's a powerful presentation that offers much insight … and which should find its way into many a college classroom as well." – Diane Donovan, *Midwest Book Review*.

"Good luck trying to pin down Rob Couteau. Name the genre, and Couteau has almost certainly been there and done that. Poet, novelist, essayist, critic, journalist, memoirist, and travel writer, Couteau is not one to be hampered by constraints. He passes easily from one form of literature to another as if the borders between them did not exist for him. Perhaps they don't.

Couteau has been called a 'literary enthusiast,' and although he certainly is enthusiastic about literature (and indeed all art), the phrase carries the smack of the amateur about it, and Couteau is anything but. He is, in fact, an undeniably consummate professional. He is an independent scholar in every meaning of the word – unaligned with any institution except for the literary and artistic canon he so loves, and a thinker who comes to his own conclusions …

This collection gives the reader a good sampling of Couteau's literary and scholarly talents, not the least of which are his interviews with writers he admires. Having spent many years as a journalist, I believe I have some ability to recognize and admire an artful interviewer, and Couteau is a master. His preparation is comprehensive, meticulous, and profound. His understanding of the process of writing in so many genres allows him insights into the particular problems faced by the writers he interviews. His style is conversational and relaxed, but deceptively so; he is always in control of the interview. This said, however, when a sudden fact or insight takes the interview down unexpected pathways, Couteau has the aesthetic nimbleness to recognize the opening and to follow it.

The collection features interviews with biographers, memoirists, historians, an inner-city antiviolence activist, and the creator of LSD. You'll also find herein Couteau's writings on literature, which I hesitate to call criticism since they lack the worst features of much literary criticism, which can be clogged with so much pretentiousness, cant, and philosophical obfuscation that it would take a plunger of Brobdingnagian proportions to restore a healthy flow. Couteau's essays are often rhapsodic appreciations and evocations of the work under study, and are stuffed with both insights and joy.

– James Dempsey, author of *The Tortured Life of Scofield Thayer*.

THE SLEEPING MERMAID

"Novelist and literary enthusiast Rob Couteau brings readers part of his love with *The Sleeping Mermaid*, a book of flowing poetry and thought that asks plenty of questions and offers plenty of answers. *The Sleeping Mermaid* is a poetry collection well-worth considering."
– Willis M. Buhle, *Midwest Book Review*.

"In Couteau's work there is no phoniness, no artifice for the sake of artifice – though in the great French tradition this poet knows so well, there is some art for the sake of art. Couteau does not venture into realms of obscurity where meaning is confined to the interior of a Klein bottle; his poems all have direct force, subjects, even verbs. He is intent on having his readers share in his observations, whether it be his artful retelling and reinterpretations of Native American story and song, or his appraisal of how a woman parades across the avenue. He does not ever sacrifice ordinary sense for an extra-ordinary significance. Instead, he speaks with fervor, with something to say, with something he wants us to hang onto and, in the process, come to an understanding of why it matters not just to him but should matter to us.

I think it was William Carlos Williams who said that poetry is belief. Couteau believes in belief, believes that poetic worth is measured in faithfulness to what is, what has been, and what could be. These are his talismans; these are the points where he begins and ends. His poetic excursions take us to many places: to the Paris of Rimbaud and Picasso, to the Native North Americans, to mythology and history and how the woman he is encountering is seducing him as he seduces her (and us), and finally, how alone, the cosmos plays itself out at 3 a.m. when the only lap dog is memory."
– Christopher Sawyer-Lauçanno.

Portraits from the Revolution: Interviews with the Protestors from Occupy Wall Street

"Most American readers will harbor a prior, casual familiarity with the Occupy Wall Street movement of 2011 based on newspaper headlines and events of the times; but for a more in-depth survey of the philosophies, approaches, and concerns of the protests, *Portraits from the* Revolution is the item of choice, offering unprecedented depth and detail on the history and lasting impact of the Occupy Wall Street movement.

Chapters explore not just each individual's actions but their backgrounds, reasons for participating in Occupy Wall Street, and their experiences. And it offers criticism of media reporting of the movement's history, intentions, and approaches.

From how participants decided to react to violent antagonism against the Occupy movement to the social and political ramifications of not just Occupy but the elements it opposed, these interviews capture participants from all walks of life, from teens to full-time workers, and turn the newspaper reports into a series of personal vignettes about Occupy's deeper meaning.
– Diane Donovan, *Midwest Book Review*

DOCTOR PLUSS, WITH AN AFTERWARD BY JIM FEAST

"Intellectual freshness, richness, and potency ... Couteau is an impressively creative writer, whom Barney Rosset urged me to review." – Jim Feast, *Evergreen Review*.

"Rob Couteau describes *Doctor Pluss* as 'fiction based on actual dialogues with schizophrenic patients, diabolically "sane" psycho-therapists, and well-meaning yet unerringly destructive social workers. It chronicles the descent of an eccentric, sardonic, and witty psychiatrist into what appears to be a state of complete madness.'

His intention to metaphorically and realistically portray and contrast the madness of psychiatric process as well as its patients is powerfully wrought in a story about patients 'surviving this holocaust of forgetfulness.' During this process, their identities and personalities are lost in the institutional morass of a center purported to excel in rehabilitation, but which actually contains many ethical and personal challenges to the new psychiatric resident at the Walt Whitman Asylum for Adults, Dr. Pluss.

It's a place of rage and despair, of ambiguity where hope and horror run close together, and daily gives Dr. Pluss pause for thought about his patients and his role in their lives: 'In her own unwitting way,' Pluss mused, Evelyn personified the dual aspects of the godhead: horror and joy; awe and fascination.'

Novellas typically are hard-hitting but often artificially succinct in their brevity. Often, one is left wanting for more. The best of them (of which *Doctor Pluss* is one) excels in taking this succinctness to its most logical conclusion, creating slices of life which are narrow enough to receive full-bodied flavor as the plot and characters develop.

One does not wish for more in *Doctor Pluss*. It's complete unto itself, exceptionally well developed, and emotionally compelling, connect-ing metaphorical traditional roles of doctor and patient, linking them in unexpected ways.

Couteau is not afraid to push the literary boundaries of convention in pursuit of a different form of descriptive truth, bringing readers along in a rollicking ride through schizophrenic experience that ultimately questions the foundations of reality and perception from both sides of the therapist's couch. His interpretations and descriptions of the schizophrenic experience are particularly astute, astonishing, and evocatively described …

Readers who choose *Doctor Pluss* are in for a treat. It's like *One Flew Over the Cuckoo's Nest* on steroids: a thought-provoking examination of sanity, insanity, and the crossover process that leaves readers thinking long after this therapeutic slice of life is consumed.

– Diane Donovan, *Midwest Book Review*.

www.ingramcontent.com/pod-product-compliance
Lightning Source LLC
Chambersburg PA
CBHW060425310726
48977CB00001B/52